Liturgical Resources 2

*Marriage Rites
for the Whole Church*

As presented to the 79th General Convention, 2018

I certify that this edition of Liturgical Resources 2 conforms to the text approved for trial use by the seventy-ninth General Convention of the Episcopal Church.

Juan M. C. Oliver
Custodian of the Book of Common Prayer.
November 2019

© 2019 by The Domestic and Foreign Missionary Society of
The Protestant Episcopal Church in the United States of America

All rights reserved.

ISBN-13: 978-1-64065-187-6 (pbk.)
ISBN-13: 978-1-64065-188-3 (ebook)

Church Publishing, Incorporated
19 East 34th Street
New York, New York 10016

www.churchpublishing.org

Table of Contents

1	I. Introduction
5	II. Liturgical Resources
9	The Celebration and Blessing of a Marriage 2
19	The Witnessing and Blessing of a Marriage
33	The Blessing of a Civil Marriage 2
35	An Order for Marriage 2
37	Prefaces for Marriage
39	III. Essays: Christian Perspectives on Marriages and Family Life Today
43	Introduction: Christian Perspectives on Marriages and Family Life Today
45	Biblical and Theological Foundations for Relationships
49	Culture, Ethnicity, and Marriage
53	Householding
61	Singleness
65	Sexual Intimacy: A Complex Gift
69	Responses to the Essays
75	For Further Reading: Marriage, Family, and Sexuality
81	Clergy, Church, and State: A Continuing Debate

89	IV. Essays on Marriage
93	Introduction: Christian Perspectives on Marriages and Family Life Today
99	1. A Biblical and Theological Framework for Thinking about Marriage
129	2. Christian Marriage as Vocation
149	3. A History of Christian Marriage
179	4. Marriage as a Rite of Passage
189	5. The Marriage Canon: History and Critique
213	6. Agents of the State: A Question for Discernment
219	7. Changing Trends and Norms in Marriage
239	V. Dearly Beloved: A Toolkit for the Study of Marriage
243	Introduction
247	Format 1: Carry-On Conversations
261	Format 2: Forums
273	Format 3: Study Groups
275	VI. Pastoral Resources for Preparing Couples for Marriage
279	Pre-Marital Preparation: Introduction
281	Presenters
283	Session One: Getting to Know You and an Overview
285	Session Two: Learning from the Past, Part 1
286	Session Three: Learning from the Past, Part 2
287	Session Four: Looking to the Future
288	Session Five: Liturgical Decisions and Wrap-up
291	Handouts
293	1. Declaration of Intention for Marriage (Canon I.18.4)
295	2. About Presenters—For the Couple
297	3. Information for Presenters
299	4. Model Congregational Guidelines
301	VII. Appendices
303	1. Marriage Canons
307	2. A Review of General Convention Legislation

I. Introduction

The materials in this volume were developed by the Standing Commission on Liturgy and Music between 2009 and 2015, by the Task Force on the Study of Marriage appointed after the 2012 General Convention, and by an expanded Task Force on the Study of Marriage appointed after the 2015 General Convention. The rites of "The Witnessing and Blessing of a Marriage" and "The Celebration and Blessing of a Marriage 2" were first authorized for trial use in 2015 by the 78th General Convention.

Liturgical Resources

In 2009, the General Convention of The Episcopal Church directed the Standing Commission on Liturgy and Music (SCLM) to "collect and develop theological and liturgical resources" for blessing same-sex relationships (Resolution 2009-C056). The commission developed "The Witnessing and Blessing of a Lifelong Covenant," which the 2012 General Convention authorized for provisional use (Resolution 2012-A049).

During the next triennium (2012-2015), the SCLM prepared an adaptation of the 2012 liturgy that can be used for the marriage of any couple ("The Witnessing and Blessing of a Marriage"), as well as "The Celebration and Blessing of a Marriage 2," a gender-neutral adaptation of the marriage rite in the 1979 Book of Common Prayer. The 2015 General Convention authorized both liturgies for trial use. The same convention revised the marriage canon to allow clergy to solemnize a marriage using any of the liturgical forms authorized by The Episcopal Church (Canon I.18.1).

Resolution 2015-A037 directed the expanded Task Force on the Study of Marriage, in consultation with the SCLM, to study and monitor the impact of the marriage of same-sex couples on The Episcopal Church, and to make recommendations to the 79th General Convention. The task force heard concerns about "separate but equal" rites, that is, that rites not included in The Book of Common Prayer are not of equal status with those that are. Accordingly, the task force recommends that the 79th General Convention authorize these liturgies for trial use as additions to The Book of Common Prayer.

In order to recognize marriage between same-sex couples, the task force also proposes a revision of the rubric "Concerning the Service" of The Celebration and Blessing of a Marriage, along with an additional Proper Preface for Marriage, for use in eucharistic prayers (Rite I and Rite II) at a nuptial eucharist. In addition, the task force proposes a revision to the Catechism to state that Christian marriage involves two people, rather than specifying a man and a woman, and adds a question concerning the requirements for those seeking to be married in The Episcopal Church, similar to a question about the requirements for those to be confirmed.

Essays

As the Standing Commission on Liturgy and Music developed liturgical resources for blessing same-sex relationships, it faced repeated questions about marriage. In response, the commission recommended to the 2012 General Convention the creation of a task force on the study of marriage. The task force that convened from 2012-2015 addressed the question, "What might The Episcopal Church have to say to today's world as to what makes a marriage Christian and holy?" Their research and reflection led to seven essays, which were presented to the 2015 General Convention.

The task force identified a number of contemporary trends and norms in marriage and family life, and the 2015 General Convention directed an expanded task force to continue to study those trends and norms. This latter task force developed a series of short essays to invite reflection about marriage and human sexuality, along with a list of resources for further study. The collections of essays from both task forces (2012-2015 and 2015-2018) are included in this volume.

The 2015 General Convention also directed the expanded task force to study the debate about clergy acting as "agents of the state" at marriages. In response, the task force prepared an essay that includes historical background and contemporary perspectives, and concludes with a suggestion to consider clergy as "agents of the couple," acting as advocates for those entering both the sacred and civil commitments of marriage.

A Toolkit for the Study of Marriage

The Task Force on the Study of Marriage created in 2012 began its work by creating a toolkit for the study of marriage that was released in June 2014. An updated version of the toolkit was included in the report of the task force to the 2015 General Convention, and the convention requested that congregations and dioceses use the toolkit.

Pastoral Resources

The material for premarital preparation was originally developed as part of the resources for blessing same-sex relationships prepared by the SCLM during the 2009-2012 triennium. It has been revised to be suitable for use with any couple preparing for marriage. While Canon I.18.3(c) requires that couples be instructed "in the nature, purpose, and meaning, as well as the rights, duties and responsibilities of marriage," the use of these resources for preparation is not required.

Conclusion

The Task Force on the Study of Marriage offers this material to The Episcopal Church in the hopes that these resources will enable us as Christians to deepen our understanding of marriage and will strengthen our witness to the Gospel.

The Task Force on the Study of Marriage
December 2017

II. Liturgical Resources

proposed for trial use

as presented to the 79th General Convention

II. LITURGICAL RESOURCES

Contents

The Celebration and Blessing of a Marriage 2 **
The Witnessing and Blessing of a Marriage **
The Blessing of a Civil Marriage 2 **
An Order for Marriage 2 **
Prefaces for Marriage *

* Prepared by the Task Force on the Study of Marriage, 2015-2018
** Prepared by the Standing Commission on Liturgy and Music, 2012-2015

II. LITURGICAL RESOURCES

The Celebration and Blessing of a Marriage 2

Concerning the Service

At least one of the parties must be a baptized Christian; the ceremony must be attested by at least two witnesses; and the marriage must conform to the laws of the State.

A priest or a bishop normally presides at the Celebration and Blessing of a Marriage, because such ministers alone have the function of pronouncing the nuptial blessing, and of celebrating the Holy Eucharist.

When both a bishop and a priest are present and officiating, the bishop should pronounce the blessing and preside at the Eucharist.

A deacon, or an assisting priest, may deliver the charge, ask for the Declaration of Consent, read the Gospel, and perform other assisting functions at the Eucharist.

Where it is permitted by civil law that deacons may perform marriages, and no priest or bishop is available, a deacon may use the service which follows, omitting the nuptial blessing which follows The Prayers.

It is desirable that the Lessons from the Old Testament and the Epistles be read by lay persons.

In the opening exhortation (at the symbol of N. N.), the full names of the persons to be married are declared. Subsequently, only their Christian names are used.

Additional Directions are on page 18.

The Celebration and Blessing of a Marriage 2

At the time appointed, the persons to be married, with their witnesses, assemble in the church or some other appropriate place.

During their entrance, a hymn, psalm, or anthem may be sung, or instrumental music may be played.

Then the Celebrant, facing the people and the persons to be married, addresses the congregation and says

> Dearly beloved: We have come together in the presence of God to witness and bless the joining together of N. and N. in Holy Matrimony. The joining of two people in a life of mutual fidelity signifies to us the mystery of the union between Christ and his Church, and so it is worthy of being honored among all people.
>
> The union of two people in heart, body, and mind is intended by God for their mutual joy; for the help and comfort given one another in prosperity and adversity; and when it is God's will, for the gift of children and their nurture in the knowledge and love of the Lord. Therefore marriage is not to be entered into unadvisedly or lightly, but reverently, deliberately, and in accordance with the purposes for which it was instituted by God.
>
> Into this holy union N. N. and N. N. now come to be joined.
>
> If any of you can show just cause why they may not lawfully be married, speak now; or else for ever hold your peace.

Then the Celebrant says to the persons to be married

> I require and charge you both, here in the presence of God, that if either of you knows any reason why you may not be united in marriage lawfully, and in accordance with God's Word, you do now confess it.

The Declaration of Consent

The Celebrant says to one member of the couple, then to the other

N., will you have this woman/man/person to be your wife/husband/spouse; to live together in the covenant of marriage? Will you love her/him, comfort her/him, honor and keep her/him, in sickness and in health; and, forsaking all others, be faithful to her/him as long as you both shall live?

Answer   I will.

The Celebrant then addresses the congregation, saying

Will all of you witnessing these promises do all in your power to uphold these two persons in their marriage?

People   We will.

If there is to be a presentation or a giving in marriage, it takes place at this time.

See Additional Directions, p. 19.

A hymn, psalm, or anthem may follow.

The Ministry of the Word

The Celebrant then says to the people

The Lord be with you.

People   And also with you.

Celebrant   Let us pray.

O gracious and everliving God, you have created humankind in your image: Look mercifully upon N. and N. who come to you seeking your blessing, and assist them with your grace, that with true fidelity and steadfast love they may honor and keep the promises and vows they make; through Jesus Christ our Savior, who lives and reigns with you in the unity of the Holy Spirit, one God, for ever and ever. *Amen.*

Then one or more of the following passages from Holy Scripture is read. Other readings from Scripture suitable for the occasion may be used. If there is to be a Communion, a passage from the Gospel always concludes the Readings.

Genesis 1:26–28 (Male and female he created them)
Song of Solomon 2:10–13; 8:6–7
   (Many waters cannot quench love)
Tobit 8:5b–8 (New English Bible)
   (That she and I may grow old together)

1 Corinthians 13:1–13 (Love is patient and kind)
Ephesians 3:14–19
   (The Father from whom every family is named)
Ephesians 5:1–2 (Walk in love, as Christ loved us)
Colossians 3:12–17
   (Love which binds everything together in harmony)
1 John 4:7–16 (Let us love one another, for love is of God)

Between the Readings, a psalm, hymn, or anthem may be sung or said. Appropriate psalms are Psalm 67, Psalm 127, and Psalm 128.

When a passage from the Gospel is to be read, all stand, and the Deacon or Minister appointed says

> The Holy Gospel of our Lord Jesus Christ according to _____.

People   Glory to you, Lord Christ.

> Matthew 5:1–10 (The Beatitudes)
> Matthew 5:13–16
>   (You are the light ... Let your light so shine)
> Matthew 7:21, 24–29
>   (Like a wise man who built his house upon the rock)
> John 15:9–12 (Love one another as I have loved you)

After the Gospel, the Reader says

> The Gospel of the Lord.

People   Praise to you, Lord Christ.

A homily or other response to the Readings may follow.

II. LITURGICAL RESOURCES

The Marriage

Each member of the couple, in turn, takes the right hand of the other and says

> In the Name of God, I, N., take you, N.,
>   to be my *wife/husband/spouse*,
> to have and to hold from this day forward,
> for better for worse, for richer for poorer,
> in sickness and in health, to love and to cherish,
> until we are parted by death.
> This is my solemn vow.

The Priest may ask God's blessing on rings as follows

> Bless, O Lord, these rings to be signs of the vows
> by which N. and N. have bound themselves to each other;
> through Jesus Christ our Lord. *Amen.*

The giver places the ring on the ring finger of the other's hand and says

> N., I give you this ring as a symbol of my vow,
> and with all that I am, and all that I have, I honor you,
> in the Name of the Father, and of the Son,
> and of the Holy Spirit [or in the Name of God].

Then the Celebrant joins the right hands of the couple and says

> Now that N. and N. have given themselves to each other
>   by solemn vows,
> with the joining of hands and the giving and receiving
>   of rings,
> I pronounce that they are wed to one another,
> in the Name of the Father, and of the Son,
>   and of the Holy Spirit.
> Those whom God has joined together let no one put asunder.

People Amen.

The Prayers

All standing, the Celebrant says

> Let us pray together in the words our Savior taught us.

People and Celebrant

Our Father, who art in heaven,	Our Father in heaven,
hallowed be thy Name,	hallowed be your Name,
thy kingdom come,	your kingdom come,
thy will be done,	your will be done,
on earth as it is in heaven.	on earth as in heaven.
Give us this day our daily bread.	Give us today our daily bread.
And forgive us our trespasses,	Forgive us our sins
as we forgive those	as we forgive those
who trespass against us.	who sin against us.
And lead us not into temptation,	Save us from the time of trial,
but deliver us from evil.	and deliver us from evil.
For thine is the kingdom,	For the kingdom, the power,
and the power, and the glory,	and the glory are yours for
ever and ever. Amen.	now and for ever. Amen.

If Communion is to follow, the Lord's Prayer may be omitted here.

The Deacon or other person appointed reads the following prayers, to which the People respond, saying, Amen. If there is not to be a Communion, one or more of the prayers may be omitted.

Leader   Let us pray.

Eternal God, creator and preserver of all life, author of salvation, and giver of all grace: Look with favor upon the world you have made, and for which your Son gave his life, and especially upon N. and N. whom you make one flesh in Holy Matrimony. *Amen.*

Give them wisdom and devotion in the ordering of their common life, that each may be to the other a strength in need, a counselor in perplexity, a comfort in sorrow, and a companion in joy. *Amen.*

Grant that their wills may be so knit together in your will, and their spirits in your Spirit, that they may grow in love and peace with you and one another all the days of their life. *Amen.*

Give them grace, when they hurt each other, to recognize and acknowledge their fault, and to seek each other's forgiveness and yours. *Amen.*

Make their life together a sign of Christ's love to this sinful and broken world, that unity may overcome estrangement, forgiveness heal guilt, and joy conquer despair. *Amen.*

Bestow on them, if it is your will, the gift and heritage of children, and the grace to bring them up to know you, to love you, and to serve you. *Amen.*

Give them such fulfillment of their mutual affection that they may reach out in love and concern for others. *Amen.*

Grant that all married persons who have witnessed these vows may find their lives strengthened and their loyalties confirmed. *Amen.*

Grant that the bonds of our common humanity, by which all your children are united one to another, and the living to the dead, may be so transformed by your grace, that your will may be done on earth as it is in heaven; where, O Father, with your Son and the Holy Spirit, you live and reign in perfect unity, now and for ever. *Amen.*

The Blessing of the Marriage

The People remain standing. The couple kneel, and the Priest says one of the following prayers

Most gracious God, we give you thanks for your tender love in sending Jesus Christ to come among us, to be born of a human mother, and to make the way of the cross to be the way of life. We thank you, also, for consecrating the union of two people in his Name. By the power of your Holy Spirit, pour out the abundance of your blessing upon N. and N. Defend them from every enemy. Lead them into all peace. Let their love for each other be a seal upon their hearts, a mantle about their shoulders, and a crown upon their foreheads. Bless them in their work and in their companionship; in their sleeping and in their waking; in their joys and in their sorrows; in their life and in their death. Finally, in your mercy, bring them to that table where your saints feast for ever in your heavenly home; through Jesus Christ our Lord, who with you and the Holy Spirit lives and reigns, one God, for ever and ever. *Amen.*

or this

> O God, you have so consecrated the covenant of marriage that in it is represented the spiritual unity between Christ and his Church: Send therefore your blessing upon these your servants, that they may so love, honor, and cherish each other in faithfulness and patience, in wisdom and true godliness, that their home may be a haven of blessing and peace; through Jesus Christ our Lord, who lives and reigns with you and the Holy Spirit, one God, now and for ever. Amen.

The couple still kneeling, the Priest adds this blessing

> God the Father, God the Son, God the Holy Spirit, bless, preserve, and keep you; the Lord mercifully with his favor look upon you, and fill you with all spiritual benediction and grace; that you may faithfully live together in this life, and in the age to come have life everlasting. *Amen.*

The Peace

The Celebrant may say to the People

> The peace of the Lord be always with you.

People   And also with you.

The newly married couple then greet each other, after which greetings may be exchanged throughout the congregation.

When Communion is not to follow, the wedding party leaves the church. A hymn, psalm, or anthem may be sung, or instrumental music may be played.

At the Eucharist

The liturgy continues with the Offertory, at which the newly married couple may present the offerings of bread and wine.

Preface of Marriage 2, or of the Season

At the Communion, it is appropriate that the newly married couple receive Communion first, after the ministers.

In place of the usual postcommunion prayer, the following is said

> O God, the giver of all that is true and lovely and gracious:
> We give you thanks for binding us together
> in these holy mysteries of the Body and Blood
> of your Son Jesus Christ.
> Grant that by your Holy Spirit,
> N. and N., now joined in Holy Matrimony,
> may become one in heart and soul,
> live in fidelity and peace,
> and obtain those eternal joys prepared for all who love you;
> for the sake of Jesus Christ our Lord. Amen.

As the wedding party leaves the church, a hymn, psalm, or anthem may be sung, or instrumental music may be played.

Additional Directions for
The Celebration and Blessing of a Marriage 2

If Banns are to be published, the following form is used

> I publish the Banns of Marriage between N. N. of _____ and N. N. of _____. If any of you know just cause why they may not be joined together in Holy Matrimony, you are bidden to declare it. This is the first [or second, or third] time of asking.

The Celebration and Blessing of a Marriage 2 may be used with any authorized liturgy for the Holy Eucharist. This service then replaces the Ministry of the Word, and the Eucharist begins with the Offertory.

After the Declaration of Consent, if there is to be a giving in marriage, or presentation, the Celebrant asks,

> Who presents [gives] these two people to be married to each other?

The appropriate answer is, "I do." If more than one person responds, they do so together.

For the Ministry of the Word it is fitting that the couple to be married remain where they may conveniently hear the reading of Scripture. They may approach the Altar, either for the exchange of vows, or for the Blessing of the Marriage.

It is appropriate that all remain standing until the conclusion of the Collect. Seating may be provided for the wedding party, so that all may be seated for the Lessons and the homily.

The Apostles' Creed may be recited after the Lessons, or after the homily, if there is one.

When desired, some other suitable symbol of the vows may be used in place of the ring.

At the Offertory, it is desirable that the bread and wine be presented to the ministers by the newly married persons. They may then remain before the Lord's Table and receive Holy Communion before other members of the congregation.

The Witnessing and Blessing of a Marriage

Concerning the Service

This rite is appropriately celebrated in the context of the Holy Eucharist and may take place at the principal Sunday Liturgy. This rite then replaces the Ministry of the Word. A bishop or priest normally presides. Parallel texts from Enriching Our Worship 1 are included as options for elements of this rite.

At least one of the couple must be a baptized Christian, and the marriage shall conform to the laws of the state and canons of this church.

Two or more presenters, who may be friends, parents, family members, or drawn from the local assembly, may present the couple to the presider and the assembly.

As indicated in the opening address, the consent, and the blessing of the rings, the rite may be modified for use with a couple who have previously made a lifelong commitment to one another.

The Witnessing and Blessing of a Marriage

The Word of God

Gathering

The couple joins the assembly.

A hymn of praise, Psalm, or anthem may be sung, or instrumental music may be played.

The Presider says the following, the people standing
Presider   Blessed be God: Father, Son, and Holy Spirit.
People   Blessed be God, now and for ever. Amen.

In place of the above may be said
Presider   Blessed be the one, holy, and living God.
People   Glory to God for ever and ever.

From Easter Day through the Day of Pentecost
Presider   Alleluia. Christ is risen.
People   The Lord is risen indeed. Alleluia.

In place of the above may be said
Presider   Alleluia. Christ is risen.
People   Christ is risen indeed. Alleluia.

Then may be said
Presider   Beloved, let us love one another,
People   For love is of God.

II. LITURGICAL RESOURCES

Presider Whoever does not love does not know God,
People For God is love.

Presider Since God so loves us,
People Let us love one another.

The Presider may address the assembly in these words

> Dear friends in Christ, *or* Dearly beloved,
> in the name of God and the Church
> we have come together today with N. N. and N. N.,
> to witness the vows they make,
> committing themselves to one another
> in marriage [according to the laws of the state
>   [or civil jurisdiction of X].
> Forsaking all others,
> they will bind themselves to one another
> in a covenant of mutual fidelity and steadfast love,
> remaining true to one another in heart, body, and mind,
> as long as they both shall live.
>
> The lifelong commitment of marriage
> is not to be entered into lightly or thoughtlessly,
> but responsibly and with reverence.
> Let us pray, then, that God will give them the strength
> to remain steadfast in what they vow this day.
> Let us also pray for the generosity
> to support them in the commitment they undertake
> and for the wisdom to see God at work in their life together.

Or this, for those who have previously made a lifelong commitment to one another

> Dear friends in Christ, *or* Dearly beloved,
> in the name of God and the Church
> we have come together today with N. N. and N. N.,
> to witness the sacred vows they make this day
> as they are married [according to the laws of the state
>   or civil jurisdiction of X],
> and reaffirm their commitment to one another.
> Forsaking all others,
> they will renew their covenant of mutual fidelity
>   and steadfast love,
> remaining true to one another in heart, body, and mind,
> as long as they both shall live.

Let us pray, then, that God will give them the strength
to remain steadfast in what they vow this day.
Let us also pray for the generosity
to support them in the commitment they undertake,
and for the wisdom to see God at work in their life together.

The Collect of the Day

Presider   The Lord be with you.   *or*   God be with you.
People   And also with you.
Presider   Let us pray.

The Presider says one of the following Collects

> God of abundance:
> assist by your grace N. and N.,
> whose covenant of love and fidelity we witness this day.
> Grant them your protection, that with firm resolve
> they may honor and keep the vows they make;
> through Jesus Christ our Savior,
> who lives and reigns with you in the unity of the
>   Holy Spirit,
> one God, for ever and ever. *Amen.*

or this

> Almighty and everliving God:
> look tenderly upon N. and N.,
> who stand before you in the company of your Church.
> Let their life together bring them great joy.
> Grant them so to love selflessly and live humbly,
> that they may be to one another and to the world
> a witness and a sign of your never-failing love and care;
> through Jesus Christ your Son our Lord,
> who lives and reigns with you and the Holy Spirit,
> one God, to the ages of ages. *Amen.*

or this

> O God, faithful and true,
> whose steadfast love endures for ever:
> we give you thanks for sustaining N. and N. in the life
>   they share
> and for bringing them to this day.
> Nurture them and fill them with joy in their life together,

continuing the good work you have begun in them;
and grant us, with them, a dwelling place eternal in
    the heavens
where all your people will share the joy of perfect love,
and where you, with the Son and the Holy Spirit, live
    and reign,
one God, now and for ever. *Amen.*

or this

For those who bring children

Holy Trinity, one God,
three Persons perfect in unity and equal in majesty:
Draw together with bonds of love and affection
N. and N., who with *their families*
seek to live in harmony and forbearance all their days,
that their joining together will be to us
a reflection of that perfect communion
which is your very essence and life,
O Father, Son, and Holy Spirit,
who live and reign in glory everlasting. *Amen.*

The Lessons

The people sit. Then one or more of the following passages of Scripture is read. If the Holy Communion is to be celebrated, a passage from the Gospels always concludes the Readings. When the blessing is celebrated in the context of the Sunday Eucharist, the Readings of the Sunday are used, except with the permission of the Bishop.

    Ruth 1:16-17
    1 Samuel 18:1b, 3, 20:16-17, 42a;
        or 1 Samuel 18:1-4
    Ecclesiastes 4:9-12
    Song of Solomon 2:10-13, 8:6-7
    Micah 4:1-4

    Romans 12:9-18
    1 Corinthians 12:31b-13:13
    2 Corinthians 5:17-20
    Galatians 5:14, 22-26
    Ephesians 3:14-21
    Colossians 3:12-17
    1 John 3:18-24
    1 John 4:7-16, 21

When a biblical passage other than one from the Gospels is to be read, the Reader announces it with these words

Reader   A Reading from _____.

After the Reading, the Reader may say
> The Word of the Lord.

or
> Hear what the Spirit is saying to God's people.

or
> Hear what the Spirit is saying to the Churches.

People   Thanks be to God.

Between the Readings, a Psalm, hymn, or anthem may be sung or said. Appropriate Psalms are

Psalm 65	Psalm 126
Psalm 67	Psalm 127
Psalm 85:7-13	Psalm 133
Psalm 98	Psalm 148
Psalm 100	Psalm 149:1-5

Appropriate passages from the Gospels are

Matthew 5:1-16	John 15:9-17
Mark 12:28-34	John 17:1-2, 18-26
Luke 6:32-38	

All standing, the Deacon or Priest reads the Gospel, first saying
> The Holy Gospel of our Lord Jesus Christ according to _____.

or
> The Holy Gospel of our Savior Jesus Christ according to _____.

People   Glory to you, Lord Christ.

After the Gospel, the Reader says
> The Gospel of the Lord.

People   Praise to you, Lord Christ.

The Sermon

The Witnessing of the Vows and the Blessing of the Covenant

The couple comes before the assembly. If there is to be a presentation, the presenters stand with the couple, and the Presider says to them

Presider Who presents N. and N., as they seek the blessing of God and the Church on their love and life together?

Presenters We do.

Presider Will you love, respect, and pray for N. and N., and do all in your power to stand with them in the life they will share?

Presenters We will.

The Presider then addresses the couple, saying

Presider N. and N., you have come before God and the Church to exchange and renew solemn vows with one another and to ask God's blessing.

The Presider addresses one member of the couple, saying

Presider N., do you freely and unreservedly offer yourself to N.?

Answer I do.

Presider Will you live together in faithfulness and holiness of life as long as you both shall live?

Answer I will, with God's help.

The Presider addresses the other member of the couple, saying

Presider N., do you freely and unreservedly offer yourself to N.?

Answer I do.

Presider Will you continue to live together in faithfulness and holiness of life as long as you both shall live?

Answer I will, with God's help.

The assembly stands, the couple faces the people, and the Presider addresses them, saying

Presider Will all of you gathered to witness these vows do all in your power to uphold and honor this couple in the covenant they make?

People We will.

Presider	Will you pray for them, especially in times of trouble, and celebrate with them in times of joy?
People	We will.

The Prayers

The Presider then introduces the prayers

Presider	Then let us pray for N. and N. in their life together and for the concerns of this community.

A Deacon or another leader bids prayers for the couple.

Prayers for the Church and for the world, for the concerns of the local community, for those who suffer or face trouble, and for the departed are also appropriate. If the rite takes place in the principal Sunday worship of the congregation, the rubric concerning the Prayers of the People on page 359 of the Book of Common Prayer is followed.

Adaptations or insertions may be made to the form that follows. A bar in the margin indicates a bidding that may be omitted.

Leader	For N. and N., seeking your blessing and the blessing of your holy people; Loving God, *or* Lord, in your mercy,
People	Hear our prayer.
Leader	For a spirit of loving-kindness to shelter them all their days; Loving God, *or* Lord, in your mercy,
People	Hear our prayer.
Leader	For friends to support them and communities to enfold them; Loving God, *or* Lord, in your mercy,
People	Hear our prayer.
Leader	For peace in their home and love in their family; Loving God, *or* Lord, in your mercy,
People	Hear our prayer.
Leader	For the grace and wisdom to care for the children you entrust to them [*or may entrust to them*]; Loving God, *or* Lord, in your mercy,
People	Hear our prayer.

II. LITURGICAL RESOURCES

Leader   For the honesty to acknowledge when they hurt each other, and the humility to seek each other's forgiveness and yours;
Loving God,   *or*   Lord, in your mercy,

People   Hear our prayer.

Leader   For the outpouring of your love through their work and witness;
Loving God,   *or*   Lord, in your mercy,

People   Hear our prayer.

Leader   For the strength to keep the vows each of us has made;
Loving God,   *or*   Lord, in your mercy,

People   Hear our prayer.

The leader may add one or more of the following biddings

Leader   For all who have been reborn and made new in the waters of Baptism;
Loving God,   *or*   Lord, in your mercy,

People   Hear our prayer.

Leader   For those who lead and serve in communities of faith;
Loving God,   *or*   Lord, in your mercy,

People   Hear our prayer.

Leader   For those who seek justice, peace, and concord among nations;
Loving God,   *or*   Lord, in your mercy,

People   Hear our prayer.

Leader   For those who are sick and suffering, homeless and poor;
Loving God,   *or*   Lord, in your mercy,

People   Hear our prayer.

Leader   For victims of violence and those who inflict it;
Loving God,   *or*   Lord, in your mercy,

People   Hear our prayer.

Leader   For communion with all who have died [especially those whom we remember this day: _____];
Loving God,   *or*   Lord, in your mercy,

People   Hear our prayer.

The Presider concludes the Prayers with the following or another appropriate Collect

> Giver of every gift, source of all goodness,
> hear the prayers we bring before you
> for N. and N., who seek your blessing this day.
> Strengthen them as they share in the saving work of Jesus,
> and bring about for them and for all you have created
> the fullness of life he promised,
> who now lives and reigns for ever and ever. *Amen.*

If the Eucharist is to follow, the Lord's Prayer is omitted here.

Leader	And now, as our Savior Christ has taught us, we are bold to say,	As our Savior Christ has taught us, we now pray,

People and Leader

Our Father, who art in heaven,	Our Father in heaven,
hallowed be thy Name,	hallowed be your Name,
thy kingdom come,	your kingdom come,
thy will be done,	your will be done,
on earth as it is in heaven.	on earth as in heaven.
Give us this day our daily bread.	Give us today our daily bread.
And forgive us our trespasses,	Forgive us our sins
as we forgive those	as we forgive those
who trespass against us.	who sin against us.
And lead us not into temptation,	Save us from the time of trial,
but deliver us from evil.	and deliver us from evil.
For thine is the kingdom,	For the kingdom, the power,
and the power, and the glory,	and the glory are yours for
ever and ever. Amen.	now and for ever. Amen.

The Marriage

The people sit. The couple stands, facing the Presider.

Presider   N. and N., I invite you now, illumined by the Word of God and strengthened by the prayer of this community, to make your covenant before God and the Church.

Each member of the couple, in turn, takes the hand of the other and says

> In the name of God,
> I, N., give myself to you, N. and take you to myself.
> I will support and care for you by the grace of God:
> in times of sickness, in times of health.
> I will hold and cherish you in the love of Christ:
> in times of plenty, in times of want.
> I will honor and love you with the Spirit's help:
> in times of anguish, in times of joy,
> forsaking all others, as long as we both shall live.
> This is my solemn vow.

or this

> In the name of God,
> I, N., give myself to you, N. and take you to myself.
> I will support and care for you:
> in times of sickness, in times of health.
> I will hold and cherish you:
> in times of plenty, in times of want.
> I will honor and love you:
> in times of anguish, in times of joy,
> forsaking all others, as long as we both shall live.
> This is my solemn vow.

If rings are to be exchanged, they are brought before the Presider, who prays using the following words

> Let us pray.
> Bless, O God, these rings
> as signs of the enduring covenant
> N. and N. have made with each other,
> through Jesus Christ our Lord. *Amen.*

The two people place the rings on the fingers of one another, first the one, then the other, saying

> N., I give you this ring as a symbol of my vow,
> and with all that I am, and all that I have, I honor you,
> in the name of God.   *or*   in the name of the Father, and of
> the Son, and of the Holy Spirit.

If the two have previously given and worn rings as a symbol of their commitment, the rings may be blessed on the hands of the couple, the Presider saying

> Let us pray.
> By the rings which they have worn, faithful God,
> N. and N. have shown to one another and the world
> their love and faithfulness.
> Bless now these rings, that from this day forward
> they may be signs of the vows N. and N. have exchanged
> in your presence and in the communion of your Church,
> through Christ our Lord. *Amen.*

Pronouncement

The Presider joins the right hands of the couple and says

> Now that N. and N. have exchanged vows of love
>   and fidelity
> in the presence of God and the Church,
> I pronounce that they are married [according to the laws
> of the state *or* civil jurisdiction of X].
> and bound to one another
> as long as they both shall live. *Amen.*

Blessing of the Couple

As the couple stands or kneels, the Presider invokes God's blessing upon them, saying

>Let us pray.
>Most gracious God,
>we praise you for the tender mercy and unfailing care
>revealed to us in Jesus the Christ
>and for the great joy and comfort bestowed upon us
>in the gift of human love.
>We give you thanks for N. and N.,
>and the covenant of faithfulness they have made.
>Pour out the abundance of your Holy Spirit upon them.
>Keep them in your steadfast love;
>protect them from all danger;
>fill them with your wisdom and peace;
>lead them in holy service to each other and the world.

The Presider continues with one of the following

>God the Father,
>God the Son,
>God the Holy Spirit,
>bless, preserve, and keep you,
>and mercifully grant you rich and boundless grace,
>that you may please God in body and soul.
>God make you a sign of the loving-kindness and
>   steadfast fidelity
>manifest in the life, death, and resurrection of our Savior,
>and bring you at last to the delight of the heavenly banquet,
>where he lives and reigns for ever and ever. *Amen.*

or this

>God, the holy and undivided Trinity,
>bless, preserve, and keep you,
>and mercifully grant you rich and boundless grace,
>that you may please God in body and soul.
>God make you a sign of the loving-kindness and
>   steadfast fidelity
>manifest in the life, death, and resurrection of our Savior,
>and bring you at last to the delight of the heavenly banquet,
>where he lives and reigns for ever and ever. *Amen.*

The Peace

The Presider bids the Peace.

Presider   The peace of the Lord be always with you.
People   And also with you.

In place of the above may be said

Presider   The peace of Christ be always with you.
People   And also with you.

The liturgy continues with the Holy Communion. When the Eucharist is not celebrated, the Presider blesses the people. The Deacon, or in the absence of a Deacon, the Priest, dismisses them.

At the Eucharist

The liturgy continues with the Offertory, at which the couple may present the offerings of bread and wine.

The following proper preface may be used.

>Because in the giving of two people to each other in
>   faithful love
>you reveal the joy and abundant life you share
>   with your Son Jesus Christ and the Holy Spirit.

The following postcommunion prayer may be used.

>God our strength and joy,
>we thank you for the communion of our life together,
>for the example of holy love that you give us in N. and N.,
>and for the Sacrament of the Body and Blood
>   of our Savior Jesus Christ.
>Grant that it may renew our hope
>and nourish us for the work you set before us,
>to witness to the presence of Christ in the world,
>through the power of your Spirit,
>to the glory of your Name. Amen.

The Blessing of a Civil Marriage 2

The rite begins as prescribed for celebrations of the Holy Eucharist, using the Collect and Lessons appointed in the Marriage service.

After the Gospel (and homily), the couple stand before the Celebrant, who addresses them in these or similar words

> N. and N., you have come here today to seek the blessing of God and of his Church upon your marriage. I require, therefore, that you promise, with the help of God, to fulfill the obligations which Christian Marriage demands.

The Presider then addresses the couple, saying

> N., you have taken N. to be your *wife/husband/spouse*. Do you promise to love *her/him*, comfort *her/him*, honor and keep *her/him*, in sickness and in health, and, forsaking all others, to be faithful to *her/him* as long as you both shall live?

Answer   I do.

The Celebrant then addresses the congregation, saying

> Will you who have witnessed these promises do all in your power to uphold these two persons in their marriage?

People   We will.

If rings are to be blessed, the members of the couple extend their hands toward the Priest [or Bishop], who says

> Bless, O Lord, these rings to be signs of the vows by which N. and N. have bound themselves to each other; through Jesus Christ our Lord. *Amen.*

The Celebrant joins the right hands of the couple and says

        Those whom God has joined together let no one put asunder.

People   Amen.

The service continues with The Prayers on page 14.

An Order for Marriage 2

If it is desired to celebrate a marriage otherwise than as provided on page 423 of The Book of Common Prayer, or in the trial-use liturgies "The Witnessing and Blessing of a Marriage" or "The Celebration and Blessing of a Marriage 2," this Order is used.

Normally, the celebrant is a priest or bishop. Where permitted by civil law, and when no priest or bishop is available, a deacon may function as celebrant, but does not pronounce a nuptial blessing.

The laws of the State and the Canons of this Church having been complied with, the couple, together with their witnesses, families, and friends assemble in the church or in some other convenient place.

1. The teaching of the Church concerning Holy Matrimony, as it is declared in the formularies and Canons of this Church, is briefly stated.

2. The intention of the couple to enter the state of matrimony, and their free consent, is publicly ascertained.

3. One or more Readings, one of which is always from Holy Scripture, may precede the exchange of vows. If there is to be a Communion, a Reading from the Gospel is always included.

4. The vows are exchanged, using the following form In the Name of God,

    I, N., take you, N., to be my
    wife/husband/spouse, to have and to hold
    from this day forward,
    for better for worse, for richer for poorer,

in sickness and in health, to love and to cherish,
until we are parted by death.
This is my solemn vow.

or this

I, N., take thee N., to my wedded
wife/husband/spouse, to have and to hold from
this day forward,
for better for worse, for richer for poorer,
in sickness and in health, to love and to cherish,
till death us do part, according to God's holy
ordinance; and thereto I plight [or give] thee my troth.

5. The Celebrant declares the union of the couple, in the Name of the Father, and of the Son, and of the Holy Spirit.

6. Prayers are offered for the couple, for their life together, for the Christian community, and for the world.

7. A priest or bishop pronounces a solemn blessing upon the couple.

8. If there is no Communion, the service concludes with the Peace, the couple first greeting each other. The Peace may be exchanged throughout the assembly.

9. If there is to be a Communion, the service continues with the Peace and the Offertory. The Holy Eucharist may be celebrated either according to Rite One or Rite Two, or according to the Order on page 400 of the Book of Common Prayer 1979.

Prefaces for Marriage

Note: The following Proper Preface is proposed for trial use as an addition to the Preface for Rite I, BCP p. 349.

Marriage 2

Because in the marriage of two people in faithful love thou dost reveal unto us the joy and abundant life thou sharest with thy Son Jesus Christ and the Holy Ghost.

Note: The following Proper Preface is proposed for trial use as an addition to the Preface for Rite II, BCP p. 381.

Marriage 2

Because in the marriage of two people in faithful love you reveal the joy and abundant life you share with your Son Jesus Christ and the Holy Spirit.

III. Essays: Christian Perspectives on Marriages and Family Life Today

prepared by the
Task Force on the Study of Marriage 2015-2018

Contents

Introduction: Christian Perspectives on Marriages and Family Life Today
Biblical and Theological Foundations for Relationships
Culture, Ethnicity, and Marriage
Householding
Singleness
Sexual Intimacy: A Complex Gift
Responses to the Essays
For Further Reading: Marriage, Family, and Sexuality
Clergy, Church, and State: A Continuing Debate

Introduction: Christian Perspectives on Marriages and Family Life Today

Six years ago, the 2012 General Convention of the Episcopal Church created a Task Force on the Study of Marriage charged with exploring "biblical, theological, historical, liturgical, and canonical dimensions of marriage," and to "consider issues raised by changing societal and cultural norms and legal structures" (Resolution 2012-A050). The task force produced several essays, including one on "Changing Trends and Norms in Marriages." In its executive summary, the task force reported:

> The main issue that we identified for our reflection as a church has to do with the current drop in marriage rates, and for those who do marry, a delay until a later age than ever before. Cohabitation, as a temporary option or alternative to marriage, is significantly on the rise.

The task force also explored "differences in marriage trends among groups identified by race and ethnicity: African Americans, Hispanics and Latinos, Native Americans, and Asian Americans."[1]

The 2015 General Convention called for an expanded task force to continue this work, including further exploration of "those contemporary trends and norms identified by the Task Force on the Study of Marriage in the previous triennium," and to "explore biblical, theological, moral, liturgical, cultural, and pastoral perspectives on these matters, and develop written materials about them which represent the spectrum of understanding in our Church and which include responses from theologians, ethicists, pastors, liturgists, social scientists, and educators who are not members of the expanded Task Force, and whose perspectives represent the spectrum

---

1 Introduction, Appendix 1: Essays on Marriage, in Report of the Task Force on the Study of Marriage to the 78th General Convention (Reports to General Convention, 1976-2015, Archives of the Episcopal Church), p. 12, https://www.episcopalarchives.org/e-archives/gc_reports/reports/2015/bb_2015-R044.pdf (accessed 8/19/17). Essay 7, "Changing Trends and Norms in Marriages," is on pp. 88-98 of the report. The essays are included below in their entirety.

of understandings on these matters in our Church" (Resolution 2015-A037).

The task force has responded to this charge by producing a series of short essays that are intended to invite reflection and conversation about marriage, intimate human relationships, and human sexuality from a Christian perspective. The essays in this series build on the essays produced by the earlier task force, and they rely on the data in the essay "Changing Trends and Norms in Marriages."

In summer 2017, the task force sent first drafts of these essays to scholars, pastors, and educators and invited responses. The twenty replies we received informed the final revisions of the essays. A final essay lists the respondents and summarizes the critiques and suggestions that were not incorporated into the essays.

The task force also circulated a survey in fall 2016 that invited Episcopalians to tell us about their experiences of marriage and other intimate human relationships. We have incorporated a few of these responses in the essays to illustrate some of the realities of marriage, singleness, and family life in our contemporary contexts.

We encourage congregations and other groups to discuss these essays. Several questions for reflection follow each essay, and a bibliography offers resources for further study.

Over the centuries, Anglicans have developed theology that is rooted in Scripture, draws upon the breadth of Christian tradition, and is in dialogue with its contemporary context. These brief essays seek to do the same. They offer a foundation for a Christian understanding of human relationships, and they explore how we understand God to be at work in the complexity of intimate human relationships, including marriage, in our time, in the various contexts in which the Episcopal Church is located today. We invite Episcopalians to join us in this theological reflection, seeking to understand the blessings of lifelong committed relationships and to discern how to respond pastorally to individuals and couples in the midst of changing social and cultural norms.

Biblical and Theological Foundations for Relationships

Even before we are born, we are in relationship, as God knits us together in our mother's womb (Psalm 139:13). We grow and develop in a network of relationships, including but not limited to family, friendship, and marriage. Because we are created in the image of God (Genesis 1:27-28), human beings are created for relationship.

Christians understand ourselves to be drawn into relationship with God and with one another through Christ. Faith in the incarnate Word awakens us to the promise of right relationship that is God's desire for all humankind.

"The heart of Christian faith is the encounter with the God of Jesus Christ who makes possible both our union with God and communion with each other. In this encounter God invites people to share in divine life and grace through Jesus Christ by the power of the Holy Spirit; at the same time, we are called to live in new relationship with one other, as we are gathered together by the Spirit into the body of Christ."[2]

God's love is revealed in Jesus, the Word who became flesh and lived among us (John 1:14). From Jesus, we learn that loving God with our whole being is integrally connected with loving our neighbor as ourselves (Matthew 22:36-40). In his life and teaching, Jesus taught and embodied the love of neighbor commanded in Jewish Law (Leviticus 19:18). Jesus enacted God's self-giving love, for example, by feeding the multitudes (Matthew 15:32-38). After taking on the role of a servant and washing the feet of his disciples (John 13:1-15), Jesus then gave his disciples a new commandment: to love one another as he loved them (John 13:34-35).

Loving one another is not limited to family or the Christian community, as the Baptismal Covenant in the 1979 Book of Common Prayer indicates: "Will you seek and serve Christ in all persons, loving your neighbor as yourself?" (p. 305) Love of neighbor requires

---
[2] Catherine Mowry LaCugna, "The Practical Trinity," Christian Century (July 15-22, 1992), 679.

concern for the whole human family: "Will you strive for justice and peace among all people, and respect the dignity of every human being?" (p. 305) The Baptismal Covenant thus calls us to a way of life that is not only loving but also liberating and life-giving.

We make these baptismal promises in response to the affirmation of faith (the Apostles' Creed) that proclaims God's mission of creating, redeeming, and sanctifying love for the world. Through baptism, we become members of a community of faith that recognizes God at work in the world, from the beginning of creation to the promised new creation, a community that extends through time as the communion of saints. Baptism signifies God's claim on us as beloved children of God and marks us as Christ's own (BCP p. 308). Our participation in baptism and eucharist sustains us in our relationships with people and communities throughout the world, and with all creation.[3]

While Christians strive to love as Christ loved us, following the way of Jesus is difficult. All too often Christians fall short as we wrestle with the evil powers of this world and our own sinful desires (BCP p. 302), as the Baptismal Covenant recognizes: "Will you persevere in resisting evil, and whenever you fall into sin, repent and return to the Lord?" (BCP p. 304).

Like Christians today, the earliest Christian communities struggled to fulfill Jesus' new commandment of love. Writing to the Christian community in Corinth, a community that was divided among themselves (I Corinthians 1:11-12), the apostle Paul exhorted them to recognize their unity in the body of Christ through baptism (I Corinthians 12:12-13), then called them to love one another. In a passage frequently read at wedding ceremonies, though originally intended for the entire Christian community at Corinth, Paul explained, "Love is patient; love is kind; love is not envious or boastful or arrogant or rude. It does not insist on its own way; it is not irritable or resentful; it does not rejoice in wrongdoing, but rejoices in the truth. It bears all things, believes all things, hopes all things, endures all things" (I Corinthians 13:4-7).

In his letter to the Philippians, Paul made clear that our love for one another is to be a selfless love that is rooted in Christ's incarnation. "Be of the same mind, having the same love, being in full accord and of one mind. Do nothing from selfish ambition or conceit, but in humility regard others as better than yourselves. Let each of you look not to your own interests, but to the interests of others. Let the same

---

[3] "Faith, Hope, and Love: Theological Resources for Blessing Same-Sex Relationships," in "I Will Bless You, and You Will Be a Blessing," Liturgical Resources 1, revised and expanded edition (New York: Church Publishing, Inc., 2015), 39-43.

mind be in you that was in Christ Jesus, who… emptied himself… being born in human likeness" (Philippians 2:2-7). God's self-giving love, revealed most especially in the incarnation, not only casts down the mighty, it also lifts up the lowly (The Song of Mary, Luke 1:46-55; see also The Song of Hannah, I Samuel 2:1-10).

It is evident in Jewish teaching that this love extends beyond our family and nearest neighbors. The Law of Moses states, "You also shall love the stranger, for you were strangers in the land of Egypt" (Deuteronomy 10:19), a principle that Jesus extended in radical ways when he redefined his family not as those with whom he shared ties of blood but as those "who hear the word of God and do it" (Luke 8:21, also Matthew 12:50 and Mark 3:35) and taught that those who would be children of God must care at great personal cost for those whom they have been taught are unworthy of such attention (Luke 10:25-37).

Like all human beings, Christians do not always live in the way of love. Striving for power or position, jealousy, factionalism, destructive uses of substances, spiritual manipulation, and loveless or indiscriminate sexual behavior are just a few of the ways that relationships are distorted and sinful. When Christians fail to live in the way of love, they can seek forgiveness from one another, and from God, an essential part of baptismal living. Christians are able to acknowledge their faults and seek forgiveness through Jesus Christ, who makes known God's love and offers forgiveness of sins.

By the power of the Holy Spirit, God continues to be present among us, saving us from sin, seeking communion with us and all creation, drawing us toward the promised new creation. The fruit of the Spirit, the apostle Paul tells us, is "love, joy, peace, patience, kindness, generosity, faithfulness, gentleness, and self-control" (Galatians 5:22-23). Those who live by the Spirit grow in holiness of life as they embody these qualities in their relationships, including marriage and family.

Questions for Consideration

1. Is there anything of Jesus' own character or teachings that has taught you something about "right relationship" in your life?

2. The church speaks of "communion with God and one another." In the Eucharist, do you sense a communion with God and other people? If so, what is that like? How has this affected how you are in relationship with others?

3. We are urged to "love and serve one another as Christ loved and served us." Can you think of times when Christ's example of love and service affected your love and service to others?

4. How have you tried to live out the Baptismal Covenant's call to "resist evil" in yourself and/or the world around you?

5. Do you sense a connection between God's forgiveness of you and your forgiving or being forgiven by others in relationship? If so, what is that like?

Culture, Ethnicity, and Marriage

Resolution 2015-A037 asked the Task Force on the Study of Marriage to "explore... differences in marriage patterns between ethnic and racial groups."[4] An early effort to summarize data on marriage patterns among differing racial and ethnic groups ran into two insurmountable problems. First was the impossibility of including all the racial and ethnic groups present in The Episcopal Church.[5] Second, and more significant, was the overwhelmingly negative response from many on the Task Force, who found that this approach reinforced harmful, offensive stereotypes. Especially in a time of increased harassment of and hate crimes against non-white persons, we believed it was irresponsible and un-Christian to add to the burden of racism that people of color bear.[6] A third important factor was that the Task Force had already addressed the data in the previous triennium. The Blue Book report of 2015 discussed varying relationship patterns among different groups throughout The Episcopal Church.[7] Therefore, this essay takes up what was largely unexamined in 2015: the importance of understanding power and culture. We seek to offer the Church a tool that could be valuable to couples and to clergy ministering with them, and so we turned to the need for cultural

---

4 Resolution 2015-A037, "Appoint an Expanded Task Force on the Study of Marriage," https://www.episcopalarchives.org/cgi-bin/acts/acts_resolution.pl?resolution=2015-A037 (accessed March 30, 2017). Some of the racial and ethnic differences in marriage patterns are explored in "Essay Seven: Changing Trends and Norms in Marriages," Essays on Marriage, appendix to the Report of the Task Force on the Study of Marriage to the 78th General Convention (2015), 575-78, https://www.episcopalarchives.org/e-archives/gc_reports/reports/2015/bb_2015-R044.pdf (accessed March 30, 2017).
5 Our denomination consists of congregations in more than a dozen countries, and the Task Force's best efforts to solicit input from the whole Episcopal Church, in all its geographical, racial, ethnic, and cultural diversity, unfortunately did not yield responses from Province IX.
6 Southern Poverty Law Center, "Hate Groups Increase for Second Consecutive Year as Trump Electrifies Radical Right," February 15, 2017, https://www.splcenter.org/news/2017/02/15/hate-groups-increase-second-consecutive-year-trumpelectrifies-radical-right (accessed March 25, 2017).
7 Task Force on the Study of Marriage, Blue Book 2015, pp. 93ff, https://extranet.generalconvention.org/staff/files/download/12485.pdf (accessed September 26, 2017).

competency among all people interacting with couples, including the partners themselves.

We start with the simple definition found in the Merriam-Webster dictionary. Culture is "the integrated pattern of human knowledge, belief, and behavior that depends upon the capacity for learning and transmitting knowledge to succeeding generations." Culture is dynamic and fluid; elders and peers transmit culture to us across the span of our lifetimes. For our purposes, culture shapes the norms and expectations of individuals, couples, and families. Culture is one more element to consider during premarital counseling. A focus on culture might expand the work done with couples with respect to their family of origin. For couples in an interracial or inter-cultural relationship, and for families formed by interracial adoption, the development of cultural competency is both a product of the relationship and vital to its strength. A Swedish woman married to an American man says:

> I've been married to the same man for 48½ years (½ is important according to my granddaughter), and we've had our ups and downs—some of the downs as a result of my massive culture shock when arriving in the US as a newly-wed in 1968... The only person I could be myself with was my husband...[8]

Everyone is part of a culture; it conditions what we think of as normal. For those who are part of a majority culture, their distinctive cultural identity may be unexamined, and all other cultures are thought of as "abnormal" or "other." For some it may take time and encouragement to see and name their cultural heritage, especially for those who are accustomed to thinking of culture as something other people have, or who have limited experience with a diversity of cultures. Traveling to a different region or country can help us to see our own culture, as we recognize that "they do things differently here." By encouraging couples and clergy to explore their cultures, we hope our work will be useful across all racial and ethnic groups.

Every marriage is a complex interplay of culture, family systems, and individual personalities. We offer these questions for couples to consider, for clergy to use when preparing couples for marriage or counseling married couples—really, for anyone to use in a variety of contexts in deepening their own cultural competency.

---

[8] This story is taken from narratives obtained through a survey on relationships circulated throughout The Episcopal Church in fall, winter, and spring of 2016-17 by the Task Force on the Study of Marriage. We were moved by these glimpses of relationship, and they have allowed writers of this series of essays to add a personal context. Through stories we are led to deeper truths about relationship and a profound appreciation of each writer's dignity. We understand that each story is a glimpse of one person's experience and realize that there are many stories to tell.

Questions for Consideration

1. What would you name as your culture or ethnicity? What makes you glad to be a part of that culture or ethnicity? What are the challenges of that culture or ethnicity? In what ways is your culture or ethnicity the same as that of your spouse, and in what ways is it different?

2. What norms and expectations of family relationship and marriage are familiar to you from your own family of origin, geography, and culture or ethnicity?

3. What have you learned from your culture or ethnicity about gender roles? Money? Sexuality? Raising children? Religion?

4. How does racism—the intersection of prejudice and power—affect your daily life? What advantages have you received as a result of your race or ethnicity, and how does that affect your daily life? If you are married or preparing for marriage, what support would you welcome from your spouse as you live with racism, and what would you resist? If your spouse is from a different race or ethnicity, what do they need to know and understand to keep you and themselves safe? How does your experience of power in your cultural context compare to that of your partner? What do you need your spouse to know about your experience of power or authority?

5. In your cultural or ethnic context, what role do parents expect to play in their grown child's marriage? Do your parents expect you to care for them and/or live with them as they grow older? If you are married or preparing for marriage, how involved will your parents be in the lives of your children? Are there special roles that family members are expected to play, either in your wedding ceremony or in your life as a couple?

6. How is emotion communicated in your culture or ethnicity?

7. How is conflict addressed, or not addressed, in your culture or ethnicity?

8. What attitudes towards alcohol, licit or illicit substance use, gambling, etc. have you absorbed from your culture or ethnicity?

9. What role do honor and shame play in your culture or ethnicity? What's the worst thing that could happen to a person of your culture or ethnicity?

10. How are holidays celebrated in your culture or ethnicity? What cultural or ethnic traditions are most important to you?

11. In what ways are the norms of your culture or ethnicity congruent with Christian teachings? Where is your culture or ethnicity in conflict with Christianity, and how do you navigate those areas?

12. What would a person need to know about your culture or ethnicity to understand you?

13. What gifts might your culture or ethnicity give to your friendships and relationships? To your marriage? To your spouse? To your children?

14. What parts of your cultural or ethnic norms do you wish to keep in your life together? What parts would you like to change or leave behind?

Householding

For Christians, the Holy Trinity is an important foundation for understanding relationships. In the Trinity, each member gives to the others and receives from them, creating a dynamic whole that honors and upholds the unique personhood of each. This ideal of community is reflected in the real relationships of human households in which our shared lives, loves, and responsibilities create an atmosphere that is sacred and sanctifying.[9]

In a household that manifests the holiness of the triune God, two or more people join in a common life in which they practice love of neighbor.[10] By sharing space, meals, fellowship, labor, and love, and through the behaviors fostered by such sharing, including mutual service, hospitality, mercy, kindness, gentleness and self-control, the shared life can foster mutual affection and generosity of spirit.[11] As members of a household participate in giving and receiving love with one another, they may grow in the love of God, and their love may extend beyond their household.

Households also provide opportunity to practice forgiveness and reconciliation. In the nearness of a household, its members—finite, imperfect, sinful human creatures—inevitably fail from time to time to treat each other with the love of neighbor that God requires. For example, the marriage service in the 1979 Book of Common Prayer includes this prayer for the couple: "Give them grace, when they hurt each other, to recognize and acknowledge their fault, and to seek each other's forgiveness and yours" (*p. 429*). Bishop Thomas Breidenthal cautions that this prayer does not condone physical or emotional abuse but rather is concerned with "ordinary, everyday unpleasantness: the petty, unkind acts we commit even against those

---

[9] Thomas Breidenthal, *Christian Households* (Boston: Cowley Publications, 1997), p. 159.
[10] Some single persons identify themselves as a household. See the accompanying essay on Singleness for more on this subject.
[11] Breidenthal, *Christian Households*, pp. 1-2, 16.

we love, simply because we are self-centered and sinful."[12] By seeking and offering forgiveness, members of a household can participate in God's mission "to restore all people to unity with God and each other in Christ" (*BCP* p. 855).

Marriage

Christian marriage, as understood today, embodies an equality and mutual service that demonstrate the transformative power of holy householding. Expression of this can be found throughout the liturgies approved for marriage and in The Episcopal Church's teaching on marriage as laid out in the canonical Declaration of Intention signed by a couple prior to the solemnization of their marriage:

> We understand the teaching of the church that God's purpose for our marriage is for our mutual joy, for the help and comfort we will give to each other in prosperity and adversity, and, when it is God's will, for the gift and heritage of children and their nurture in the knowledge and love of God. We also understand that our marriage is to be unconditional, mutual, exclusive, faithful, and lifelong; and we engage to make the utmost effort to accept these gifts and fulfill these duties, with the help of God and the support of our community.[13]

The lifelong nature of this commitment is key to the couple's continuing growth in holiness, as a man married to his wife for 33 years explains:

> In those years we have had times of liking one another and times of hating one another, times of deep and passionate lust for one another and times when the flames of passion have burned cool and low. But through it all we have remained deeply and profoundly in love with one another. This kind of lasting love is, I believe, a choice. I didn't choose to fall in love with my wife, but I have chosen to remain in love with her. Why? Because she helps me become more of the person God intended me to be. She challenges me to reach beyond what I thought I could grasp and to discover the true extent of my reach. She sees me with eyes that are not limited by my poor vision, not clouded by the pain and self-doubt that builds up in life. And being seen through her eyes allows me to achieve more than I would have without her present in my world.[14]

---

12 Thomas Breidenthal, *Sacred Unions: A New Guide to Lifelong Commitment* (Cambridge, MA: Cowley Publications, 2006), p. 101.
13 Canon I.18.4, *The Constitution and Canons of the Episcopal Church* (New York: Church Publishing, Inc., 2015).
14 The stories found in this essay are taken from narratives contained in a survey on relationship

The church's teaching on marriage applies to all couples marrying in The Episcopal Church, including same-sex couples. After several decades of grassroots change and official action, the 2015 General Convention authorized two trial-use liturgies for marriage that can be used by any couple, same-sex or different-sex, with the permission and under the direction of the diocesan bishop. However, our church is not of one mind on this; for example, one married man comments,

> There is a significant number of people who do not believe that tradition or the Bible supports marriage between two people of the same sex. It may be appropriate for civil rights but dubious for the church. I know a priest whose vestry asked him to leave because he would not perform a same-sex marriage.

Although Episcopalians and other Christians have different theological understandings of human sexuality, including same-sex relationships, the Convention directed bishops to make provision for all couples seeking to be married in The Episcopal Church to have access to these liturgies.[15] This has allowed same-sex couples in longtime relationships to solemnize their marriages in church. A man who recently married his husband on the fifteenth anniversary of the date they first met describes their relationship:

> I understand our relationship to be God-given, and sacred. Ours is a committed, monogamous and life-long relationship based upon mutual love and respect. People who know us understand that we bring out the best in each other and those around us. In this sense we live sacramentally as a married couple symbolizing through our love for each other the love that God has for the Church and the World.

As a "natural estate," marriage is created by the intention and vows of a couple to one another, apart from any liturgy of the Church or license by the State. The State's license provides legal protections for the couple, while in the sacramental rite of marriage, the couple make a public commitment to one another and receive the community's prayer and support as well as "the grace and blessing of God to help them fulfill their vows" (*BCP p. 861*). In addition, the Church's canonical requirements for marriage ensure that the couple is

---

circulated throughout The Episcopal Church in fall, winter, and spring of 2016-17 by the Task Force on the Study of Marriage. We were moved by these glimpses of relationship, and they have allowed writers of each of these essays to add a personal context. Through stories we are led to deeper truths about relationship and a profound appreciation of each writer's dignity. We understand that each story is a glimpse of one person's experience and realize that there are many stories to tell.

15 Resolution 2015-A054, "Authorize for Trial Use Marriage and Blessing Rites Contained in 'Liturgical Resources I'," https://www.episcopalarchives.org/cgi-bin/acts/acts_resolution.pl?resolution=2015-A054.

instructed "in the nature, purpose, and meaning, as well as the rights, duties, and responsibilities of marriage."[16] Thus, Christian marriage is to be recommended and affirmed.

Yet Christian marriage is not the only form of household in which participants can experience God's blessing. Moreover, abuse is never God's will, and marriage is not appropriate in relationships that are abusive or exploitative. In the realm of healthy relationships, households take many forms in addition to marriage, and commitments to love, service, and a common life come in many forms.

Cohabitation

In cohabitation, a couple form a household based on implicit or explicit promises to contribute to their common good, share responsibilities, influence one another, and ease one another's burdens. The union of household may be "for as long as we can" or "for as far as we can see." The couple may understand the arrangement as a time of discernment about marriage, as an alternative to marriage, or as a prelude to marriage, in which the partners come to know themselves as they grow in knowledge and love of another. Such cohabitation of intimate sexual partners is increasingly common, challenging the church to respond pastorally while also affirming norms for relationship.

In 2000, the General Convention acknowledged couples living in lifelong committed relationships other than marriage and identified qualities expected of these couples as well as married couples: "fidelity, monogamy, mutual affection and respect, careful, honest communication, and the holy love which enables those in such relationships to see in each other the image of God."[17] These characteristics can also provide norms for the relationships of cohabiting couples who have not made a lifelong commitment to each other. A couple who make an examined choice to cohabit and seek to build a loving and life-giving relationship marked by these characteristics may experience God's blessing in their relationship.

The church might consider various pastoral and/or liturgical responses to couples who cohabit. Recognizing the number of Christian couples who live together before marriage, Adrian Thatcher proposes a pastoral approach: "to thank God for the marital values their

---

16 Canon I.18.3c
17 Resolution 2000-D039, "Acknowledge Relationships Other Than Marriage and Existence of Disagreement on the Church's Teaching," https://www.episcopalarchives.org/cgi-bin/acts/acts_resolution.pl?resolution=2000-D039. The resolution also states that these same characteristics apply to other lifelong committed relationships.

togetherness already expresses, and to guide them to the solemnization and deepening of those values in the sacrament of Christian marriage."[18] Rosemary Radford Ruether suggests different forms of covenantal vows for sexual friendships: temporary vows, for younger cohabiting couples who are "not yet ready for permanent commitment personally or economically," and life vows, for those making a lifelong commitment.[19] Michael Lawler and Todd Salzman distinguish between non-nuptial and nuptial cohabiters. For the latter group, who are committed to marry one another, Salzman and Lawler call for a process of nuptial commitment, beginning with a public betrothal ceremony, followed by "nuptial cohabitation" and eventually, a wedding ceremony.[20]

Some cohabiting couples in some legal jurisdictions do not desire any kind of church blessing of their relationship because the state may then consider them to be legally married. The church should be sensitive to this concern.

Households with Children

In a household with children the dynamics of householding take on new dimensions. Adults enter a household with one another as equals in authority, but parents and children have different levels of authority to ensure the healthy upbringing of children. Beyond these differences in authority, many aspects of a household remain the same when adults and children are involved. All can serve, love, and support in ways appropriate to their maturity and capacity. All serve the common good by their participation in the household. New depths of wonder and partnership can be revealed between parents as they partner to raise a child. Sharing roles, stepping in when the other is overwhelmed, communicating joys and concerns associated with the child — all of these open new ways for Christ to be revealed and realized in the household. At the same time raising children is hard work; all parents need the church's support and affirmation.

---

18 Adrian Thatcher, *Theology and Families* (Oxford: Blackwell Publishing, 2007), pp. 135-36.
19 Rosemary Radford Ruether, *Christianity and the Making of the Modern Family* (Boston: Beacon Press, 200), p. 215. In the course of this work the Task Force has heard a desire for a form of life vows for i) older couples who desire to form and to formalize a relationship that is monogamous, unconditional, and lifelong, but is nevertheless something different than a marriage in that it does not include the merging of property, finances, and other legal encumbrances, and for ii) couples for whom the requirement to furnish identification to obtain a marriage license could result in state penalties including deportation, because of their immigration status.
20 Michael G. Lawler and Todd A. Salzman, "People Beginning Sexual Experience," in *The Oxford Handbook of Theology, Sexuality, and Gender*, edited by Adrian Thatcher (Oxford: Oxford University Press, 2015), pp. 566, 568-70.

While the church and society have not always been supportive of same-sex couples raising children, social-science research over the past quarter century has yielded overwhelming evidence "that children of same-sex parents do not differ from those of heterosexual or single parents on a range of social and behavioral outcomes."[21] Same-sex as well as different-sex parents face similar concerns, "such as providing appropriate structure for children, while also being warm and accepting, setting limits, teaching open and honest communication, healthy conflict resolution, and monitoring of child's peer network and extracurricular activities." However, same-sex parents and their children may face challenges because of social stigma and disagreement with extended family members about the validity of the couple's relationship.[22]

The loving self-sacrifice associated with parenting is as true in the adoptive household as it is in every child-rearing household. Perhaps because adoption happens only when parents explicitly desire a child and pursue that good, many adoptive households bring special benefits of engagement and preparation to their child-rearing. In many of these households, children are read to more often and are encouraged more often to participate in extracurricular activities.[23]

Parenting can be especially challenging for a single parent raising one or more children. While some become single parents by choice, for others divorce or the death of a partner may result in the necessity of single-parenting. Single parents do not have the support of a partner with whom to share responsibility, and divorced parents may face particular challenges of co-parenting with a former spouse. Thus the support and affirmation of extended family and community, including the church community, becomes especially important. A great-grandmother reports:

> Of my three grandchildren and two great-grandchildren, only one was born to parents married to each other. We would have preferred that our children and grandson had made different decisions about sexual intimacy and becoming parents. But when faced with unplanned pregnancies, we chose to welcome the births and support these new families.

---

[21] Robert Preidt, "'Overwhelming' Evidence That Same-Sex Parenting Won't Harm Kids," US News and World Report, June 26, 2015, http://health.usnews.com/health-news/articles/2015/06/26/overwhelming-evidence-that-same-sexparenting-wont-harm-kids.

[22] Deanna Linville and Maya O'Neil, "Same Sex Parents and Their Children" (American Association for Marriage and Family Therapy), http://www.aamft.org/imis15/aamft/Content/Consumer_Updates/Samesex_Parents_and_Their_Children.aspx.

[23] Sharon Vandivere, Karin Malm, and Laura Radel, "Adoption USA: A Chartbook Based on the 2007 National Survey of Adoptive Parents" (US Department of Health and Human Services) https://aspe.hhs.gov/pdf-report/adoption-usachartbook-based-2007-national-survey-adoptive-parents.

> We cherish our grandchildren and great-grandchildren, and their parents (our children and grandson) have grown as they have faced the challenges and joys of parenting.

Many families in our communities are blended, including step-parents and children from previous relationships. Blending families is often hard work, but it can also be richly rewarding, as a woman who has been married for 52 years reports:

> We raised three of his children from a previous (extremely unhappy) marriage, and two boys of our own. All have turned out to be strong, wonderful people. This marriage has been very positive and happy, and I am glad to have been married to my husband.

Insights into Householding

Living together shapes us. Whether the household is formed by marriage, cohabitation, parenting, or in some other way, such as monastic communities, roommates, or multigenerational families, the intimacies that come from close contact can create networks of trust and mutuality in which the fruit of the Spirit[24] can be known and shared.

Whatever the form of household, its members have the potential to experience God's grace in their relationships, for God follows love just as surely as love follows God. What is telling is not the type of household we consider, but its nature. Do the members willingly engage love and service? Is the preciousness of all members honored? Is the household free of promiscuity, exploitation, and abusiveness?[25] Are patience and kindness manifest? Or is the household marked by envy, boasting, arrogance, or rudeness? Do members insist on their own way? Are they irritable or resentful? Do they rejoice in wrongdoing, or do they rejoice in the truth?[26] No household will perfectly manifest the love of God, for surely all sin. A commitment to acknowledge occasions of hurt and to seek one another's forgiveness, and God's, is key to growth in holiness.

In the intimacy and mutual responsibility of a household, Christians have an opportunity to participate in God's self-giving love, which is demonstrated in the communion of persons in the triune God. As the members of the household practice love of neighbor, recognizing others in the household as their nearest neighbors, they may deepen their relationships not only with one another but also with God.

24 Galatians 5:22-23
25 Resolution 2000-D039.
26 1 Corinthians 13.

Questions for Consideration

1. What pastoral response and guidance should the church offer to persons who are cohabitating, or are considering cohabitation?

2. How can the church support families who are raising children?

3. What employment practices (e.g. health care, paid family leave, child care, living wage) should the church adopt to support its employees and their families? What public policies should the church advocate to support families?

4. When an unmarried woman becomes pregnant unintentionally, what factors should be weighed in making a moral choice about adoption, abortion, or raising the child as a single parent? What pastoral response and guidance can the church offer to the pregnant woman as she considers this choice, and to the man who has fathered the child?

5. For a woman or man considering becoming a single parent through pregnancy, adoption, or foster parenting, what guidance can the church offer? Under what circumstances is intentional single-parenting a just, moral choice?

6. The Church teaches that Christian Marriage has the qualities of fidelity, monogamy, and lifelong commitment.
    a. Why is emotional and sexual faithfulness essential for a Christian Marriage?
    b. Why is the covenantal relationship between two parties (and two parties only—commonly called monogamy) essential for a Christian Marriage?
    c. Why is lifelong commitment essential for a Christian Marriage?

7. For people considering intimate relationships that do not have all three qualities of fidelity, monogamy, and lifelong commitment, or for people already in such relationships, what pastoral response and guidance should the church offer?

Singleness

Any commentary on single people is inherently challenging because of the diversity present within singleness.[27] Single people may choose to be single and understand this choice as a call from God. Others are unattached involuntarily, either via the death of a spouse, a divorce not of their choosing, physical or mental illness that complicates being in relationship, not having found a partner, or any number of reasons. A single person's primary relationships may be with their family, their friends, an intentional or monastic community, their children and grandchildren, or any combination thereof. Single people may live alone, with roommates, or with family. Adults of all ages can be single. Although society and the church often assume singleness to be a temporary state, a kind of "pre-married" phase, it may last for decades or the entirety of a person's life. Many of the older adults in our congregations will be single for the rest of their lives after the loss of a spouse. Singleness should not then be viewed as a waiting period or as a state less desirable than marriage; it is not "tragic, embarrassing and freakish," as one single priest describes the common stereotype of single people.[28] Singleness is hardly unusual in our time, for that matter. The United States Census Bureau reported in 2015 that 49.7 percent of people age 15 and older were either never married, widowed, divorced, or separated.[29] For some Christians, singleness can be a vocation to which God calls a person for a season or for life. For others, it is a source of grief and pain, a state they would never have chosen for themselves. And for some, singleness

---
[27] A good, though dated, illustration of this diversity is the narratives in Kay Collier-Slone, *Single in the Church: New Ways to Minister with 52% of God's People* (Washington, DC: Alban Institute, 1992), 2-7.
[28] Stephanie Couvela, *Celebrating Celibacy: Sexuality, Intimacy and Wholeness for the Single Adult* (Cambridge: Grove Books, 2007), author's biography.
[29] This age category is defined by the Census Bureau. This figure includes unmarried adults who cohabit with a romantic partner, who are not considered single for the purposes of this essay. United States Census Bureau, "America's Families and Living Arrangements: 2015: Adults," http://www.census.gov/hhes/families/data/cps2015A.html (accessed September 3, 2016).

brings both advantages and disadvantages, just as marriage does for some couples. One single person explains:

> I am single and celibate. Having been this way for most of my life I can't say whether this is more positive or more negative than any other status. It has been simpler, I suspect, in some ways, I only have my own opinion to consider when discerning a move or a change. On the other hand, it can be lonely; and has been more difficult since my parents and brother have all died—I always appreciated a friendly voice on the phone (or in person) of someone who has known me all my life.[30]

Theological reflection on singleness has attempted to lift up the positive qualities of singleness, in contrast to common stereotypes of single people as desperate, lonely, and miserable. Such theological reflection tends to consider singleness from the individualistic viewpoint of white American culture. For example, singleness, to Marie Theresa Coombs and Francis Kelly Nemeck, is a middle course between marriage and celibacy (a vowed state of abstaining from all sexual and romantic relationships); a person who has chosen to be single for the sake of Christ and the Gospel possesses an independence that gives them the freedom for complete dependence on God.[31] Stephanie Couvela asserts that the freedom of celibacy is, at its best, "freedom for a full and creative life."[32] Wesley Hill finds that friendship is the appropriate form of love for him as a gay Christian committed to celibacy, and indeed, many single people possess the spiritual gift of being a remarkable friend.[33] Single people bring many other gifts to the church: self-sufficiency, the creativity born of independence, and often the time and emotional energy to commit to their faith communities that can be in short supply for couples, especially those with young children. The apostle Paul recognized that the devotion of single people to the affairs of the Lord held the Corinthian church together (1 Cor. 7:32-35). The Episcopal Church would benefit from perspectives on singleness drawn from cultures that emphasize community or family over the individual.

---

[30] This story is taken from narratives obtained through a survey on relationships circulated throughout The Episcopal Church in fall, winter, and spring of 2016-17 by the Task Force on the Study of Marriage. We were moved by these glimpses of relationship, and they have allowed writers of this series of essays to add a personal context. Through stories we are led to deeper truths about relationship and a profound appreciation of each writer's dignity. We understand that each story is a glimpse of one person's experience and realize that there are many stories to tell.
[31] Marie Theresa Coombs and Francis Kelly Nemeck, *Discerning Vocations to Marriage, Celibacy and Singlehood* (Collegeville, MN: Liturgical Press, 1994), 186-190.
[32] Couvela, 17.
[33] Wesley Hill, *Spiritual Friendship: Finding Love in the Church as a Gay Christian* (Grand Rapids: Brazos, 2015).

Singleness does not have to mean aloneness. These authors all stress the universal human need for intimacy and particularly for physical touch, which single people may find difficult to fulfill.[34] Everyone requires meaningful human interactions to counteract loneliness and isolation. Many single people receive these interactions through their families, especially in cultures that prize close extended family systems. Some single people are in romantic relationships, yet live by themselves. For other single persons, faith communities can be important in meeting this fundamental need. The sacramentality of human touch found in the exchange of the Peace, the hand of blessing laid on the shoulder, and the hug at coffee hour may be of particular emotional significance for a single person. This may be the only physical touch they receive over the course of the week.

Singleness inevitably raises questions of sexual ethics, and the Task Force's essay "Sexual Intimacy: A Complex Gift" addresses this in more depth. Here, it should be acknowledged that single people have a variety of experiences of sexuality, both with a partner and with themselves, and some single people find grace in sexual intimacy. Pastors, theologians, and ethicists might ask, "What does a healthy theology and ethic of sexuality look like for a single person? How does sexuality fit into holiness of life for a single Christian?" The Task Force essay "Theological Foundations for Christian Relationships" provides a starting point for this kind of reflection.

Though nearly half the population is unmarried, churches often appear unmindful of single people. Any survey of profiles prepared by congregations searching for clergy reveals that parishes' most sought-after demographic is families with young children. This seems to be the consequence of our denominational anxiety about the shrinking and aging of The Episcopal Church: if our Sunday schools and youth groups are full, it must mean that the church isn't failing and it has a future. Yet the often-relentless focus on families with young children sends a message to anyone who does not fit that mold. In a culture in which "family" often means "married couple with children," website banners that declare "We love families! All families welcome!" can inadvertently communicate to single people, as well as couples without children or with grown children, that they are unwanted in the church. Significant resources devoted to family ministry while nothing is offered for adults without children tell a similar story. Congregations, dioceses, and The Episcopal Church must be vigilant that our tag line—The Episcopal Church Welcomes You—does not become a lie for half the population. The vision of church communities that Couvela holds, "where marriages are strengthened and enriched by friends

---

34 Coombs and Nemeck, 198; Couvela, 12.

from outside, where single people can find closeness and touch, where children can have friendships with adults as they grow in faith," is possible only if we acknowledge and celebrate the single people in our midst.[35]

Questions for Consideration

1. In a culture centered around the nuclear family, how does the church acknowledge the dignity of singleness?
2. How does the church teach young people about intimate relationships? What does the church teach young people about intimate relationships?
3. In what ways is it possible for sexual intimacy to be a means of grace for a single person?
4. What practices of discernment can the church provide to people considering the vocations of singleness, marriage, or celibacy? How do we listen for God's call to us regarding intimate relationships?

---

35 Couvela, 25.

Sexual Intimacy: A Complex Gift

During the course of our work, members of the Task Force for the Study of Marriage began to see the subject of sexual intimacy required further study and reflection. While this topic may be broached within the context of preparation for Holy Matrimony, current trends suggest the need to expand the church's teaching and thinking beyond marriage preparation.

Census data reported 6 million households maintained by unmarried couples in 2006.[36] By 2016 the same type of households had increased to 7.2 million.[37] Coupled with the growing numbers of single adults[38] in the United States, the need to provide discussion and potentially guidelines for sexual intimacy seems warranted.

The Task Force is not of one mind about how the church might engage the subject of sexual intimacy. Nor do we have adequate data to confirm the trends cited above in dioceses beyond the United States of America. Still, we see a growing need to teach, counsel, and prepare single individuals, unmarried couples, and married couples to contemplate sexual intimacy as religious people.

When the church considers Holy Scripture for marriage preparation, the church could do the same in teaching and counseling about sexual intimacy for adults. For example, the description of "naked and were not ashamed" could be as important as citing the "one flesh" of the man and his wife in the second chapter of Genesis (Genesis 2:25). Further, a wealth of poetic descriptions of erotic love is found in the

---

[36] United States Census Bureau, "American Community Survey: 2006: Unmarried Partnered Households by Sex of Partner," https://factfinder.census.gov/faces/tableservices/jsf/pages/productview.xhtml?src=bkmk (accessed November 5, 2017).
[37] United States Census Bureau, "American Community Survey: 2016: Unmarried Partnered Households by Sex of Partner," https://factfinder.census.gov/faces/tableservices/jsf/pages/productview.xhtml?src=bkmk (accessed November 5, 2017).
[38] United States Census Bureau, "Facts For Figures: Unmarried and Single Americans Week: Sept. 18-24, 2016," https://www.census.gov/newsroom/facts-for-features/2016/cb16-ff18.html, (accessed November 5, 2017).

Song of Songs. Even if the poems of two lovers found in this book are read as symbolism or metaphor, the poetry remains a sensitive and sensual description of sexual intimacy. Passages such as these may give us insight about God's vision for sexual intimacy.

If we were to consider sexual intimacy a blessing, given by God for the good of God's people, then this blessing is a complex gift. A gift able to bestow joy, deepen love, give pleasure, and kindle the holy in relationship. Like so many of God's gifts, this gift can be more than we could think to ask or imagine on our own. Yet unlike other gifts, this one requires maturity, consent, vulnerability, respect for one's self, and respect for another person. For some, this blessing or gift may require compassionate and skilled teaching from the church.

The church seems to have an understandable desire to speak a single truth for all, or even for a majority, as sexuality is discussed, taught, and addressed in church governance. Still, circumstances require nuanced teaching and theology in response to the variety of situations presented by consenting adults. Sexual expression includes a wide range of behaviors from a casual one-time encounter to a life-long committed relationship where sexual intimacy is one of many types of intimacy.

For some Christians, sexual intimacy is only to be expressed within monogamous heterosexual marriage.[39] From this perspective the gift of sexual intimacy is one of the blessings of marriage. The bodily expression is underscored in the first English Book of Common Prayer (1549). Thomas Cranmer, himself a married man, included among the purposes of marriage, "mutual society, help, and comfort…both in prosperity and adversity." At the giving of the ring the husband said to his wife, "With my body, I thee worship."

For others, sexual intimacy outside of marriage can be an experience of grace.[40] An unmarried woman in a long-time relationship wrote of a robust love life with her partner. "We functioned as a true pair in many ways…that was an aspect of life lacking for me basically all my years…There are people who merely want companionship — a domestic or activity partner. I, however, believe that most of us yearn to be chosen by one other person, and to transcend convenience and/

---

[39] "My understanding of sexual ethics has been that, regardless of whether it's gay or straight, sex outside marriage is wrong." Archbishop of Canterbury Justin Welby, interview with Dominic Lawson, "So Many Crosses to Bear," thetimes.co.uk, March 17, 2013.

[40] "An absolute declaration that every sexual partnership must conform to the pattern of commitment or else have the nature of sin and nothing else is unreal and silly." Former Archbishop of Canterbury Rowan Williams, "The Body's Grace," 10th Michael Harding Memorial Address, Institute for the Study of Christianity and Sexuality, , 1989, reprinted in *Theology and Sexuality: Classic and Contemporary Readings*, edited by Eugene F. Rogers, Jr. (Oxford: Blackwell, 2002), 315-16.

or convention by knowing and being known intimately and uniquely. Such relationships give each partner wings."[41]

Whether sexual relationships are between married or unmarried people, sexual intimacy can be a blessing drawing a couple into deeper bonds of trust, love, vulnerability, and holiness.[42] Such intimacy can also be a source of sorrow, a tool for manipulation, and a method of exploitation. By saying nothing to those in sexually intimate relationships who are not married, the church endorses this grace as only meant for and experienced by married people. It may also assume that all married people have healthy consensual sexual relationships. The church could promote a healthy and holy approach to sexual intimacy with teaching, guidance, and pastoral care for this complex gift.

Resolution 2000 - D039, sets an expectation that life-long committed relationships are to "be characterized by fidelity, monogamy, mutual affection and respect, careful, honest communication, and the holy love which enables those in such relationships to see in each other the image of God." Further, the resolution denounces "promiscuity, exploitation, and abusiveness in the relationships of any of our members." In it the church pledges "to hold all its members accountable to these values, and will provide for them the prayerful support, encouragement, and pastoral care necessary to live faithfully by them."

For those seeking guidance for the expression of sexual intimacy, the values held in this resolution have the potential to inform, support, and guide decision making. This resolution also can provide direction to the church as it seeks to develop pastoral and formational resources regarding sexual intimacy.

---

41 This story is taken from narratives obtained through a survey on relationships circulated throughout The Episcopal Church in fall, winter, and spring of 2016-17 by the Task Force on the Study of Marriage. We were moved by these glimpses of relationship, and they have allowed writers of this series of essays to add a personal context. Through stories we are led to deeper truths about relationship and a profound appreciation of each writer's dignity. We understand that each story is a glimpse of one person's experience and realize that there are many stories to tell.
42 Williams, "The Body's Grace."

Questions for Consideration

1. In what ways does Holy Scripture inform your experience of sexual intimacy?
2. How have you experienced sexual intimacy as God's blessing or gift to you? to your relationship?
3. What does the existence of sexual pleasure teach us about being made in the image of God?
4. What should the Church teach about sexual intimacy for married and unmarried people?
5. How should the church teach young people about the gift of sexual intimacy and the right use of this gift?
6. What support from the Church is needed by older adults in sexually intimate relationships?

Responses to the Essays

In the summer of 2017, an early draft of these essays was shared with the faculty of all ten Episcopal seminaries and an additional group of theologians, ethicists, pastors, liturgists, social scientists, and educators[43] from a broad range of backgrounds for feedback. Twenty individuals or organizations offered responses:

1. Thomas Breidenthal, Bishop of Southern Ohio
2. Isaiah Brokenleg, MDiv student (Diocese of Fond du lac), Church Divinity School of the Pacific
3. Matthew Burdette, Episcopal Church of the Good Shepherd, Dallas
4. Chad Gandiya, Bishop of Harare, Zimbabwe (whose archdeacon responded to each of the questions)
5. Mary Gray-Reeves, Bishop of El Camino Real
6. Scott Gunn, Executive Director of Forward Movement
7. Tobias Haller, 2012-2015 task force member
8. Wesley Hill, Assistant Professor of Biblical Studies, Trinity School for Ministry
9. Anne Hodges-Copple, Bishop Suffragan, Diocese of North Carolina
10. Deon Johnson, St. Paul's Episcopal Church, Brighton, Michigan
11. Lam Chun Wai, Vice Principal and Lecturer in Liturgical Studies, Ming Hua Theological College, Hong Kong
12. Robert MacSwain, Associate Professor of Theology, School of Theology, University of the South
13. Dale B. Martin, Woolsey Professor Emeritus of Religious Studies, Yale University

---

43 2015-A037 Continue the work of the Task Force; Resolve 5.

14. Kevin Moroney, Associate Professor of Liturgics, General Theological Seminary

15. Jane Patterson, Associate Professor of New Testament, & Director of Community Care, Seminary of the Southwest

16. Jenny Te Paa Daniel, Anglican Church in Aotearoa, New Zealand, and Polynesia

17. Adrian Thatcher, Honorary Professor in the Department of Theology and Religion at the University of Exeter, UK; Honorary Fellow in Medical Humanities in the Plymouth University Peninsula Schools of Medicine and Dentistry, UK

18. Kwasi Thornell, Lecturer in Pastoral Theology, Church Divinity School of the Pacific

19. Gerald West, Professor of Biblical Studies, University of Kwazulu-Natal, South Africa

20. The faculty of the Church Divinity School of the Pacific

Responses fell into three general categories:

A. Appreciations of the work;

B. Critiques and suggestions that were incorporated into the final essays;

C. Critiques and suggestions not incorporated into the essays, which are summarized and paraphrased in the six sections below.

1. Personal narratives appear elevated.

Many responders commented on the personal narratives interspersed throughout the essays. Some supported their use. Others wondered:

- Are the personal narratives too supportive of the points in the essays?

- Do the personal narratives paint too rosy a picture of some kinds of relationship, not adequately expressing the challenges some may face?

- Are the personal essays given too central a position in the essays?

- Are the personal narratives truly representational?

- Is there enough balance in the narratives, as between pro and con, male and female, young and old, success and failure in relationship, heterosexual and same-sex, married and unmarried, various cultures, various regions of the church, et cetera?

2. The church should stand for something.

Some responders expressed concern about the approach of the essays, wishing they had taken on a mantle of moral teaching:

- These essays do not speak in a clear moral voice.
- In a regressive world, the church needs to stand for something.
- The very concept of "contemporary trends and norms" is troubling.
- Human society's whims are irrelevant to the calling of the church.
- We should question the validity of contemporary norms.
- We should question where contemporary norms are originating.
- Human life and human sexuality have a specific purpose: we are made for a reason; we are given the gift of sexual expression for a reason.
- Why does a person's sense of "experiencing a blessing" through a certain life-choice, life-style, or activity matter?
- God creates goods for a specific purpose.
- When we misuse these goods harm is done.
- These goods and their purpose have been fully revealed to the Church.
- Our job is not discernment but duty.

3. Culture: strengths and challenges

In these essays, an entire piece is dedicated to culture. Some responders were grateful for the essay's approach, while others expressed concerns:

- Culture is the problem. Culture is relative, while God is the same yesterday, today, and forever.
- The Church will lose its moorings if we begin comparing cultures and bowing to cultural dictates.
- The Church should speak in a clear voice across all cultures.
- In the generation of these essays were enough voices across cultures heard? If not, that undermines the work that has been done.
- The Church is not separate from culture; the Church is and has always been a part of culture.

- Culture is of primary importance if you want to appreciate the richness and diversity of the Body of Christ.
- Aspects of culture can profoundly affect relationships—power dynamics, unique social pressures, effects of continued racism, stressors related to one's living environment, historical injustices, and more. These elements could have been included in the essays.

4. When is sexual intimacy appropriate?

These essays consider foundations for relationship and sexual intimacy. Responders had a number of thoughts in these areas:

- The Church should teach that sexual intimacy is only ever appropriate between married persons.
- The Church should teach that sexual expression between same-sex persons is never acceptable; people with such attraction should concentrate on having lots of good friendships.
- The Church should teach that sexual intimacy is acceptable between persons when their relationship is on a trajectory toward marriage.
- Sexuality is not a particular "gift," but part of the broad giftedness of being human.
- Is "consent" the only firm moral norm underlying the essays?
- What must be present in a relationship for the Church to be able to call sexual expression in that relationship good?
- Do the promises, character, or intent of a relationship determine when sexual expression is appropriate?

5. Regarding pregnancy

These essays do not consider the potential of pregnancy and childbirth, several responders noted:

- Discussions of sexual intimacy should always keep in mind the serious implication of pregnancy.
- Becoming a single parent by choice is an immoral and unjust decision with serious negative implications for the child.
- Marriage is better for the raising of children than cohabitation or separated households. The Church should stand for this.

6. Marriage and sanctification

Several responders expressed a desire to probe Christian Marriage more deeply to understand what makes it special:

- What makes marriage so special among human relationships?
- What makes marriage sacred?
- What makes marriage sanctifying?
- Grace might be found in other kinds of relationships, but it is a sure bet in Christian marriage.
- If we could understand the spiritual process underlying marriage we could open doors in our attempt to understand how God is at work in other forms of relationship.

For Further Reading: Marriage, Family, and Sexuality

Adichie, Chimamanda Ngozi. "The Danger of a Single Story." TED talk, July 2009, https://www.ted.com/talks/chimamanda_adichie_the_danger_of_a_single_story. "The single story creates stereotypes, and the problem with stereotypes is not that they are untrue, but that they are incomplete. They make one story become the only story." Adichie calls us to seek out alternative stories—particularly important when we consider marriage and family patterns across different races, ethnicities, and cultures.

Bradbury, John, and Susannah Cornwall, eds. *Thinking again about Marriage: Key Theological Questions*. London: SCM Press, 2016. The essays in this book explore biblical, historical, theological, and liturgical perspectives on marriage, gender, and sexuality. The authors represent a broad ecumenical spectrum of theologians, pastors, and a social worker.

Breidenthal, Thomas E. Christian *Households: Sanctification of Nearness*. Cambridge, MA: Cowley Publications, 1997. Breidenthal draws upon scripture and, to a lesser extent, Christian tradition to develop a theology of the Christian household, and he proposes criteria to determine which forms of household are holy.

Breidenthal, Thomas E. *Sacred Unions: A New Guide to Lifelong Commitment*. Cambridge, MA: Cowley Publications, 2006. Building on his earlier work on Christian households, Breidenthal considers romantic love as a form of love of neighbor. He explores precedents in Scripture and Christian tradition for a positive value of romantic love based on the command to love one's neighbor and discusses disciplines necessary to build a lifelong relationship.

Cahill, Lisa Sowle. *Sex, Gender, and Christian Ethics*. New York: Cambridge University Press, 1996. Cahill seeks to draw together scripture, ethics, and contemporary approaches, like feminism and postmodernism, and apply them to sexual ethics.

Choplin, Leslie, and Jenny Beaumont. *These Are Our Bodies: Talking Faith and Sexuality at Church and Home.* New York: Church Publishing, 2016. This resource offers a guide to conversation about sexuality from theological, ethical, biological, and practical perspectives. In addition to a foundation book for educators, clergy, parents, youth leaders, and others, the program includes leader's guides, participant books, and parent guides designed for use with different age levels.

Coakley, Sarah. *The New Asceticism: Sexuality, Gender, and the Quest for God.* New York: Bloomsbury Continuum, 2015. Coakley suggests that we need to re-examine our theology of desire, understanding eros in a broad sense, which goes beyond simple sexual attraction to a desire for the good in society, the good for the poor, and a desire for God. This theological grounding, she suggests, will help get us out of a binary conflict on sexual issues.

Coates, Ta-Nehisi. *Between the World and Me.* Spiegel & Grau, 2015. This book-length letter from a father to his son illustrates the stress that racism puts on black Americans' marriages and families while challenging common stereotypes of African-Americans.

Coontz, Stephanie. *Marriage, a History: From Obedience to Intimacy or How Love Conquered Marriage.* New York: Viking, 2005. This history of marriage speaks to marriage in the ancient world, in early Christianity, and up to the present time, including especially the "Love Revolution" which brought a new paradigm to the purpose of marriage (and new questions).

DeGenova, Mary Kay, ed. *Families in Cultural Context: Strengths and Challenges in Diversity.* McGraw Hill, 1997. This textbook, with chapters written by different authors, offers a comparative view of families from different ethnic groups. Chapters explore changes and adaptations made by families following their immigration into the US.

Demo, David, Katherine Allen, and Mark Fine, eds. *The Handbook of Family Diversity.* Oxford: Oxford University Press, 1999. This textbook discusses different aspects of family, including race, socioeconomic status, family structure, sexual orientation, and gender. Each chapter introduces recent research and theoretical developments; the book does not consider religion.

Edin, Kathryn, and Maria Kefalas. *Promises I Can Keep: Why Poor Women Put Motherhood Before Marriage.* Berkeley: University of California Press, 2005. This sociological study of three high-poverty neighborhoods—one largely white, one Hispanic, one African-American—in Philadelphia with high rates of unmarried mothers argues that poor women value marriage so highly that they are reluctant to enter into it, having realistically assessed that the men in their lives are not strong prospects for a lifelong commitment.

Farley, Margaret. *Just Love: A Framework for Christian Sexual Ethics.* New York: Continuum, 2006.

Haller, Tobias. *What About Sex? A Little Book of Guidance.* New York: Church Publishing 2015. This book draws upon Scripture as well as science and psychology to discuss how we use our bodies sexually.

Hill, Wesley. *Spiritual Friendship: Finding Love in the Church as a Celibate Gay Christian.* Grand Rapids: Brazos, 2015. Part memoir, part biblical and theological reflection. Hill diagnoses our modern condition as one of loneliness, in which traditional communal and familial bonds have in large part broken down, leaving the sexual bond and the nuclear family to carry much more weight than they should have to bear. Hill calls on the church to be a genuine family, a community in which the sexual and marital bonds can take their place among other committed and communal forms of love.

Hymowitz, Kay, Jason S. Carroll, W. Bradford Wilcox, and Kelleen Kaye. *Knot Yet: The Benefits and Costs of Delayed Marriage in America.* University of Virginia: The National Marriage Project, 2013. http://nationalmarriageproject.org/wp-content/uploads/2013/03/KnotYet-FinalForWeb.pdf. This study considers why American twenty-somethings are delaying the age of marriage and the benefits and costs of this delay. It concludes that America must bring childbearing and marriage back into sync.

Jeal, Roy R., ed. *Human Sexuality and the Nuptial Mystery.* Eugene, OR: Cascade Books, 2010. This collection of essays, originally presented at the St. Margaret's Consultation on Doctrine, Liturgy, and Preaching held at St. Margaret's Anglican Church in Winnipeg, Canada in 2008, considers human sexuality and marriage from a theological standpoint.

Lerman, Robert I., and W. Bradford Wilcox. *For Richer, For Poorer: How Family Structures Economic Success in America.* Institute for Family Studies, American Enterprise Institute, 2014. http://www.aei.org/wp-content/uploads/2014/10/IFS-ForRicherForPoorer-Final_Web.pdf. American Enterprise Institute policy paper advocating for marriage, as better for children, partners, and the family.

Long, Kimberly Bracken. *From This Day Forward: Rethinking the Christian Wedding.* Louisville: Westminster John Knox Press, 2016. Addressing the question of whether the church should be in the "wedding business," Long argues for marriage as part of the church's mission. Includes historical overview of marriage.

McCarthy, David Matzko. *Sex and Love in the Home.* New edition. London: SCM Press, 2004. From his Roman Catholic perspective, McCarthy critiques a "closed suburban home" and argues instead for "an open, socially reproductive household" interdependent with its neighbors, standing in contrast to the market economy.

McCleneghan, Bromleigh. *Good Christian Sex: Why Chastity Isn't the Only Option—And Other Things the Bible Says about Sex.* New York: HarperOne, 2016. McCleneghan, a pastor serving a congregation in the United Church of Christ, brings Scripture into conversation with the work of theologians, ethicists, and psychologists, to offer a positive view of human sexuality and explore how Christians can practice their sexuality in light of their faith.

McGoldrick, Monica, Elizabeth A. Carter, and Nydia Garcia-Perez. *The Expanding Family Life Cycle: Individual, Family, and Social Perspectives.* This textbook for family therapists offers perspectives on human development and developmental tasks, taking account of societal changes influencing life-cycle patterns; it does not offer a theological perspective.

Prichard, Robert W. *Cohabiting Couples and Cold Feet: A Practical Marriage-Preparation Guide for Clergy.* New York: Church Publishing, 2008. The first part of this book delves deeply into statistics about relationships, marriage, cohabitation, etc. in the United States. The second part looks at the process of encountering, pastoring, counseling and performing services for people seeking marriage in the Episcopal Church.

Rogers, Eugene F., Jr., ed. *Theology and Sexuality: Classic and Contemporary Readings.* Malden, MA: Blackwell Publishing, 2002. This is a collection of readings from both classical and contemporary sources, encompassing Roman Catholic, Eastern Orthodox, and Protestant sources. Rogers provides a brief introduction for each. The focus is the question of what marriage is for, beyond procreation of children and legitimation of sexual intercourse. The resources he includes present marriages as signs to the community of the faithful of God's reconciliation, and sexuality as a means of sanctification that draws us into God's life.

Sawhill, Isabel V. *Generation Unbound: Drifting into Sex and Parenthood without Marriage.* Washington, DC: Brookings Institution Press, 2014. Sawhill explores changing patterns of marriage and family, focusing on increase in single parenting, but does not offer a theological perspective. She attempts to offer an even-handed assessment, considering perspectives of both "traditionalists" and "village builders," and argues for two-parent families.

Thatcher, Adrian. *Marriage after Modernity: Christian Marriage in Postmodern Times*. Washington Square, NY: New York University Press, 1999. Thatcher offers a vision for Christian marriage that is based in Scripture and history and responds to contemporary social and cultural changes.

Thatcher, Adrian, ed. *The Oxford Handbook of Theology, Sexuality, and Gender*. Oxford: Oxford University Press, 2015. This comprehensive collection of essays explores gender and sexuality in scripture and Christian tradition, as well as providing perspectives from other faiths and offering insights from biology and social sciences.

Thatcher, Adrian. *Theology and Families*. Malden, MA: Blackwell Publishing, 2007. Thatcher considers how Christian faith and theology can contribute to the thriving of families and children.

Witte, John, Jr. *From Sacrament to Contract: Marriage, Religion, and Law in the Western Tradition*. Second edition. Louisville, KY: Westminster John Knox Press, 2012. Study of the interplay of law, theology, and marriage from classical times through the Reformation. Traces "the millennium-long reduction of marriage from a complex spiritual, social, contractual, and natural institution into a simple, private contract with freedom of entrance, exercise, and exit for husband and wife alike." Extended discussion of the theology of marriage in patristic, medieval Catholic, Lutheran, Calvinist, Anglican, and Enlightenment traditions.

Witte, John, Jr. *The Sins of the Fathers: The Law and Theology of Illegitimacy Reconsidered*. New York: Cambridge University Press, 2009. Witte applies his legal and historical acumen to the development of a "doctrine of illegitimacy," for which he finds no biblical justification. He argues that early Christian and rabbinical teaching did not stigmatize illegitimacy, and that a doctrine of illegitimacy developed in medieval Roman canon law. Witte calls for more attention to adoption as well as stronger laws to require birth parents, absent adoption, to support children born out of wedlock.

Clergy, Church, and State:
A Continuing Debate

The first Task Force on the Study of Marriage presented an essay titled, "Agent of the State: A Question for Discernment" in its report to the 78th General Convention.[44] This essay presented a series of topics for consideration in discussing the dual role of clergy in marriage, acting on behalf of both the church as an officiant in the sacramental rite of marriage and on behalf of the state as an authorized officiant to certify and register a marriage.

Predating the debate about legalizing marriage of same-sex couples, clergy would occasionally assert their discomfort in acting on behalf of the state in signing marriage licenses and at times would declare the church should not be in "the marriage business." Some of this discussion reflected views in support of the separation of church and state and a desire to disentangle the sacramental from the secular view of marriage. During the preceding triennium, there was some discussion, chiefly among clergy, centered around responses to the increasing number of court decisions extending marriage to same-sex couples. Some clergy were voicing their support for marriage for same-sex couples by pledging not to officiate at any marriages until all could be married. Others were responding to perceived pressure to change their deeply held views that marriage of same-sex couples is wrong, whether theologically or legally based. The latter group expressed their view in The Marriage Pledge: refusing to sign government issued marriage licenses and agreeing only to bless a civil marriage in opposition to the definition of marriage from "one man, one woman" to two people of same or opposite sex.

Anne Hodges-Copple described her discernment of her role in officiating marriages, considering these questions:

---

44 Appendix 1: Essays on Marriage, in Report of the Task Force on the Study of Marriage to the 78th General Convention (Reports to General Convention, 1976-2015, Archives of the Episcopal Church), pp. 85-87, https://www.episcopalarchives.org/e-archives/gc_reports/reports/2015/bb_2015-R044.pdf (accessed 8/19/17).

- As a priest, if I sign a marriage license, issued by the county clerk, am I acting as an agent of the State?
- If I refuse to sign such a license have I afforded some greater measure of justice to all couples who seek God's nuptial blessing?
- If I sign a marriage license have I privileged some married couples over others?
- If I decline to sign a marriage license will I give couples a great "teachable moment" about the importance of separation between Church and State?
- Do I need to protect the Sacrament of Marriage from the tarnish of the State's interference?[45]

Hodges-Copple's discernment led her to continue to sign state licenses for couples whose marriages she officiates.

Missing in this list of questions is discernment in community, the traditional way The Episcopal Church seeks to understand how God may be leading us in new directions. Such discernment ought to include lay leadership as well as clergy. The laity, after all, are the ones who bear the burden when the clergy decline to officiate a marriage, a burden rarely acknowledged when the clergy stand on their personal principles.

History: Church, State and Marriage

Who has the power to declare a marriage valid: the Church or secular authorities?[46] There is no consistent answer across the scope of Western Christianity. In some times and places, civil authorities have held sole jurisdiction over marriage matters. In others, marriage was the province exclusively of the Church. In still others—as in the contemporary United States, where judges or clergy may solemnize a marriage—secular and religious authorities shared authority over marriage.

In the first several centuries of Christianity, marriage was strictly a civil matter, and clergy had a limited role, if at all, in the formation of marriage. Patristic writers did not demand that secular authorities should submit to the Church in marriage cases, but rather exhorted

---

45 Anne Hodges-Copple, "Signing Marriage Licenses? Yes," in Greg Jones, ed., *Writings on Marriage: The Journal of the Bishop's Task Force on Marriage*, Convention Edition (Raleigh: The Episcopal Diocese of North Carolina, 2009), p. 99.
46 "Secular authorities" and "civil authorities" are used here in acknowledgment that "state" is an anachronistic term before at least the seventeenth century.

Christians to obey the secular laws.[47] No liturgies related to marriage survive before the late fourth or early fifth century, when clergy began blessing the couple or the marriage bed, but not solemnizing the marriage itself.[48] Even when the Church did claim jurisdiction over marriage formation, neither a public wedding liturgy nor a priest was required to contract a valid marriage. Twelfth-century canon law held that "a valid marriage might be contracted either by the free and voluntary exchange of present consent between parties of legal age who were free to marry each other, or by the free and voluntary exchange of future consent between two parties legally able to marry each other, if that consent was ratified by subsequent sexual intercourse."[49] The canons also decreed that banns should be proclaimed and a marriage should be solemnized in facie ecclesiae; a couple could be disciplined for not following the rules, but the Church still recognized their marriage as valid.[50] In their insistence on vows made in the present tense ("I take you to be my wife..."), Peter Lombard and other scholastics may have been trying to teach the laity how to contract a marriage properly without a priest.[51]

Yet couples continued to marry with little involvement of the Church. Florentine couples in the Renaissance usually exchanged vows in the bride's home, then the bride and her goods, the groom, and their friends processed to his house, where a priest might bless the marriage bed. That was the extent of the Church's role in marriage formation.[52] A compromise between Christian and civil authorities evolved in nineteenth-century Spanish and Mexican Texas, where the state recognized only Roman Catholic marriage ceremonies officiated by a priest, but most Anglo settlements did not have a priest. Stephen F. Austin proposed, and civil authorities agreed, to the solution of marriage by bond: the couple signed a marriage contract obligating them to have a priest solemnize their vows as soon as possible, or else pay a substantial fine.[53] This separation between civil marriage and a church wedding is the norm in modern-day France, where a

---

47 Edward Schillebeeckx, *Marriage: Secular Reality and Saving Mystery*, vol. 2, trans. N. D. Smith (London: Sheed and Ward, 1965), pp. 54-55.
48 Philip L. Reynolds, "Marrying and Its Documentation in Pre-Modern Europe: Consent, Celebration, and Property," in Philip L. Reynolds and John Witte, Jr., eds., To Have and to Hold: Marrying and Its Documentation in Western Christendom, 400-1600 (Cambridge: Cambridge University Press, 2007), p. 19.
49 James A. Brundage, *Law, Sex, and Christian Society in Medieval Europe* (Chicago: University of Chicago Press, 1987), p. 334.
50 R. H. Helmholz, *Marriage Litigation in Medieval England* (Cambridge: Cambridge University Press, 1974), p. 524.
51 Reynolds, "Marrying and Its Documentation in Pre-Modern Europe," p. 27.
52 Thomas Kuehn, "Contracting Marriage in Renaissance Florence," in Philip L. Reynolds and John Witte, Jr., *To have and to Hold: Marrying and Its Documentation in Western Christendom*, 400-1600 (Cambridge: Cambridge University Press, 2017), pp. 394, 396-400.
53 Hans W. Baade, "Form of Marriage in Spanish North America," Cornell Law Review, vol. 61, no. 1 (1975), p. 8.

couple must marry in a civil ceremony for their marriage to be legally binding; most couples hold a religious service the following day. The understanding of marriage as a sacrament evolved in the early twelfth century among scholastics in Paris.[54] Peter Lombard clarified the concept of sacramentality and applied it to marriage; Thomas Aquinas argued that the couple's exchange of consent conferred grace.[55] The 1563 Tridentine decree on marriage, Tametsi, held that marriage is one of the seven sacraments, confirming local synodical statements dating back to 1184.[56] As the medieval Western Church came to understand marriage as a sacrament, it also gained exclusive jurisdiction over marriage. Historians disagree on when this happened; dates range from the ninth century to the thirteenth.[57] Regardless of the date, R. H. Helmholz, the authority on this subject, cautions against thinking of the jurisdiction question as a contest between civil and ecclesiastical structures. He asserts, "It was not a question of competition between secular and ecclesiastical jurisdictions. The problem was to ensure that ordinary marriage disputes went to any court at all. The real hurdle was the persistent idea that people could regulate marriages for themselves."[58] Examples abound of medieval people who contracted marriages of dubious legality outside the purview of any authority, secular or religious. Any children born in such unions were likely illegitimate. Once a question was raised about the legality of a marriage—which often happened after the couple were estranged—the parties could find themselves unable to marry anyone else. This put women in particular at economic risk. In these circumstances, Helmholz implies, the church's willingness to assume jurisdiction over marriage cases was a benefit to the civil authorities. The Church was the only universal sovereign in the medieval West, and few medieval monarchs could claim either the Church's universal reach or its administrative capacity.[59] It should not surprise us that medieval authorities determined that church courts were better suited to investigate and judge matrimonial cases.

This history suggests that it is inaccurate to frame the question of authority over marriage as church versus the secular authorities. For most of Western Christianity, this was not an adversarial relationship, but something closer to a partnership. Both church and civil authorities preferred public wedding ceremonies because both

---

54 Reynolds, "Marrying and Its Documentation in Pre-Modern Europe," p. 9.
55 Brundage, *Law, Sex, and Christian Society in Medieval Europe*, pp. 270, 433.
56 John Witte, Jr., *From Sacrament to Contract: Marriage, Religion, and Law in the Western Tradition*, 2nd ed. (Louisville: Westminster John Knox Press, 2012), p. 106.
57 Christopher N. L. Brooke, The Medieval Idea of Marriage (Oxford: Oxford University Press, 1989), pp. 127, 140; Brundage, *Law, Sex, and Christian Society in Medieval Europe*, pp. 223, 319.
58 Helmholz, *Marriage Litigation in Medieval England*, p. 5.
59 Witte, *From Sacrament to Contract*, p. 97.

had an interest in knowing who was married to whom: the Church wished to identify fornication and adultery and reify the concept of marriage as a sacrament; secular authorities needed to determine the property rights established through marriage.[60] Both church and civil authorities also had an interest in protecting unwitting spouses and innocent children from bigamists. Who was supervising the formation of marriage mattered less than that some authority was doing so. In this context, clergy may be seen less as agents of the state and more as agents of the couple, ensuring that their marriage was valid in the eyes of any authority.

Agent of the State or Agent for the Couple?

Arriving at an understanding that the historic interplay between clergy and civil authority has been one of mutually beneficial partnership and appreciating the intent and context of recent concerns about clergy feeling tainted or somehow compromised by their partnership with the State in marriage, the Task Force is open to consider the role of clergy in a new way.

In a memorandum offered by Christopher Hayes, Chancellor of the Diocese of California, the Task Force received the image of clergy as advocates for the marrying couple—agents of the couple, as Chancellor Hayes described it.

He likens the role of a wedding officiant to that of an Officer of the Court. As an attorney, identified as an agent of any court, he is empowered to act in the name of the court, but only on behalf of his client. The court authorizes his role, but any and all work done is in support of his client's best interests, not the court's.

Therefore, extending this analogy, the Task Force is convinced to offer the clergy of our Church the more appropriate assertion that they actually serve as agents, or advocates, of the marrying couple. Clergy vouch for the marriage partners to the civil authority that all necessities for a marriage contract have been completed. Recognition as agents of the couple is consistent with the traditional role of clergy in marriage: as officiants, the clergy do not marry the couple; the couple marries themselves with the blessing of the Church and the State. The requirements for the State to recognize a marriage include consent of two persons to marry, freely, seriously and plainly expressed by each in the presence of the other and in the presence of a defined officiant, and with a declaration by the officiant that

---

60 Lawrence Stone, *The Road to Divorce: England 1530-1987* (Oxford: Oxford University Press, 1990), p. 54.

the persons are married. Likewise the Marriage Canon requires the couple to assert each is legally free to marry and consent to do so "freely, without fraud, coercion or mistake as to the identity of either, or mental reservation" (Canon I.18.3[a]). Signing the State-issued marriage license merely verifies to the State official that a marriage ceremony between the two named people occurred on a specific date at a specific time and place, just as entering the required information into the Parish register certifies to the Church that the marriage took place.

Clergy are not enforcers of contract law, but rather are advocates for the persons entering into both sacred and civil commitments. Indeed, as signatories of marriage licenses, clergy enjoy the confidence expressed by civil authorities (for centuries) in their ability to provide helpful discernment to the couple as well as secure the necessities of a marriage contract.

Anecdotally, most clergy's issues around officiating at marriages have more to do with unpleasant or compromising wedding experiences than they do with complicity in any state legality. Clergy experiences of being dismissed by wedding planners, exploited by exuberant parents, disrespected by unchurched guests, along with abuse of parish property and holy spaces, all contribute to reluctance on the part of some clergy to participate in a marriage ceremony.

Some of these experiences can be ameliorated:

- Establish and publish written guidelines and policies for weddings that honor the sacred space and the sacred occasion;
- Train one or two members of the congregation to act as wedding planners and require couples to make their arrangements through them;
- Engage the Vestry in setting building use guidelines, including weddings;
- Educate the congregation regularly on all marriage requirements and policies;
- Develop and commit to a robust pre-marital counseling plan.

This more expansive frame of reference invites the Church not to step away from these opportunities, but rather to engage them more deeply. To recommit to formation of each couple, as well as the community they come from, the cleric fulfills her or his basic calling to be a pastor and teacher. Therefore, the Task Force invites the Church not to distance or withdraw from its views on the importance of marriage, but rather renew its commitment to the words of the opening address of the marriage rite:

> Therefore marriage is not to be entered into unadvisedly or lightly, but reverently, deliberately, and in accordance with the purposes for which it was instituted by God. (*Book of Common Prayer*, p. 423)

References cited

Baade, Hans W., "Form of Marriage in Spanish North America," *Cornell Law Review*, vol. 61, no. 1 (1975).

Brooke, Christopher N. L., *The Medieval Idea of Marriage* (Oxford: Oxford University Press, 1989)

Brundage, James A., *Law, Sex, and Christian Society in Medieval Europe* (Chicago: University of Chicago Press, 1987)

Hayes, Christopher, "Agents of the State," Memo to the Task Force on the Study of Marriage, August 30, 2016

Helmholz, R. H., *Marriage Litigation in Medieval England* (Cambridge: Cambridge University Press, 1974)

Helmholz, R. H., *The Oxford History of the Laws of England, Vol. 1, The Canon Law and Ecclesiastical Jurisdiction from 597 to the 1640s* (Oxford: Oxford University Press)

Hodges-Copple, Anne, "Signing Marriage Licenses? Yes," in Greg Jones, ed., *Writings on Marriage: The Journal of the Bishop's Task Force on Marriage, Convention Edition* (Raleigh: The Episcopal Diocese of North Carolina, 2009)

Kuehn, Thomas, "Contracting Marriage in Renaissance Florence," in Philip L. Reynolds and John Witte, Jr., *To Have and to Hold: Marrying and Its Documentation in Western Christendom, 400-1600* (Cambridge: Cambridge University Press, 2017)

Reynolds, Philip L., "Marrying and Its Documentation in Pre-Modern Europe: Consent, Celebration, and Property," in Philip L. Reynolds and John Witte, Jr., ed., *To Have and to Hold: Marrying and Its Documentation in Western Christendom, 400-1600* (Cambridge: Cambridge University Press, 2007)

Schillebeeckx, Edward, *Marriage: Secular Reality and Saving Mystery*, vol. 2, trans. N. D. Smith (London: Scheed and Ward, 1965)

Stone, Lawrence, *The Road to Divorce: England 1530-1987* (Oxford: Oxford University Press, 1990)

Witte, John, Jr., *From Sacrament to Contract: Marriage, Religion, and Law in the Western Tradition,* 2nd ed. (Louisville: Westminster John Knox Press, 2012)

IV. Essays on Marriage

prepared by the
Task Force on the Study of Marriage 2015-2018

Contents

Introduction
1. A Biblical and Theological Framework for Thinking about Marriage
2. Christian Marriage as Vocation
3. A History of Christian Marriage
4. Marriage as a Rite of Passage
5. The Marriage Canon: History and Critique
6. Agents of the State: A Question for Discernment
7. Changing Trends and Norms in Marriage

Introduction: Christian Perspectives on Marriages and Family Life Today

One of the defining characteristics of our Anglican tradition is how we approach significant matters that require faithful discernment. We rely upon three interrelated resources that provide a holistic and balanced method of consideration: Scripture, tradition, and reason.

The resolution that defined the work for the Task Force on the Study of Marriage (2012-A050) was broad, to say the least. It asked us to consider the historic, theological, biblical, canonical, legal, liturgical, and social dimensions of marriage. Our budget and our time together were, however, very limited.

Nevertheless, the advantage of having such a broad charge was to ensure that we would approach this important subject holistically, from all three of the traditionally Anglican viewpoints. In some of the seven essays that follow, one viewpoint may be more evident than another, but throughout them all, we have attempted to engage deeply with Scripture, tradition, and reason.

This introduction summarizes a few of the highlights of each essay, in order that the reader might see where we are headed. Those who take the time to read the essays themselves, however, will find a much richer and more nuanced treatment than what this introduction provides. We begin with a biblical and theological foundation in the first two essays, examine our history in the following three, and conclude with two on contemporary issues: whether clergy should act as agents of the state in performing marriages, and some data and reflections on the current state of marriage in our society and Church.

Please keep in mind that these seven essays, however holistic, are not an attempt to be comprehensive, and we do not consider them to be the final word. They are simply our present, admittedly limited contribution to a process of study and discernment that has gone on, and will continue to go on, for a long time.

It is our hope that these essays will provide something more than interesting reading for those who take the time. Given the changing norms and practices around marriage, blessing, singlehood, and other forms of what people consider to be "family," the subject bears close and faithful consideration by our Church on a broad basis.

Therefore, we encourage the use of the essays, alongside our "Dearly Beloved" toolkit, as study materials in diocesan, congregational, and other settings. After assigning them as reading, facilitators might use the discussion and reflection questions that are provided in some of the essays or come up with other questions of their own.

As we begin our first essay, **"A Biblical and Theological Framework for Thinking about Marriage,"** we make it clear that we approach the subject of marriage — as has the Church for centuries — not as a matter of dogma or core doctrine, but as a concern of pastoral or moral theology. While the former is considered to be unchanging, the latter can, and does, evolve considerably over time.

Our lead-up to the subject also includes an overview of the wide range of values and regulations for marital relations that are found in biblical texts. This overview shows just how complex, evolving, and contradictory our Scriptures are on the subject, and therefore how tricky it is to speak of "the biblical view of marriage." We demonstrate how different biblical views and practices of marriage have variously formed and influenced different parts of the faith community through history, even into our own day.

The paper then moves to the heart of the matter: a theological framework that we offer for thinking about marriage. This framework includes several powerful biblical models that serve as analogies for the relationship of marriage: God's unconditional faithfulness and forgiveness; the paradox of union and difference in Christ; and Christ's self-offering in love that is at the heart of the Paschal Mystery.

Finally, the essay concludes with a discussion about the marriage of same-sex couples, making four points. The first is that when our criteria for a holy marriage are based upon the moral values of self-offering love, our conclusion is that same-sex couples are as capable of a holy marriage as are different-sex couples.

Second, the essential quality of marital unity in difference outlined previously can be present for same-sex couples in ways other than the often-cited "complementarity" of different-sex couples.

Third, "it is not in the sex-difference, or in sex itself (whether understood as the sex of the bodies involved or the sexual act) that moral value lies," since moral value is determined by "the context and relationship of the actors," rather than by actions alone.

And last, the clear expectations that General Convention resolution 2000-D039 set forth for any committed lifelong relationship, including same-sex couples, are seen as central to our understanding of the very nature of marriage and its vows.

In our second essay, **"Christian Marriage as Vocation,"** we consider marriage itself as "a calling, a spiritual practice, a particular, vowed manner of life …, a way of being in and engaging the world, of ordering our life in ways that facilitate our participation in the wider purposes for which God created us, redeemed us, and brings us into newness of life." This vocation is not for everyone, for Scripture itself reminds us that not all are called to marriage. However, it is set within, and as a part of, the more fundamental, universal vocation of love.

A section follows that more fully examines the notion of union-in-difference and "complementarity" that the previous essay introduced. Relying upon Paul's understanding of the "new creation" that is made in Christ, where traditional binary distinctions of male/female, slave/free, Jew/Gentile are broken down, we can then see the gift of marital difference in terms much broader and more complex than those of sex. It is the mystery of union and difference that matters in marriage, rather than the sex of the partners.

Gospel and Pauline themes provide depth to our understanding of the vocation of marriage, as they show how "particular graces or charisms gifted to each of us from God can come to their fullest fruition through the relationships and commitments we form," including marriage. The theme of "abiding" in John 15 helps us see marriage as a form of avowed stability, a vessel that God uses to help us to bear the fruit of love. Paul emphasizes the transformational quality of life in Christ in which we are made anew, and in marriage we can see the possibility of gradual, lifelong metamorphosis. As such, the vocation of marriage can be "a way of participating in the ongoing renewal of creation."

IV. ESSAYS ON MARRIAGE

The following three essays are historical. The first of these, **"A History of Christian Marriage,"** demonstrates, as do our sections on Scripture, just how complex and diverse the beliefs and practices about marriage have been within the faith community.

The various practices of early Jewish and Roman Hellenistic marriage are discussed, with themes including marriage as a partnership within a social context, procreation, belovedness, divorce, polygamy, patriarchy, and power.

In the early Church, we see a countercultural shift that "invites Christians to imagine a different kind of family from the paternalistic families of either Judaism or Rome," as family was now found through spiritual identification rather than through blood lines and social status. In the late New Testament era and beyond, the Church began, on the one hand, to commend abstinence and singleness over marriage, and on the other, to align more closely with the values of the empire.

In medieval times, familial and tribal partnerships are paramount; and in the High Middle Ages, an emphasis on chivalric romance — along with its objectification of women as noble, chaste, and pure beings — becomes a part of the backdrop for marriage. The Reformation rejected the primacy of the celibate life and emphasized companionship and the family as the central building blocks of the Christian life. In the New World, there were "numerous ways in which marriage law was used to oppress, and ... numerous ways in which subjugated people continued to find means to establish intimate bonds of familial relationship, despite the impediments to volitional marriage."

The modern age brought a new call for rights and freedoms for women, and this, in turn, led to dramatic changes in the nature of marriage and family life, including a more peer-based relational model. At the same time, "the imperative to develop a theologically sound and culturally sensitive response to the question of the sanctity of a same-sex marriage has heightened."

A part of this complex history of marriage is the closer focus of **"Marriage as a Rite of Passage,"** our next essay. Beginning with a model introduced by 20th-century anthropological studies, we see how marriage, like other rites of passage, consists of a formal ritual action designed "to help individuals or communities transition from one life state to a new one."

This time of transition serves as a "liminal state," wherein the participants are separated from their old way of life and yet are not fully incorporated into their new one. This liminal space can provide an experiential context, allowing for greater freedom, intimacy, and reinvention.

In the past, this liminal space between singleness and marriage was marked by rites of betrothal. As these practices have gone out of use, new ones have somewhat replaced them: the publishing of banns, premarital counseling, and, increasingly in our day, cohabitation as a stepping-stone to marriage. From an anthropological point of view, one could see this latter development as "a potential correction" to the loss of liminal space prior to marriage, recapturing something of the sense that marriage is something "that can and should be eased into rather than jumped into."

The essay concludes with the assertion that marriage can, at times, be a rite that subverts the status quo, a prophetic act. Examples given are interfaith and interracial marriages and new familial bonds that are created across class lines, political affiliations, and ethnicities. As younger generations cross these boundaries more easily than those before them, we now have greater potential to incarnate a Gospel vision of the world as it can be — a world marked by more equality, richness, and diversity.

The third in our series of historical essays is **"The Marriage Canon: History and Critique,"** which shows that discussions in The Episcopal Church about marriage have largely been about remarriage after divorce. As is often the case, changes in canon law have followed changes in practice. And so the essay traces some of these changes in society that forced issues resulting in canonical responses.

At first, remarriage after divorce was prohibited entirely, then only in the case of adultery, and then finally in other cases, but by petition to the bishop. In addition, other regulations were introduced after society experienced a significant rise in the divorce rate: requirements for pastoral preparation and instruction, verification that the couple had a legal right to be married, the presence of witnesses, the entry of information into the parish register, and so on.

The essay concludes with a series of questions that offer a critique of the current marriage canon. Included in this critique are explanations for each of the changes to the marriage canon that this Task Force proposes in resolution form.

Our essays now shift to two contemporary subjects. The first of these is discussed in **"Agents of the State: A Question for Discernment,"** which directly addresses the question that many today are asking: "Should the Church be in the marriage business at all?" — that is, as agents of the state. Without drawing a firm conclusion, we note that whatever the Church may decide on this matter, our discernment must include practical and ethical considerations about whether our participation in civil marriage enables us to be better agents of social transformation, makes us complicit in furthering injustice, or potentially does both.

Our final essay is **"Changing Trends and Norms in Marriages."** As required by our enabling resolution 2012 A050, we consulted broadly with individuals, couples, scholars, and ecclesial partners; and we considered current social research and data on marriage. These consultations and the information we uncovered were extremely helpful in gaining a clearer picture of the state of marriage today.

The main issue that we identified for our reflection as a church has to do with the current drop in marriage rates, and for those who do marry, a delay until a later age than ever before. Cohabitation, as a temporary option or alternative to marriage, is significantly on the rise. Possible historical causes, as well as costs and benefits of these trends, are outlined, including possible impacts that the Church may consider in its mission and pastoral ministry.

The essay concludes with a section on differences in marriage trends among groups identified by race and ethnicity: African Americans, Hispanics and Latinos, Native Americans, and Asian Americans. Finally, we included some statistics regarding same-sex marriage that were current as of the time that this document was submitted.

Note: the Task Force on the Study of Marriage wishes to thank Peggy Van Antwerp Hill, who expertly and promptly edited the essays that follow.

ESSAY 1:
A Biblical and Theological Framework for Thinking about Marriage

1. Introduction

One of the charges of the A050 Task Force on the Study of Marriage was to assist the Church and its members in engaging with the complexity of marriage. As Resolution A050 puts it, the Task Force was asked to "develop tools for theological reflection and norms for theological discussion at a local level."

In this first part of our report, the Task Force offers some starting points for reflection on the theological aspects of marriage. As heirs to the Anglican tradition of rooting theology in the Scripture and in the liturgies of the Church (themselves informed and formed by that Scripture) we begin with a look to how marriage is seen in the light of those rich resources.

A first word on "marriage"

One question that ought to be addressed at the outset, but which may at first appear trivial, is, "What constitutes marriage?" The traditional answer — "Marriage is the lifelong union of one man and one woman" — is, like many simple answers to complex questions, only partially true. As the historical essay that forms a part of this report shows, there has been a great deal of variation as to what constitutes "marriage" throughout the world, and even within the traditions of Christianity and Judaism, there are variations and discontinuities as to what makes a marriage.

One of the issues facing the Church of the seventh through the twelfth centuries was the difference of opinion on what constituted a marriage. Some theologians, influenced by Germanic traditions as well as by an understanding expressed in the Jewish law that when a man "takes" a woman she becomes his wife, held that it was coitus that constituted the marriage and made it indissoluble. Other theologians, particularly in Italy, rested on a more contractual notion (related to, but differing from, Roman civil law in some details) that it was the consent of the couple that constituted the marriage. The eventual papal ruling settled the debate (for Roman Catholics) by taking a middle ground: consent makes the marriage, but consummation seals it (Brundage, 331).

As noted, the concept of consent was not particularly biblical. Given the power dynamics that favored men over women under Jewish law, women had little control over their marital destiny. Perhaps the most extreme example of this is the biblical law that allows for marriage by rape and purchase (Deuteronomy 22:28-29); but even in demonstrably loving and caring settings, the wife had little control over her husband's right to a second wife (1 Samuel 1:2). The asymmetry of the boundaries in marriage is perhaps best revealed in the unequal understanding of adultery: a man could commit adultery only by violating another man's marriage; a woman, only by violating her own (Leviticus 20:10).

A discontinuity settled early in the life of the Church concerned the number of wives a man might have, although the trend toward monogamy had as much to do with ascetical thinking in Greco-Roman and sectarian Jewish circles as with early Christian thought. Monogamy quickly moved from a moral ideal (and under Roman law, a legal limitation) to a practical restriction. (As we will see below, some ascetical moralists in both Jewish and Christian settings felt that monogamy was absolute; even for a widow or widower to remarry was an indication of moral frailty. This thinking may underlie the limitations in the pastoral Epistles concerning marriages of clergy and enrolled widows; 1 Timothy 3:2, 12; 5:9; Titus 1:6.)

An issue that remained far less settled concerned the degree of consanguinity or affinity permitted between the parties to be married. Even within the Torah (and the Rabbinic law that supplements it) there is some inconsistency concerning degrees of relationship within which marriage is prohibited. For example, Leviticus 18:12-14 forbids a man marrying his aunt, but as the law is silent on the subject, an uncle may marry his niece. (This provision is recognized in some civil jurisdictions to this day, as in Rhode Island, which permits marriages allowed under Jewish law; see Code 15.1.1 et seq.)

Although the biblical law permits marriage of first cousins (see, for example, Numbers 36:8-13), the medieval Church extended the restrictions and prohibited marriage between parties as distant as the sixth or seventh degree of kinship. Considerable inconsistencies in definitions of what constitutes incest remain between some civil jurisdictions: many U.S. states prohibit first-cousin marriage, although in some states (Arizona, Indiana, Illinois, Utah, Wisconsin), exceptions are granted in cases of infertility or advanced age; in other states, first cousins may marry without hindrance.

Perhaps the most striking change involved the Church's prohibition of a biblical mandate: the Levirate law outlined in Deuteronomy 25:5-10, by which a man was to marry his brother's childless widow. The Church reckoned that this was incest, privileging the prohibition in Leviticus 18:16, even though the regulation in Deuteronomy is laid out as an exceptional circumstance. (This legal tangle strikes close to home for Anglicans, since this formed part of the basis for Henry VIII's marriage, and its later annulment, to Catherine of Aragon.)

Finally, whether marriage is by nature lifelong or capable of dissolution receives a mixed witness in Scripture. The Torah provides for divorce for any cause (Deuteronomy 24:1), while Jesus limits the cause to adultery (Matthew 5:31-32, 19:3-10); Paul further complicates the matter by introducing the idea that when one of a married non-Christian couple is baptized, the other has the right to divorce (1 Corinthians 7:12-13). This teaching stands in tension with Jesus' teaching that the bond of marriage is ordered in creation, rather than in Christendom. Down through the Christian centuries, the grounds for divorce expanded and contracted in both civil and canon law, to the point at which the "lifelong" character of marriage is so by "intent."

So it is that a part of the reflection with which the Church is called to engage concerns the range of possible relationships that constitute marriage. As the preceding paragraphs have indicated, many aspects of the nature of marriage have changed considerably, even within the Christian tradition. The one element that has remained stable is the relative gender of the spouses. This is a question that faces the Church in our own time, and one which has to a great extent brought us to this closer examination of what is meant by *marriage*.

The Church and the wider society are facing the question: Is the "male and female" of marriage an essential or yet another variable element in marriage? Is it a permitted variable in a civil context but not a religious one? So much has changed or varied in what constitutes marriage. Is the gender difference the sole unchangeable characteristic that makes a marriage a marriage, regardless of any and all other variations? This paper will seek to provide a framework for thinking about this question, to see if there is a theological rationale for maintaining this element as essential to marriage, or to see it as a characteristic in which grounds for variation can be not only explored, but formalized as well.

A second word on "theology"

However, before going further, it is also important at the outset to be clear about what is meant by "theology" — and what sort of theology we are addressing. Marriage is not a subject of dogmatic theology, but of moral or pastoral theology. This means that there is no core dogmatic doctrine concerning marriage, although there is a long history of regulation concerning who may (or can) marry whom, when and where, and under what circumstances; and considerable reflection on the morals and goods of marriage. There is also a rich banquet of biblical and traditional symbolism surrounding marriage — as there is surrounding banquets themselves — a fact which serves to demonstrate how human activities, particularly activities that foster community, illuminate and are illuminated by theological reflection.

Apart from these symbolic applications — some of them embodied in the liturgies of marriage — the Church did not engage in much strictly doctrinal thinking on the topic for centuries, until the later debates concerning the nature and number of the sacraments. Prior to the time of those debates, the Church engaged (as noted above) in considerable discussion about legal and moral issues, such as the marriage of a Christian with a nonbeliever, and remarriage after divorce or in widowhood, but there was no dogmatic reflection on marriage itself; it was marriage discipline that occupied the attention of the Church.

The scope of doctrinal or dogmatic theology, particularly as formed in the Anglican tradition, is limited. Doctrine ("believed as an article of the Faith") is constrained by that which can be proved by Scripture (Article VI of the Articles of Religion, BCP, 868). This way of looking at doctrine affirms *sufficiency* rather than *detailed elaboration* and is focused on, but not confined by, the Creeds (in particular the Nicene Creed, which is described as a *"sufficient* statement of the Christian Faith" in the Lambeth Quadrilateral).

As with the understanding of "the sufficiency of the Holy Scriptures for salvation" (Article VI), the concept is that not every theological issue need be addressed in detail, and that a set of basic guiding principles can set the ground rules within which the Church has authority to act. The Creeds, of course, say nothing of matrimony; moreover, the classical Anglican catechisms are also silent on it, while the 1979 BCP catechism gives only a brief description of it on page 861.

The Articles of Religion decline to name matrimony a sacrament (as it "lacks any visible sign or ceremony ordained of God"), and classify it as an estate allowed (Article XXV), while holding it to be available to clergy (as to all Christians) as they judge it to be conducive to a moral life (Article XXXII). Given the relatively sparse attention given to marriage, the principal doctrinal formularies of the early Church and later Anglicanism, we are left with what the Scripture and the liturgies of the Church tell us about it.

When we look to those sources, what we find, in addition to the occasional symbolic application of marriage, is a narrative encompassing several different forms of marriage, along with a record of changing rules and laws, rites, and ceremonies — all of which, as the Articles of Religion (XX, XXXIV) also remind us, are subject to amendment by the Church, as questions of discipline rather than of doctrine. It is not so much a matter of the Christian faith as it is of living a Christian *life*.

As noted above, and as reference to the historical paper that forms a part of this report demonstrates, the discipline of marriage has changed considerably through the centuries both in biblical times and after the biblical canon closed. Examples of amendment already cited include Jesus' own teaching on the indissolubility of marriage, setting aside a permissive statute in the Law of Moses (Matthew 5 and 19), and the Church's later prohibition of a biblical mandate (the Levirate Law expounded in Deuteronomy 25:5-10, but recorded as being in force as early as Genesis 38:8 as well as being foundational in Jesus' family tree in the story of Ruth).

In keeping with all of the foregoing, the theological approach taken here is not dogmatic but pastoral, and it will focus on the moral issues raised by marriage. It will serve to provide a basis for consideration by the Church the primary question that has shaped our work as a task force: "What might our Church want to say to the world today about what it is that makes a marriage holy and particularly Christian?"

2. A Theological Arc

The question raised by marriage

Any discussion of Christian marriage is helpfully guided by asking the question, "What makes a marriage Christian?" What is it about this nearly universal human phenomenon, which exists in many forms and in many cultures and contexts, to which the Church feels confident in pointing as a sign of God's action in the world?

Up until relatively recently in church history, the answer to the question of "What makes a marriage Christian?" was relatively simple. In the apostolic period, attested by Paul in 1 Corinthians 7 (the longest and most detailed reflection on marriage in Scripture), marriage was a social institution regarded with toleration rather than encouragement, and for which no liturgical ceremony was prescribed. A marriage was considered Christian if it took place between two baptized persons. A pagan couple, one of whom became baptized, was allowed to end the marriage if the pagan member did not wish to remain (vv. 12-15).

One who was already baptized was not to marry a nonbeliever; Paul alludes to this discipline in verse 39, and it became a matter of church law fairly quickly, and remained so for centuries with varying degrees of enforcement or toleration, from excommunication or capital punishment in the early fourth century (Watkins, 495-96), to dispensation under current Roman Catholic regulations (see the current Code of Canon Law at 1086.2).

The understanding became (and remains) that the bond and covenant of marriage is enacted by the couple themselves, and the function of the Church is to solemnize the event with a degree of formality, with the three aspects of *testimony, blessing,* and *recording.* The Church took on the civil responsibilities (and is still permitted so to do in many places, though not all) of ensuring that the marriage is attested by witnesses and recorded, and added its own function of imparting a blessing.

Since the ministers of the rite are the couple themselves, the tradition in place since the apostolic era required that they both be baptized. This requirement came to be seen as less than absolute, and dispensations became available in the Roman Catholic tradition as early as 1669 (Watkins, 575).

In 1946 The Episcopal Church went a step further, when the canons were amended to permit marriage when one of the parties was not baptized. There was strong objection to the introduction of this change, given the intensity of early and historic church opposition to such marriages. It brought into question the meaning of another part of the marriage canon that described marriage as being "entered into within the community of faith."

As many, if not most, marriages are not necessarily parish functions but involve the friends and family of the couple — many of whom may also not necessarily be baptized — this clause appears to be aspirational rather than absolute (see White and Dykman, 414). In short, the old, easy definition of what made a marriage Christian came to be no longer applicable in all cases.

An icon for the Church or of the Church

The traditional answer to the question of holiness in marriage, however, lies in the prologue to the marriage rite as it has come down to us, through many modifications, simplifications, and elaborations, but which, in its present form in The Episcopal Church, states that marriage "signifies to us the mystery of the union between Christ and his Church" (BCP, 423).

This role of *signification* has been a part of Anglican marriage liturgies since 1549. It rests on a much older principle with roots in the Hebrew Scripture, which analogized the love of spouses with the love of the Lord for the Chosen People. However, it is important to note that the biblical analogy is used for faithful as well as unfaithful relationships, recognizing that marriage in itself is morally neutral and can be good or bad to the extent the spouses are faithful to each other.

For example, from the negative side, Jeremiah 3, Ezekiel 16 and 23, and Hosea 2 and 3 present us with imagery of the Lord as the loving husband of an unfaithful spouse (or spouses, as in Jeremiah and Ezekiel the Lord is married to the two sisters, Israel and Judah). Jeremiah 3:6-8 presents this image:

> Have you seen what she did, that faithless one, Israel, how she went up on every high hill and under every green tree, and played the whore there?7 And I thought, "After she has done all this she will return to me"; but she did not return, and her false sister Judah saw it.8 She saw that for all the adulteries of that faithless one, Israel, I had sent her away with a decree of divorce; yet her false sister Judah did not fear, but she too went and played the whore.

Ezekiel 16:7-21 portrays a vivid image of a loving and indulgent husband betrayed by his unfaithful spouse. (Note the resonance between verse 9 and the imagery of Ephesians 5:25-27).

> You grew up and became tall and arrived at full womanhood; your breasts were formed, and your hair had grown; yet you were naked and bare.8 I passed by you again and looked on you; you were at the age for love. I spread the edge of my cloak over you, and covered your nakedness: I pledged myself to you and entered into a covenant with you, says the Lord GOD, and you became mine.9 Then I bathed you with water and washed off the blood from you, and anointed you with oil ...13 ... You grew exceedingly beautiful, fit to be a queen.14 Your fame spread among the nations on account of your beauty, for it was perfect because of my splendor that I

had bestowed on you, says the Lord GOD.15 But you trusted in your beauty, and played the whore because of your fame, and lavished your whorings on any passer-by ...20 You took your sons and your daughters, whom you had borne to me, and these you sacrificed to them to be devoured. As if your whorings were not enough!21 You slaughtered my children and delivered them up as an offering to them.

Ezekiel 23:2-18 follows Jeremiah in portraying the Lord as the husband of two unfaithful sisters:

> Mortal, there were two women, the daughters of one mother; ...4 Oholah was the name of the elder and Oholibah the name of her sister. They became mine, and they bore sons and daughters. As for their names, Oholah is Samaria, and Oholibah is Jerusalem.5 Oholah played the whore while she was mine; she lusted after her lovers the Assyrians ...9 Therefore I delivered her into the hands of her lovers, into the hands of the Assyrians, for whom she lusted.10 These uncovered her nakedness; they seized her sons and her daughters; and they killed her with the sword. Judgment was executed upon her, and she became a byword among women.11 Her sister Oholibah saw this, yet she was more corrupt than she in her lusting and in her whorings, which were worse than those of her sister ...18 When she carried on her whorings so openly and flaunted her nakedness, I turned in disgust from her, as I had turned from her sister.

As a final example, Hosea 2:2-19 lays out the prophetic figure of infidelity representing apostasy and idolatry, but with a hope of eventual redemption and the beginnings of a transformation of the husband from "Lord" to "spouse." This is also carried forward in Ephesians, where the husband is called to love his wife not as "Lord-over" but as "servant-of."

> Plead with your mother, plead — for she is not my wife, and I am not her husband — that she put away her whoring from her face, and her adultery from between her breasts, ...15 ... I will give her her vineyards, and make the Valley of Achor a door of hope. There she shall respond as in the days of her youth, as at the time when she came out of the land of Egypt.16 On that day, says the LORD, you will call me, "My husband," and no longer will you call me, "My Baal."17 ... 19 And I will take you for my wife forever; I will take you for my wife in righteousness and in justice, in steadfast love, and in mercy.

In the context of prophetic metaphor of the relation between God and the Chosen People, marriage can be portrayed as good or bad. This reflects the human reality that while marriage may be good or holy in and of itself as an institution, a particular marriage can be, and of right ought to be, a vehicle for holy living, for which the only guarantors are the couple themselves, aided by God and the community of support in which their marriage is set. Turning from the negative imagery of the prophetic writers, many Christian authors through the years drew on the happier imagery, such as that in the Song of Songs, in an allegorical light, applied to the Church as the people of God.

However, the ultimate touchstone for Christian reflection on holy marriage is the passage from Ephesians (5:28-32) in which the author attempts to express how it is that the many become one in Christ. He draws on the tradition of the Hebrew prophets and poets and uses marriage as an analogy to this "mystery" of the Church — not, contrary to the language of the prologue to the marriage liturgy, primarily for symbolic value ("marriage tells us something about Christ and the Church") but as a teaching example ("married couples should be one in love, just as Christ in loving the Church is one with it"). The issue is not, "if you want to know something about Christ and the Church, look to marriage," but "if you want to know how to make your marriage holy, look to Christ." Here is the actual text, including a portion of a verse that appears only in some manuscripts:

> Husbands, love your wives, just as Christ loved the church and gave himself up for her,26 in order to make her holy by cleansing her with the washing of water by the word,27 so as to present the church to himself in splendor, without a spot or wrinkle or anything of the kind — yes, so that she may be holy and without blemish.28 In the same way, husbands should love their wives as they do their own bodies. He who loves his wife loves himself.29 For no one ever hates his own body, but he nourishes and tenderly cares for it, just as Christ does for the church,30 because we are members of his body [of his flesh and of his bones].31 "For this reason a man will leave his father and mother and be joined to his wife, and the two will become one flesh."32 This is a great mystery, and I am applying it to Christ and the church. (Ephesians 5:25-32, with bracketed text from the notes; also note that the Greek of the final clause is perhaps more simply stated as, "but I speak of Christ and of the church.")

This passage and its larger context of instruction to households have become problematical in an era in which the equality of the sexes is with few exceptions either unchallenged or championed. The author writes from and to a context in which the secondary status of women was accepted as the norm. However, even within that context, the author — identified as "Paul" in keeping with the tradition, while noting the lack of consensus on the authorship of this epistle — is attempting to shift toward a more equal understanding in the relation of the sexes.

Note, for example, the paschal notion of the man giving himself for the woman (rather than the more conventional call for the woman to surrender to the man) in 5:25. This is less revolutionary than the statement in the undoubtedly Pauline 1 Corinthians 7:4, in which mutual authority is explicitly laid out, each spouse holding "authority" over the body of the other. (Perhaps Ephesians 5 reveals some authentic Pauline liberation showing through the gloss of later applications of household codes.)

Still, the language of male headship is part of the text before us, and, as unpalatable as it is for most of the present generation, it cannot be denied. What is significant is that the role of the head over the body is directed not to domination, but to care, redemption, and self-giving — a kind of kenotic lordship that agrees well with the broader understanding of Christ as head of the Church, who gave his life for it. This destabilizes the traditional notion of male superiority and female submission, much as Jesus himself, as "master," inverted the normative role assigned to him by taking the role of a servant on the night before he suffered, and called on the disciples to engage in just this reciprocal ministry of mutual submission (John 13:13-15).

So the tradition of reading this passage as laying out marriage as an allegory or signifier for Christ and the Church is likely missing a crucial part of Paul's intent, explored at length in this report's essay, "Christian Marriage as Vocation." Paul's reflects on a far greater mystery: the mystery described earlier in the epistle, the eschatological "mystery of his will, according to his good pleasure that he set forth in Christ, as a plan for the fullness of time, to gather up all things in him, things in heaven and things on earth" (Ephesians 1:9-10).

It is in this Church (the "assembly" that by its very nature unifies the plural) that Jew and Gentile are made one out of two through the flesh and blood of Christ (Ephesians 2:13-14, 21-22). This is crucial in the sense both of important and paschal — the cross underscores the Pauline teaching that it is in, with, and through Christ, and him crucified, that God's mystery of union is made plain. Paul places his household instructions within this larger context: husbands are to model their relationship with their spouses on the love of Christ for the Church; it is not that earthly marriages are mere symbols of the heavenly union, but that the heavenly union is the model which earthly marriages should emulate in order to be holy.

By employing this rhetoric, Paul reaches back long before the Incarnation and the Song of Songs, to the primal story of the first spouses described in Genesis 2. Just as Adam recognizes "himself" in Eve — "of his flesh and of his bones" — so too the Church shares a corporeal identity with Christ. Christ loves the church, his body — and the language of both Baptism and Eucharist (in both Word and Sacrament) is echoed in Ephesians: "Christ loved the church and gave himself up for her, in order to make her holy by cleansing her with the washing of water by the word" and Christ "nourishes and tenderly cares for" this body (5:25-26, 29).

Paul builds on his image of the Church as both Bride of Christ and Body of Christ, in his own way creating a bridge between the imagery of Genesis and Revelation. Marriage can indeed give us a glimpse of heaven, when and to the extent that it is modeled upon the heavenly archetype of Christ and his self-giving relationship with the Church, his body on earth. It is not marriage in the abstract or as an institution that "signifies" the relation between Christ and the Church, but more that a particular good marriage, when modeled on the love of Christ for the Church, incarnates the archetype on which all love is based.

So in response to the question, "What makes a marriage holy?" the answer that it "signifies …the mystery of the union between Christ and the Church" provokes a second question: "how do we understand this significance?" or "what are the signs of this holiness, this Christian identity?" For obviously, it is not just any marriage that is holy, any more than just any marriage is Christian.

Just as there are good and bad marriages portrayed in Scripture, there is a qualitative difference between the quickly engaged and quickly ended Hollywood or Las Vegas marriage, and that of a couple who have spent a lifetime together, sharing their lives with each other and with a wider community. So what are the signs that indicate the holiness of a marriage? And in what ways do these signs proclaim that a marriage is Christian?

Returning once more to Ephesians for guidance, note the verse that comes as an introduction to the chapter addressing marriage: "Live in love, as Christ loved us and gave himself up for us, a fragrant offering and sacrifice to God." This verse perhaps suffers from being too often heard as an offertory sentence, familiarity blunting the force of the call to paschal, loving self-offering that lies at the heart of the Christian vocation, following the kenotic path laid out by Christ himself.

It might be helpful to look at similar language from the Gospel of John, in the long reflection on the nature of the love of God and the mystery of Christ's union in and with the Church. Jesus expounds on this at the Last Supper: "This is my commandment, that you love one another as I have loved you. No one has greater love than this, to lay down one's life for one's friends" (15:12-13); "I in them and you in me, that they may become completely one, so that the world may know that you have sent me and have loved them even as you have loved me" (17:23).

As noted in the paper, "Christian Marriage as Vocation," this quality of union through loving and mutual self-offering is central to the vocation of marriage, recognized as a particular call within the universal call for Christians to love one another, and in terms of Ephesians, with Christ and his gift of himself as the template or model for the self-giving of spouses in marriage. For in marriage, the spouses literally "take" each other and "give" each other, reciprocally, exclusively, unreservedly, wholly, and unconditionally: as the declaration of consent and the vows so eloquently state: to "love ... honor ... comfort ... and keep ... forsaking all others ... to have and to hold from this day forward, for better for worse, for richer for poorer, in sickness and in health, to love and to cherish, until we are parted by death" (BCP, 424, 427).

The reciprocal nature of the vows — the commitment of each spouse to do for the other as they would be done by — reflects the Golden Rule as well as the transformative "giving" of Jesus for the Church, elaborated in Ephesians and signified in the Maundy foot washing, and most starkly in the painful glory of the cross.

As spouses love each other "as Christ did the church" they incarnate the values of "fidelity, monogamy, mutual affection and respect, careful, honest communication, and the holy love which enables those in such relationships to see in each other the image of God" (2000 - D039). As they live out this love, the wider community of the faithful, and those beyond it, will be able to see "a sign of Christ's love to this sinful and broken world, that unity may overcome estrangement, forgiveness heal guilt, and joy conquer despair" and "that all married persons ... may find their lives strengthened and their loyalties confirmed" (BCP, 429-30).

Marriage, as an icon for and of the Church, reaffirms that we do not live for ourselves alone, or die for ourselves alone (Romans 14:7) — nor do we marry for ourselves alone, but as a sign and emulation of God's grace and to God's glory. The love of God for the world in the loving self-offering of Christ Jesus thus becomes a guiding and effective pattern in discerning how a marriage proclaims that it is a Christian marriage, an evangelical sign of that "wonderful and sacred mystery" that is Christ's body, the Church.

The relationship of marriage to that larger body is emphasized in the liturgy through the requirement that marriage take place within at least a minimal assembly. As the BCP rubric notes, "marriage is a solemn and public covenant" and there must be "at least two witnesses" (422). Couples do not make their vows privately, but before God, friends, family, and (ideally) God's community, the Church. The marriage is a union celebrated and blessed on behalf of the Church in the midst of this community that is, ideally, itself "one in Christ."

As marriage is an incarnational sign of Christ's love for the Church, so it is also an expression and sign of Christian community: our life together in and as the Body of Christ. The old patristic tag (said of the Eucharist) "become what you behold" is a powerful reminder of the way in which a marriage both draws upon the love of God and the community and fosters it. So a marriage not only is blessed by the Church, but is a source of blessing for the Church.

And this blessing does not stop at the end of the rite. The community witnesses to the couple by their presence at the marriage service and throughout their marriage journey in their support of the couple. The couple, in turn, witnesses to the community by how they live their lives together — showing Christ's love to each other, the community, and the world. If marriage is a sacrament — and that has been a topic of considerable debate — it is certainly sacramental in this: it can both express and evoke in others the graces of loving, self-giving charity inherent in the vows.

Although marriage does not have "a like nature of Sacraments with Baptism and the Lord's Supper" because it lacks "any visible sign or ceremony ordained of God" (BCP, 872), the real grace of marriage lies not in the wedding ceremony, but in the life of the couple: as with the baptismal life, and the life of the eucharistic community that is the Church, it is in the living of the vows, the putting into practice of the promises and commitments, that grace is revealed and shared.

3. The Ethics of Marriage

As noted, the *exemplary* function of marriage — as a sign and echo of Christ's self-giving love for the Church, conceived in Ephesians both as his body and spouse — is a particular vocation within the larger Christian calling. As a Christian vocation, the moral significance of a marriage will be expressed by how the spouses treat each other, how they incarnate and live out the Rule of Married Life, the disciplines and responsibilities of that life, and its joys and rewards.

In some discussions of morality, the locus of concern can lie in the acts more than the actors. In marriage these two aspects of morality — acts and actors — merge in the spouses themselves, who become spouses through the marriage. The reality of being a spouse is not ontological, but performative and relational. So the efficacy of the sign will depend on the degree to which the spouses express and live out the values intended in the vows, which constitute the substance of the marital commitment.

As the essay, "Christian Marriage as Vocation" also underscores, a marriage is a way of life, a discipline, and a discipleship within the larger community of Christian disciples who make up the Church. In this sense, it is a living out of the Gospel value of love, an evangelical witness that "preaches Christ."

To echo the language of John (1 John 4:20), those who do not love their spouse, whom they have seen, cannot claim to love God, whom they have not seen. And it is in how their love is expressed to one another that others can see the love of God. The spouse is the closest and most intimate neighbor for the enactment of the Golden Rule. The theological virtue of charity truly does begin at home.

In this light, it is helpful to examine the ethics of marriage through a principle elucidated by the eighteenth-century Prussian philosopher and ethicist, Immanuel Kant. He held that people should treat each other as ends in themselves rather than as means to some other end, valued in and for themselves rather than for their utility or productivity.

This relational notion is fully consonant with the Baptismal Covenant's call to respect the dignity of every human being, and with the understanding of each human being as a living image of God. This ethical notion has particular application to marriage conceived as a mutual covenant of two persons rather than merely as a contract between two parties for the performance of services.

The reality of marriage lies in the couple themselves, and in their mutual self-giving as it reflects and embodies the love of Christ for the Church, in that each spouse lives and strives for the good of the other. This transforms and redirects the innate trend toward self-interest that lies at the core of Original Sin, toward recovery of the Original Blessing intended by God for human flourishing, as a response to the "not good" of isolation being rectified by the discovery of the "one like himself" (Tobit 8:6).

It would be helpful at this point to be reminded of three things about self-giving:

First, the gift of oneself to and for another is not to be confused with a kind of paradoxical "selflessness." To give a self that has been reduced to a nonentity is to give nothing. Moreover, the concept of "selflessness" represents a devaluation of the "dignity of every human being" (BCP, 305). Every person is precious, and to give oneself is to offer a supremely valuable gift, only worthy to be given for the sake of another, a gift for which "the whole world" would be inadequate recompense (Matthew 16:26).

It is also a sad fact that "selflessness" has often been promoted as a particular call for women; the stereotype of the dominant husband with a "selfless" wife has even in some situations been held up as an ideal. In addition to fostering a false notion of selfhood, this represents an inversion of the imagery advanced in Ephesians 5, in which the husband is called to model Christ's sacrificial self-giving for the sake of the Church.

Second, while the ultimate paradigm in Christ's self-giving — as the highest love shown in giving up one's life for others (John 15:13) — is both costly and painful, it is also the cause of joy. The Paschal Mystery encompasses this marvelous interchange in which "the cross he bore" is "life and health" to humanity, "though pain and death to him" (Hymnal 1982, 483).

Third, each Christian participates in this Paschal Mystery, and further is called to take up his or her own cross to follow the Lord in this path of self-giving. It is a universal call, but it is given a particular form in marriage, in which the couple give themselves to each other, giving and receiving to and from each other in a paschal and a joyful exchange, incarnating the Original Blessing as they celebrate the costly paschal vanquishing of Sin.

This movement from sin to blessing is reflected in the wedding that provides a setting for the first sign by which Jesus reveals his glory (John 2:11). Jesus transforms water provided for ritual purification into an abundance of wine for celebration — not merely a movement, but a metamorphosis, from a reminder of ritual uncleanness requiring repeated purification to a celebration that reveals and anticipates the fulfilment and completion of God's promises in Christ.

This action adorns marriage not merely as a recapitulation of creation, but as a part of the "new creation" — the water of creation not simply replaced or supplemented, but transformed into the new wine of the messianic banquet (Brown, 97-111). This banquet is figured in Revelation in the wedding of the Lamb and the New Jerusalem. Thus a sort of grand rainbow arc proclaims God's goodness from Genesis to Revelation, and links beginnings and endings, hope and fulfillment.

At the same time, Scripture itself offers little insight into marriage as it is lived out — witness the relatively small part that monogamous married couples play in the Hebrew Scriptures and in the early life of the Church, which leads to the relative shortage of suitable biblical texts available for use in marriage liturgies. So it is to how the liturgies make use of Scripture that we would turn for greater insight into how the Church itself understands marriage, and the theological and ethical implications the Church draws from it. It is significant that the account of the wedding at Cana plays a principal role in this, rightly highlighting the transformative quality of marriage, in which two become one, and the relationship into which they enter gives a glimpse of the redemptive qualities of mutual self-giving, reflective of the new life in Christ that is the Church itself.

Union of heart, body, and mind

The classical Anglican marriage liturgy (1549-1662) betrays a degree of tension even in the introductory exhortation that serves as the liturgical prologue to the rite: the recollection of the transformative vision of the wedding at Cana is firmly planted next to distinctly earthly "causes" or purposes for the institution of marriage — including deliverance from the defiling snares of fornication. There is a palpable "already, but not yet" quality to this rite, which in its classical form includes the negative language alongside more positive references.

There is also significant tension between the causal or purposeful mode of the prologue and the active language of the vows themselves. The prologue — in particular, in its classical form, its emphasis on procreation — concerns itself with a productive value of what comes out of the marriage, what marriage is for. In contrast, the vows themselves focus on the performative aspect of what goes into the marriage, how marriage is actually to be lived out.

The emphasis on procreation and children — however important the former, and however crucial the welfare of the latter to human society — primarily as a purpose or end, relies on an ethic at odds with the principle outlined above, which is that people are to be treated as ends in themselves, rather than as means to another end, however good that end might be.

The same can be said for the spouses' use of each other as a "remedy for fornication," a cause for marriage that cannot help but avoid a degree of objectification. (This remedial cause — highlighted in earlier Anglican liturgies — has been downplayed or entirely omitted in more recent marriage liturgies.)

Procreation can become a problematical cause or purpose when it is understood primarily as an extrinsic end, rather than as the natural outgrowth of the loving couple treating each other as ends in themselves. It is acknowledged that as the end in this case is a human life, it has its own inestimable worth. It must also be noted that many, if not most couples, desire this end and work together toward its accomplishment; and that the generation of new life is a tangible expression of their mutual love.

However, although sometimes held as a principal end, it has never been held to be an essential one. Even the 1549 liturgy recognized that this particular end cannot be achieved by all marriages, by providing that the prayer for the couple's fruitfulness in procreation is to be "omitted where the Woman is past childbirth." These additional factors highlight that this aspect of marriage is about achieving an end, or not; and however good that end, that goodness does not remove the ethical problems that can arise when people treat each other as means by which some other end — however good — is achieved.

Children are a gift and a grace and a hope — but ought not be understood as an extrinsic expectation or demand, in the absence of which a marriage is deemed to have failed in some intrinsic way. Moreover, the greater and more fully realized the love of a couple for each other, the more likely any child who becomes part of the growing family, by birth or adoption, will be nurtured and raised in a way that expresses the familial virtues. A bad marriage is unlikely to be "saved" by the introduction of children, which may add more tensions and stresses to it: this is hardly fair to the child.

It can be observed that the emphasis on procreation represents a Genesis 1 attitude, while an emphasis on companionship reflects the narrative in Genesis 2. However, it is also helpful to note that Genesis 1 does not employ marital language, and procreation is more closely tied to sexuality (being "male and female") and to the "filling of the earth" — language echoing that applied to the birds and the fish in the previous verses, also commanded to "be fruitful and multiply" so as to "fill the waters" and the sky. The emphasis in Genesis 1 is on sex as necessary for procreation, not marriage.

The emphasis in Genesis 2, however, is companionship — that the human one should not be alone — rather than on filling the earth and subduing it. The "Adam" itself (Heb. ha Adam) is "Earth" by name and by origin, and cannot be satisfied by the companionship of the other creatures, themselves crafted from the same soil. Only one made from Adam's own substance can stand as a suitable companion, and it is Adam's recognition of this likeness that confirms the Lord God's work, the solution to the "not good-ness" of his former isolation.

The "problem" to be solved is innate in Adam, in his own solitary existence, and it is in the discovery of the "helper suitable" that the problem finds its solution, not any subsequent act or production. Variable times of "prosperity and adversity" will lie ahead, but the role of suitable — not subordinate — helper through it all is a constant. (The man's later dominion over the woman is an artifact of the fall. "In the beginning" the couple stands side by side. The Hebrew word for helper is used of God in relation to humanity, so no inferiority or subordination is implied in this term. In fact, it is the one who needs help who is arguably the inferior.)

Some have noted that Jesus combined the two Genesis accounts in his teaching on marriage in Matthew 19:4-5, citing the creation of "male and female" and the "one flesh" joining as the source for holding marriage to be indissoluble. This passage receives considerable attention in the paper on marriage as vocation. However, in terms of the ethical concerns raised here, it is important to note that the indissolubility of the relationship is the focus of Jesus' concern, not sex as such or sexuality.

Moreover, Jesus was likely teaching in Aramaic in which, as is the case with the Hebrew of Genesis 1, the words male and female are nouns, better translated as "a male and a female" so that, as Jesus says, "the two shall become one flesh" (in contrast to the Hebrew of Genesis 2:24, which includes no number). In the same way, and using the same text, the Dead Sea Qumran community also informed its teaching on marriage discipline, asserting the divine rule for monogamy on the basis of God only having created "a male and a female" (Damascus Document 4:20f). Both in the Qumran community and in the teaching of Jesus, the focus is on the couple as a couple, not on the productive value of procreation.

From the beginning of the Church's reflection on the substance of marriage, including the recorded teaching of Jesus himself, the primary emphasis of marriage, expressed in the vows — the essence or substance of the marriage — lies in the spouses themselves and in the indissoluble union of heart, body, and mind that is achieved by means of that marriage.

Still, it is fair to note that, in a way, the tension between the two creation accounts (except as harmonized by Jesus) reflects a tension that is carried forward in the classical Anglican marriage rite: a tension between the prologue and the vows. For, as with the second creation account, there is no reference to procreation in the vows themselves — unsurprising in itself, for who could make such a solemn promise?

This suggests an awareness on the part of the composers of the rite that while a productive or ends-achieving ethic of utility may underlie the expectations of the prologue (as they do the creation of humanity in Genesis 1), a duty- or virtue-based ethic informs the vows, the couple turned to face each other, finding in the other the one "suitable" to each, and fulfilling both the vows and each other in their shared lives. The tensions in the rite between prologue and vows, as in Genesis 1 and 2, reflect a distinction between two models for understanding marriage: "dynastic" — productively looking toward the next generation — and "conjugal" — performatively focused upon the love of the couple themselves.

The emphasis on procreation stands as the first "cause" of the traditional prologue, as it does in Genesis 1, and also in current discussions on marriage, even though most current marriage liturgies have reduced the emphasis upon it, noting that it is provisional rather than essential, intrinsic, or inherent in marriage as marriage. As noted above, even the earliest Anglican rite of 1549 recognized that the productive value, while important, could not be understood as necessary, since not all marriages lead to procreation.

This is perhaps a tacit admission that, as Kant would put it, the principal end of marriage must be found in the couple themselves, and in their life together, as well as in a pragmatic recognition that marriages are not always procreative even when that is the couple's intent — and a couple incapable of procreation cannot reasonably intend it — but they are always meant to be loving and faithful. As noted above, a child coming into a loving and faithful context, whether by birth or adoption, is more likely to grow to be a loving and faithful person.

Another reason for finding the locus of the sign of marriage incarnate in the couple themselves lies in language added to the vows and included in the prologue in 1549. As Diarmaid MacCulloch helpfully notes:

> ... [Cranmer] newly added the promise by the groom "to love and to cherish," and by the wife "to love, cherish and obey," as the climax of their vows to each other. And for the first time in an official liturgical marriage text, marriage was announced as being "for the mutual society, help, and comfort that the one ought to have of the other, both in prosperity and adversity." Few medieval theologians would have extended the reasons for marriage beyond the avoidance for sin and the begetting of children; the classical list of Thomas Aquinas was *fides, proles, sacramentum,* with no mention of enjoyment. However, the Archbishop had had at least 16 years' experience of Margaret Cranmer's society, help, and comfort in prosperity and adversity when he and his drafting team finalized these words. This was an innovation that his married friend Martin Bucer greatly approved so much that when Bucer was suggesting his revisions for the 1549 rite, he unsuccessfully urged that it should be moved to appear as the first of the three stated reasons for marriage. (MacCulloch, 421)

It should be noted that Bucer has finally had his way: the American BCP 1979 reordered the prologue's "causes," as has the revised version of the prologue in the English Common Worship Marriage Service. American versions of the marriage liturgy, dating back to 1785, had originally removed all causal language from the prologue, thereby placing emphasis upon the estate itself, and the couple entering it by means of their vows, rather than upon its intentions or outcomes. Causal language was reintroduced in the 1979 BCP, but reordered so as to place emphasis on mutual joy and support as the best locus for the possible procreation and nurture of children.

Unlike the language of the prologue, the vows are unconditional; they are not based on purposes, ends, or goals. The duties described in the vows all relate to the couple themselves, and to their mutual behavior toward one another. Moreover, the vows are to perform things of which they are capable in themselves and for each other; and thus the absence of a vow to have children; even if it is an intent, its fulfillment cannot be promised, or made a condition or basis for the marriage at its outset or in its continuation.

Infertility — the inability to procreate — is neither an impediment to marriage nor a cause for divorce or annulment of marriage. (It has to be acknowledged, however, that where a "dynastic" model has been primary — literally so in royal marriages — infertility has played a part in finding ways to end marriages.)

Ideally, the spouses find in each other an appropriate end, rather than the means to some other end or objective, however good. Procreation does have virtue, in the bringing to be of human life, and it is a good toward which human endeavor in marriage is well intended when possible, growing out of the love of the couple for each other, rather than simply as an intended (or unintended) consequence.

But it is also important to note that the love of a couple for each other can result in other goods for the benefit both of the couple and the society of which they form a part, even when procreation either cannot or does not take place. There is a generativity that comes with the "mutual society" of marriage and which spills over to the larger society in which the couple lives and participates. It is perhaps good to note that the water jars at Cana were filled to the brim, and that the very act of dipping out the wine must have caused some overflow. The sheer abundance of goods that flow from the good of the couple's mutual self-giving is multiplied and expanded in a social setting.

This is perhaps nowhere so eloquently expressed as in the case of couples who adopt children whose biological parents are unable or unwilling to raise them. It is no accident that adoption is also a powerful Pauline metaphor for the church, set beside marriage in Ephesians (1:15) and primary in Romans 8 and Galatians 4. The paper on marriage as vocation expands upon this understanding of generativity and fruitfulness, in particular as an acknowledgement that we are all children of God by adoption.

Love as context and fulfillment

"Love" is a loaded word. It can, in the present context, all too often be understood only in the sense of *romance* or *affection*. Love, like marriage, is not just about romance or affection, although it can and should include them.

Love is rightly to be understood in terms of the will as much as of the emotions. It is in this sense that love forms a part of both the betrothal promises and the vows. Each member of the couple is asked, "Will you love ... ?"; and promises that they will, and then vows "to love and to cherish ..." So the problem is not that love has somehow become mixed up with marriage. The problem is that love — and marriage — have been misunderstood to be primarily about romantic feelings, and not about the commitment of each to the other in a mutual self-giving to and for the other, permanently and exclusively.

Fidelity within marriage is supported by the active will to love. In this sense, marriage is love made real, literally personified in the couple who lives out those vows, just as Jesus Christ revealed the "greatest love" in giving himself for the life of his friends — not in marriage (except as understood figuratively in his marriage to the church), but in his life, passion, death, resurrection, and ascension — which is the "mysterious" message of Ephesians.

Although it has been suggested that until the 20th century, marriages were concerned primarily or narrowly with property and progeny (an impression fueled largely by a focus on legal matters and the concerns of the propertied classes, sometimes literally "dynastic" in reference to the nobility or royalty), this view tends to ignore the rich evidence that attests to the importance of love and personal attachment in marriage, even among those very propertied classes and royalty. Where, after all, would Shakespeare be without love and the marriages it leads to?

More important, the biblical testimony bears witness to the contrast between the dynastic and conjugal models. This distinction is well documented in the Genesis account of Jacob's toil for his beloved Rachel and his disappointment with the discovery that Leah has been substituted as his bride — the situation of the two women representing a conflict between personal love and cultural conventions.

Similarly, Elkanah put this in numerical terms when he comforted his childless wife Hannah with the touching reminder that he is dearer to her "than ten sons" (1 Samuel 1:8). Even in a culture and religious tradition in which procreation was seen as the first commandment, and which allowed divorce or polygamy on the basis of infertility (as in Elkanah's case), we have a poignant witness that a loving marriage is not necessarily about having children. Love is generative even when it is not procreative.

Karl Barth put this internal focus on the couple in clear terms, laying particular stress upon the account in Genesis 2. In what might be seen as a rebuttal to the causal language in the classical marriage liturgy's prologue (in particular the emphasis on procreation and avoidance of sin), he says:

> [M]arriage as a life-partnership cannot be made to subserve the mere purpose of satisfying sexual needs ... fulfilling the impulse for procreation and training of children and therefore the ends of the family ... [It] is not a means to an end, but a life-form sui generis to be maintained and developed according to its own inner meanings and claims ... Marriage is not subordinate to the family, but the family (the relationship between parents and children which is itself an independent form) to marriage ... It subsists even without

> founding a family, even as the life-partnership of a possibly
> childless marriage. Marriage is necessarily *coniugium*, but not
> necessarily *matrimonium*. (Barth, 188)

That is, the spouses, but not necessarily parents, are always joined together. The 1978 report of the Church of England Marriage Commission stated a similar conclusion. Although it begins, demurring from Barth's outright rejection, with an affirmation that marriage "caters for certain fundamental and universal human needs and potentials," among which are the provision of "a secure and stable environment for the nurture of children," it continues by observing:

> [W]e do not believe that ... marriage is best understood as
> "for" children. We, on the other hand, wish to affirm that
> marriage is best understood as "for" husband and wife.
> It is their relationship with each other which is the basis
> of marriage. On this is built their relationship with their
> children. Arguments, therefore, in favour of the life-long
> nature of the married relationship must be seen to stem from
> the character of the husband-wife relationship itself, whether
> or not there are children. (General Synod 1978; 86, 33)

This echoes the teaching of Jesus in Matthew 19: the permanence of the couple rests on the fact that they have become one in marriage. As noted earlier, in reflection on marriage as a "sign of Christ's love for the Church," marriage forms the context in which loving spouses "become who they are" — a spouse "becomes" a spouse by virtue of relation to and with the other spouse.

Children can be conceived and born and raised apart from marriage, but marriage itself only exists between the spouses and in the context of their marriage, and it is marriage that makes them spouses, as they make the marriage, and it is the commitment to a lifelong, loving, faithful relationship — stated in the vows — that distinguishes marriage from other more casual forms of relationship.

As argued earlier, there is no real abstract "institution" of marriage but only actual, realized, incarnate instances of marriage. The ethical good that resides in real marriages — like any real "good" — is not theoretical but practical; it rests on the degree to which mutual love is expressed unconditionally, faithfully, and permanently, growing out of a union of heart, body, and mind.

It might be helpful to look at another family relationship in a similar light: The estate of being a "father" or a "mother" comes to be with conception and birth — biological processes shared by humans with many species. But being a good parent involves much more than the biological; and, most important from a biblical standpoint, parenthood is an estate that can be entered into by adoption, in which a new relationship is formed based not on a genetic heritage but on a commitment to responsibilities and the acquisition of new rights. Marriage is always such a voluntary commitment. The importance of choice or being chosen is explored at greater length in the paper on marriage as vocation.

This elective or volitional understanding of marriage — based on choice rather than necessity, on will rather than compulsion — can frame marriage as an "end" in eschatological terms, an end-in-itself anticipating but also making real some of the foretaste of the consummate joy of the union of all members in Christ the head. In this it rightly reflects the celebratory wine of Cana rather than the purposeful water of purification.

Understood in this way, marriage can take a place next to celibacy as an eschatological sign, separated from the purposefulness of marriage for procreation — necessary in this world to continue the species, but no longer needed in "the resurrection" (Luke 20:34-36). An earthly marriage can serve, as Paul suggests, as a "sign" of the mystical marriage given further elucidation in Revelation (19, 21) — of the Lamb and the New Jerusalem — a marriage in which procreation is not posited, as "the children of God" (by adoption) have been incorporated into the bride herself, whom Christ loves as his own body.

So it is that the primary "good" of marriage, its primary moral and ethical value, lies in the extent to which the couple express the love with which Christ loved his body and the Church, and in how they fulfill the mutual duty to have and to hold, to love and to cherish, and to forsake all others to remain faithful until the end — as an apprehension of the eschaton, a sign of the reign of God rather than the continuation of an earthly realm. The loving context in which and by which marriage enfolds the couple becomes an enacted parable for the community of the Church, as it "preaches Christ" to a wider world.

The implications of this understanding, in light of Barth's observation that "the question of posterity has lost its decisive significance in the time of the new covenant" (Barth, 189), opens a helpful path by which to explore the moral value to be found in all marriages, including same-sex marriages, as such couples can, as spouses, fulfill all of these moral duties.

It is not the respective maleness and femaleness of a couple that make them "suitable helpers" to each other, but rather the extent to which the couple can in fact serve each other as a "help and comfort in prosperity and adversity" and in "mutual joy." As with Adam's initial choice, and God's tolerant waiting on Adam's decision, it is up to each human being to recognize the helper suitable to each.

Facing the challenge

The biblical and theological framework described in this report could be critiqued for selecting and highlighting some elements of the tradition — scriptural, liturgical, and canonical — at the expense of others. However, this is no less true of the prevailing "traditional" view of marriage, which has emphasized or downplayed different aspects of the wide range of material available, beginning with Jesus himself, who dismissed an aspect of the Law of Moses, describing it as an allowance not in keeping with the more fundamental nature of marriage. That most churches, including The Episcopal Church, have also since nuanced Jesus' teaching on the indissolubility of marriage is perhaps worth noting. See the paper on the history of the canon law for details.

This paper has attempted to examine the moral aspects of marriage. In doing so it has drawn on Scripture, emphasizing the importance of dutiful, mutual love and service rather than dominance and submission. In the past the tendency has been to fix proper roles on the basis of gender by highlighting some aspects of the scriptural testimony at the expense of other aspects. For example, in Pauline writings, concepts of male headship came to be read apart from his equally clear call to mutual submission (1 Corinthians 11:3,11-12).

It is always a challenge to distinguish between elements of the tradition — including those recorded in Scripture — that truly reflect God's will as opposed to the overlay of human culture and custom. We have tried to elucidate that moral values of love, care, fidelity, and mutuality lie at the core of the meaning of marriage. In doing so, our hope is to provide an authentic framework for reflection on the virtues that can be displayed in all marriages, thereby strengthening all marriages by this testimony.

It may seem ironic, given his negative words on homosexuality in Church Dogmatics III.4, to have brought Karl Barth back into the discussion. However, conversation from late in his life, attested in a letter from Eberhard Busch written at Barth's direction, reveal that he had second thoughts about what he referred to as his "incidental comments" about homosexuality in his earlier work, his openness to revisiting the subject, and his regrets that his health and energy did not allow him the scope to undertake a formal reevaluation (Rodgers, 114).

The Church does not have the excuse of such fatigue or lack of energy, and it is incumbent upon it to do the best it can in its careful consideration of the theology of marriage. In this effort, the questions, "Can a same-sex couple serve as an image for Christ and the church?" and "Can the moral values evident in Christ's self-sacrificing love be lived out by a same-sex couple?" will have to be answered in light of the foregoing discussion.

In that light, the answer to both questions is the same as it is for a mixed-sex couple — that is, in the affirmative, that a couple who love each other sacrificially, mutually, faithfully, and exclusively are reflective of the love of God in Christ, to the extent that human flesh is capable of bearing that reflection.

Clearly, some difficulties remain, and for some these difficulties are insuperable. It is sometimes said that the reason only a mixed-sex couple can marry is based on the fact that only such a couple demonstrates a kind of complementary "unity in difference." Proponents of traditional understandings of marriage often claim that since same-sex relationships do not reflect this complementarity, such relationships represent an intrinsic disordering of God's creative ordering of human sexuality, and so ought not to be blessed.

So too, others assert that although same-sex relationships should be blessed as a distinct good that the Church has now discerned, nevertheless traditional marriage as many now understand it should retain a privileged status in large part due to the complementarity of the couple. These ideas are explored at greater length in the essay on marriage as vocation.

However, it is worth noting once more that it is not in the sex-difference, or in sex itself (whether understood as the sex of the bodies involved or the sexual act) that moral value lies. The traditional teaching of the relationship between sexuality and marriage is that it is the latter that sanctifies the former. Sexual acts outside of marriage — whether adultery or casual sex — are culpable on moral grounds due to the lack of (or violation of) the moral values of commitment, fidelity, mutuality, and exclusivity; so it is not the sexual acts themselves, or the relative genders of the couple who engage in them, that are morally good or bad, but the context and relationship of the actors that make them so.

There is a tension between what tradition has generally deemed to be intrinsically wrong and what many in the Church discern as manifestly good in particular same-sex couples. We discern similar sins and goods in particular heterosexual relationships. In short, sexuality is not in itself the locus of morality.

Rather, the location of the goodness of the metaphorical "tree" lies in its fruit (Matthew 12:33): and "the fruit of the spirit is love, joy, peace, patience, kindness, generosity, faithfulness, gentleness, and self-control. There is no law against such things" (Galatians 5:22-23). Moreover, within the context of marriage, sexual abuse, exploitation, or domination are moral failings; so it is not marriage in itself that leads to holiness, but the faithful and mindful enactment of the loving disciplines, rights, and responsibilities expressed in the marriage vows reflecting the love of Christ for his body, the Church.

4. Reflection on the Vows

> N. and N., you have come here today to seek the blessing of God and of his Church upon your marriage. I require, therefore, that you promise, with the help of God, to fulfill the obligations which Christian marriage demands. (BCP, 433)

These words begin the liturgy for the blessing of a civil marriage in the Book of Common Prayer. This rite is used for those couples already married in a civil ceremony who desire, as the liturgy states, God's blessing and that of the Church upon that marriage, and then make promises consistent with those made in The Celebration and Blessing of a Marriage (BCP, 424).

As we explore what makes a marriage holy or what makes a marriage a Christian marriage, we can take the opening words of this liturgy as a clear indicator of what is intended in marriage — what it is upon which the blessing of God and the Church is to be invoked; the substance of the marriage that is to find concrete fulfillment in the couple's faithful living of their solemn vows, enacting the obligations which Christian marriage demands. "Obligations" and "demands" are strong words that indicate to the couple and to all who witness the rite the seriousness of that to which they are committed. These words echo the caution in the opening exhortation of the marriage rite itself, which reminds the couple that marriage "is not to be entered into unadvisedly or lightly" (BCP, 423).

This is holy and serious business — holy in part because it is held up as such by the Church as witnessed to by our liturgy. The act of blessing that which already is — in this case the marriage and the couple — is both a recognition and a consecration, a graced moment between what has been and what is to be.

In 2000, General Convention adopted Resolution D039, which sets out expectations that the Church has of lifelong, committed, monogamous relationships. These expectations witness to the "obligations which Christian marriage demands." The resolution lists the expectations that the Church holds dear in all such relationships, saying they will "be characterized by fidelity, monogamy, mutual affection and respect, careful, honest communication, and the holy love which enables such relationships to see in each other the image of God."

The resolution goes on to "denounce promiscuity, exploitation, and abusiveness in the relationships of any of our members" and emphasizes accountability by stating "this Church intends to hold all its members accountable to these values." This is a profound statement solidly based in the ethics and virtues, the demands and obligations of holy living.

In many ways, the resolution builds on and even strengthens the actual vows in the prayer book (BCP, 427). Expectations are clear, and accountability is clearly stated. Most important, God is in the midst of it all, as the kind of love needed to accomplish these expectations will be holy love that shows forth the love of God and reminds the couple to seek and serve God as imaged in each other. When they do this, they become an icon of the love of God to the wider community.

The vows in the BCP (427) are ancient and familiar, powerful in their own right. Each member of the couple proclaims the vows to the other, in the Name of God. As the true ministers of the rite, the couple makes these solemn vows before God and witnesses — but the vows are made directly to each other. The familiar words remind all couples of the difficulties they face in marriage — better or worse, sick or well, rich or poor, through all this and in spite of any subsequent conditions short of death itself, the will to love and to cherish remains as the chief obligation and duty. The use of "cherish" adds to the promise to love an implication of a tenderness of affection that gives a glimpse of that special, unconditional love that God has for us, and which Christ has for his bride, the Church.

The demands of marriage as the site of blessing

What does Christian marriage demand? Both resolution D039 and the BCP marriage liturgies link the solemn vows with God. Seeing the image of God in your spouse, asking God's blessing upon your union: these liturgical acts and exhortations wrap these powerful promises in holy language. This same holy language is even echoed in the liturgy Thanksgiving for Adoption of a Child (BCP, 441) that allows the child, if old enough, to "take" his or her mother and/or father. The taking is mutual, and a family is the result, blessed and marked liturgically.

When exploring how our marriage vows help us understand what makes a marriage holy, a brief glance at some history is helpful. The current vows in the 1979 BCP continue to use phrases such as "to have and to hold." This was originally intended to protect the rights to property and the "taking care of" the bride. Previous iterations included words about the dowry. Marriage as a contract that had to do with property, rights, and inheritance had little or no theological underpinning.

However, as deeper reflection on the moral and theological virtues was undertaken, the Church took a higher view of the vows, while retaining some of the old language. Eventually, the promise of the bride to "obey" was removed, making the vows identical for both bride and groom. The vows evolved into holy language intent on sacred promises to each other made by the true ministers of the rite, focused on covenant terms that not only bind the couple together, but also remind us of God's covenant promises to God's people.

As noted above, Cranmer's expansion of the vows in the 1549 prayer book led even more to casting the demands and obligations as sanctifying love more than as merely contractual fulfillment. The 1979 BCP moves us further in that direction, and resolution D039 from GC 2000 continues that pattern in more specific terms and extends the expectations to unmarried couples in committed relationships. It is the commitment that transforms the relationship from casual to faithful, and it is the commitment that is sanctified by the blessing of the Church.

What makes a marriage holy? For Christians, the solemn vows of fidelity and love until death are promised and made, and the gathered Church witnesses and blesses this new commitment. "From this day forward" the couple "takes" each other, creating a new reality in their union as one in heart, body, and mind. It is this relationship that has been imbued with the Holy Spirit through prayer and blessing in the Name of God, which points to what makes a marriage holy.

Works Cited

Scripture citations are from the New Revised Standard Version.

Barth, Karl. *Church Dogmatics* III.4. London: T & T Clark, 1961.

Brown, Raymond E. *The Gospel According to John I-XII*. Garden City, N.Y.: Doubleday, 1966.

Brundage, James A. *Law, Sex and Christian Society in Medieval Europe*. Chicago: University of Chicago Press, 1987.

General Synod Marriage Commission. *Marriage and the Church's Task* (GS 363). London: CIO Publishing, 1978.

MacCulloch, Diarmaid. *Thomas Cranmer: A Life*. New Haven: Yale University Press, 1996.

Rodgers, Eugene F., Jr. *Theology and Sexuality: Classic and Contemporary*. Oxford: Blackwell, 2002.

Watkins, Oscar D. *Holy Matrimony: A Treatise on the Divine Laws of Marriage*. London: Rivington, Percival, 1895.

White, Edwin Augustine, and Jackson A. Dykman. *Annotated Constitution and Canons for the Government of the Protestant Episcopal Church in the United States of America otherwise known as The Episcopal Church Adopted in General Conventions 1789-1979* (New York: DFMS, 1981)

ESSAY 2:
Christian Marriage as Vocation

Introduction: A Vocation to Study Marriage

In this moment in the life of The Episcopal Church, we are in active, church-wide discernment on several fronts about how we are called to proclaim the Good News. We do this work grounded in an array of contexts within The Episcopal Church, mindful of our membership in the Anglican Communion and the wider Body of Christ. By passing resolution A050 and forming the Task Force on the Study of Marriage, the 77th General Convention in 2012 identified the study of marriage as an important component of that wider discernment.

The work of this Task Force has emerged from a series of conversations over several decades on our understanding of human difference and how the Church is called to honor and embody that difference. This paper operates on the premise that this ongoing conversation is an important facet of our central mission: to be agents of Christ's ministry of reconciliation in the Church and in the world.

It also proposes that just as we are coming to recognize the place of this conversation in our wider ecclesial vocation at this moment, we also have an opportunity to consider — or perhaps, more accurately, to reconsider and in some ways to reinterpret — Christian marriage as a vocation. It presents marriage as a spiritual practice, a particular vowed manner of life meant to be engaged over the course of a lifetime. The sections that follow unpack that vocation more fully: a call to love, to union in the midst of difference, to fidelity and stability, to growth and generativity, and ultimately to eschatological communion with God and one another.

1. An Emerging Framework

More immediately than the Church's decades-long conversation, reflections received by the Task Force during this triennium helped crystallize this paper's vocational framework. As the Task Force met, publicized its work, and received input from various corners of the Church, one theme (among several) that surfaced repeatedly was a concern about how marriage has factored into our collective ecclesial conversations in recent years. This message was, essentially: do not overemphasize the significance of marriage within Christian life. Do not make it the absolute center, the end-all, be-all of human relationships. Remember singleness. Remember friendship. Remember the emerging web of intentional communities in which units of family, of holy households, are in various quarters being discovered anew. (Some of this feedback is also reflected in the Task Force papers on the history of Christian marriage, marriage as a rite of passage, and changing trends and norms.)

Single people asked please not to be relegated to second-class citizenship.[61] Some couples reported struggling with ecclesial pressure to marry either before they were ready to do so or despite not feeling called to do so. This strain of feedback also tended to emphasize the ways in which Christian marriage has been entangled historically with patterns of social inequality and injustice (as reflected in the Task Force papers, "A History of Christian Marriage" and "Changing Trends and Norms in Marriage").

Mindful of this particular feedback, it is important to underscore that marriage is a manner of life that should not be assumed or imposed but freely discerned. In the Gospel of Matthew, Jesus acknowledges that marriage is not a universal vocation. In response to the disciples who wonder aloud whether it might be "better not to marry" given Jesus' strong strictures against divorce, he replies that "not everyone can accept this teaching, but only those to whom it is given" (Matthew 19:11).

To assume that marriage is a universal, default manner of life to which all adults are called would implicitly devalue those who do not marry. Indeed, as David Runcorn has argued in the context of the Church of England's conversation, "part of the gift of this debate [concerning

---

61 As the Primate's Theological Commission of the Anglican Church of Canada on the Blessing of Same-Sex Unions has written, "It is clear that, while Christianity has historically upheld the sanctity of the single state, regardless of whether or not it is lived out in the context of a vow of celibacy, there have been and are now many cultures that expect each person to be part of a couple or family, and are suspicious and judgmental of any expression of the single life, including celibate clergy." The St. Michael Report, Section 18. See http://www.anglican.ca/primate/ptc/smr/.

sexuality and marriage] is that it is reminding the Church that human beings need a wider range of relationships in community than just the model of marriage."[62]

Further, to assume that marriage is a universal human vocation would belie important New Testament witnesses that critique marriage or emphasize singleness. In his first letter to the Corinthians, for instance, Paul wishes that "all were as I myself am" — that is, single and celibate. But, he continues, "each has a particular gift from God, one having one kind and another a different kind" (1 Corinthians 7:7).

In the Gospel of Luke, Jesus asserts that while "those who belong to this age marry and are given in marriage, those who are considered worthy of a place in that age and in the resurrection from the dead neither marry nor are given in marriage" (Luke 20:34-36). As much scholarship has shown (including the Task Force paper, "A History of Christian Marriage"), the New Testament is far from univocal in its portrayals of marriage, whether affirming or critical.[63]

Yet even if biblical and historical descriptions of marriage have varied, even if marriage has been critiqued justly for its long tendency to be embedded in patterns of social privilege and injustice, Christian marriage need not be summed up by this history. Neither should it be reduced to an unthinking concession to social custom or ecclesial conformity.

Indeed, Task Force feedback also reflected a desire for theologically robust reflection on how Christian marriage emerges from the richness and complexity of our tradition. Couples, as well as single people anticipating marriage down the road, reflected a desire to discern carefully whether and when they might be called to marriage. How might they know if they are ready to marry a particular person, or if they are called to marriage at all? How many of the tracks of adult life should be laid down before entering into a marriage?

Or, conversely, what role might marriage have in stabilizing and grounding lives in the midst of transition? Indeed, what relationship might marriage have to change and stability? How might discernment of a call to parenthood intersect with and remain distinct from that

---

[62] David Runcorn, Appendix 4, in *Report of the House of Bishops Working Group on Human Sexuality* (London: Church House Publishing, 2013), 193.

[63] See, for example, Adrian Thatcher, chapter 3, in *Marriage after Modernity* (Sheffield: Sheffield Academic, 1999); Elizabeth Clark, *Reading Renunciation: Asceticism and Scripture in Early Christianity* (Princeton: Princeton University Press, 1999); Dale Martin, *Sex and the Single Savior: Gender and Sexuality in Biblical Interpretation* (Louisville: Westminster John Knox Press, 2006); Mary Ann Tolbert, "Marriage and Friendship in the Christian New Testament: Ancient Resources for Contemporary Same-Sex Unions," in M. Jordan, M. Sweeney, and D. Mellott, eds., *Authorizing Marriage: Canon, Tradition, and Critique in the Blessing of Same-Sex Unions* (Princeton and Oxford: Princeton University Press, 2006), 41-51.

of marriage? These responses requested reflection on how Christian marriage might invite people more deeply into their lives of faith (a topic addressed at length in "A Biblical and Theological Framework for Thinking about Marriage").

Underlying this range of reflections and questions was a broad query: to what forms of relationship are we being called as individuals, as couples, as communities, as members of Christ's body? Routed through the charge of the Task Force, these inquiries helped raise a more focused question: how might a theological frame of marriage, understood as a vocation, aid the wider discernment of the Church as well as of individual church members?

Now more than ever, we as a church are called to articulate marriage as a living Christian vocation, to invite its discernment as a manner of life that, both like and unlike other vocations, enables its participants to engage in their wider call to love, to union, to relational fidelity and stability, and to generativity and growth as members of Christ's body.

2. Vocation and Discernment

"Vocation" in this paper refers to manners of life opened up for, and ultimately received by, God's people, both as individuals and as communal members of Christ's body. It is a way of being in and engaging with the world, of ordering our life in ways that facilitate our participation in the wider purposes for which God created us, redeemed us, and brings us into newness of life.

Vocation can speak to specific life professions, to particular messages we are challenged to convey in and to the world (as in the examples of the biblical prophets and of Jesus' disciples), to modes of relationship (as in the calls to parenthood by the patriarchs and matriarchs and to Mary the God-bearer), to broader ways of engaging the world that God created (as in Paul's enjoinder in 2 Corinthians 5:20 "be reconciled to God").

Connected to vocation is discernment: the process of receiving clarity about what one may be called to do. Discernment entails prayer and reflection, conversation, new perception, and decision. It is both individual and communal.[64] Most important, it entails creating space

---

[64] The report, To Set Our Hope on Christ (written by a group of Episcopal theologians at the request of Presiding Bishop Frank Griswold) also uses language of discernment with respect to the current church-wide conversation on sexuality and marriage. *To Set Our Hope on Christ: A Response to the Invitation of Windsor Report 135* (New York: The Episcopal Church Center, 2005), 8-9: "[W]e believe that God has been opening our eyes to acts of God that we had not known how to see before" (9).

to perceive and receive what the Holy Spirit may be prodding an individual or a community to do, as distinct from what an individual or community may feel inclined to do on their own. The phrase from Matthew 19:11 regarding those who are called to marriage and those who are not commonly is translated, "not everyone can accept this teaching, but only those to whom it is given."[65]

Yet the verb translated as "accept," *chorousin*, is also spatial. It means "to leave space, to make room," to "move forward, to advance," or "to have room for receiving" something. Space is opened for something that is "given" (*dedotai*), a gift both freely bestowed and received. Discernment creates space in a spirit of God-given freedom. As John Chrysostom (c. 347-407 C.E.) remarks regarding this Matthew 19 phrase, it is not "shut up in the compulsion of a law." Rather, because of God's "unspeakable gentleness," we are free to receive and to heed the promptings and trajectories of the God who made us and calls us.[66] Through this process the Holy Spirit ultimately leads us into all truth, sometimes in ways we never could have anticipated, and may indeed have difficulty bearing (John 16:12-13).

3. A Vocation of Love

First and foremost, marriage is caught up in the larger, more fundamental vocation of love. As Christians we are all called to respond to, to join, and to become agents of the love of God in Jesus Christ. The commandments, as Jesus summarized them, are to love God with all one's heart, soul, and mind; and to love one's neighbors as oneself (Matthew 22:37-40; Mark 12:30-31; Luke 10:27; see also Romans 13:9).[67] In the Gospel of John, Christ gives us what he calls "a new commandment that you love one another. Just as I have loved you, you also should love one another." That expression of love for one another marks us as Christ's disciples (John 13:34-35; 15:12).

The first letter of John further develops that vocation: "Beloved, let us love one another, because love is from God; everyone who loves

---

65 Matthew 19: 11, NRSV. All subsequent biblical quotations will also be from the NRSV unless otherwise specified.
66 John Chrysostom, Homily 62.3 on the Gospel of Matthew in ed. Philip Schaff, *Nicene and Post-Nicene Fathers*, Vol. 10, *Chrysostom: Homilies on the Gospel of Saint Matthew* (Peabody, Mass.: Hendrickson Publishers, 1994), 384.
67 Thomas Breidenthal has also argued that "true romantic love is a form of the love of neighbor." *Sacred Unions: A New Guide to Lifelong Commitment* (Cambridge, Mass.: Cowley Publications, 2006), 11. See especially chapter 2. Breidenthal goes on to argue that "[j]ust as the romantic tradition [of the troubadors whose lyric poetry emerged around the eleventh century C.E. in what is now southern France] helped the Christian world rediscover the marriage of man and woman as a spiritual vocation, so now, as we struggle to extend our understanding of that vocation to include partners of the same sex, that tradition emerges once again as a fruitful starting point and a rich resource for that discussion" (Sacred Unions, 26).

is born of God and knows God" (1 John 4:7). By loving, we come to know and to share the divine life of the One who "wonderfully created and yet more wonderfully restored" us.[68] "In your infinite love you made us for yourself," intones Eucharistic prayer A of the 1979 prayer book, echoing the language of Augustine of Hippo's (354-430 C.E.) Confessions. In response to that love, our whole lives form a pattern of restlessly seeking the One in whom our ultimate rest is to be found.[69]

Augustine's contemporary Gregory of Nyssa (c. 335-c. 395 C.E.) envisioned that loving search as a process of stretching forth (*epektasis*), in which we participate in God's unending desire for us. Through lives prayerfully lived, always stretching forth toward the heart of the living God, we can become vessels for the outpouring of God's desire. Throughout our lifetimes, we open our hearts and are repeatedly filled with that desire, as God continuously expands our capacity for it. This loving vocation never ends.[70]

This vocation further emerges from the fundamental Christian teachings of the Incarnation and the Paschal Mystery. To love is to offer ourselves to one another, inspired by and grounded in the love with which Christ poured himself into our midst, reconciling us to the God from whom we had grown estranged. "No one has greater love than this, to lay down one's life for one's friends," Jesus teaches in the fifteenth chapter of John. We respond to that love, he continues, as his friends, appointed to bear the fruit of that love in lives offered to God and to one another (John 15:12-17).

This love catalyzes us to live lives of solidarity and sympathy, in imitation of the One who is always able to sympathize with us in our weakness (Hebrews 4:15). In love our lives bear witness to the mystery of resurrection life, healing our death-dealing wounds of betrayal and brokenness, refreshing and renewing our very creation. In Christ we lovingly join our own lives to the bridge he reforged between creation and the God in whose image we are made.

---

68 Collect "Of the Incarnation," Book of Common Prayer (New York: Church Hymnal Corporation, 1979), 252.
69 Eucharistic Prayer A, Book of Common Prayer, 362. Augustine of Hippo, *Confessions* 1.1 in trans. F.J. Sheed, Confessions Books I-XIII (Indianapolis: Hackett Publishing Company, 1993), 3.
70 Gregory expounds this idea of *epektasis* in several texts, including the *Life of Moses and his Homilies on the Song of Songs*. Note also that Gregory does not hesitate to use the term "desire" to describe the driving force of this process. For more on Gregory of Nyssa's ideas of desire and gender, see Sarah Coakley's *Powers and Submissions: Spirituality, Philosophy and Gender* (Malden, MA: Blackwell, 2003), chapters 7-9. See also Coakley's *God, Sexuality, and the Self*, in which she argues that human desire originates in that of the Triune God who is ultimately "the means of [human desire's] transformation." *God, Sexuality, and the Self: An Essay on the Trinity* (Cambridge: Cambridge University Press, 2013), 6.

Our wider vocation to love can find a more particular expression through the love of two spouses for one another. It is a love that draws couples together in shared sexuality, affirming the goodness of our embodiment and desire. It is a love of discovery that delights in a lifetime of adventures lived, challenges faced, insights shared. It is a vocation that rejoices in seeing and being seen and known by spouses who can reveal to one another what, individually, they could never have perceived on their own. "It is not good that *ha adam* should be alone," God declares in Genesis 2:18: "I will make him a helper as his partner."

Spousal love can convey a deep sense of comfort in the ongoing partnership of assembling and maintaining a shared life. It can form the foundation for the birth and raising of children, the nurture of family. Thus, to speak of marriage as a vocation to love is to refer not simply to the affective state of being in love, or of falling in love. More fundamentally, the love in which Christian marriage is grounded is relational and lifelong. Bounded by the vows made in holy matrimony, marriage is a holy vessel in which a couple grows and changes together over the course of a lifetime. Ultimately, in these many and various ways the vocation of Christian marriage continually invites spouses to reveal to one another, and to their wider community, the love of God in Jesus Christ.

4. Union and Difference

As with love, a vocation to marriage calls couples into a particular sort of union that is always already caught up in a wider call to be one. What is often called marriage's unitive quality bears out in its own manner Jesus' "new commandment" to "love one another" and to be one just as he and the Father are one (John 17:21). This union both joins us together and rejoices in our particularity, our difference. At a fundamental, sacramental level, our call to union emerges from our baptism in which we are engrafted into the wider Body of Christ.

Throughout our lives we live out our membership in that body in various ways: as we receive communion week by week, as we seek and serve Christ in all persons, loving our neighbor as ourselves (Baptismal Covenant, 1979 BCP, 305). When we pray "that we all may be one" (1979 BCP, 387) we open our hearts to unions of affinity and difference, to friendship, to family, to wide-ranging collectives of work and home, to our Church, flung far and wide around the globe.

"Cleaving" and creation

The unitive vocation in Christian marriage emerges in important ways from how we have read the creation stories. As Christians, we read the stories of our creation through New Testament as well as Hebrew biblical lenses. These include Jesus' own interpretive citations. Despite his own life of (apparent) singleness and his critical reflections on ideas of family in his imperial Roman context (again, see "A History of Christian Marriage" and footnote 3 above), Jesus clearly also respects and envisions a place for marriage. As mentioned earlier, he goes on to imply in Matthew 19 that marriage is a vocation "given" (*dedotai*) to many, even as there are others to whom it is not.[71]

Jesus' explanation of this vocation (in 19:3-12, paralleled by Mark 10:2-12) emerges in response to a question from the Pharisees about divorce. While Moses allowed divorce "because of your hardness of heart," Jesus replies, "from the beginning it was not so." Citing the conclusion of the first creation story, Genesis 1:27, he asserts that "the one who made them at the beginning 'made them male and female.'" Without citing the Genesis 1:28 command "be fruitful and multiply," he then continues directly with a citation from Genesis 2:24: "For this reason a man [*anthropos*] shall leave his father and mother and be joined [*kollethesetai*] to his wife [*gynaiki*], and the two[72] shall become one flesh [*hoi duo eis sarka mian*]."[73]

When we marry one another as Christians we take up this created possibility of shared embodiment. We reverence God's own creative

---

[71] In Matthew 19, Jesus goes on to explain that there are those to whom what he has just said about marriage and divorce does not apply, or is not given: "For there are eunuchs who have been so from birth, and there are eunuchs who have been made eunuchs by others, and there are eunuchs who have made themselves eunuchs for the sake of the kingdom of heaven. Let anyone accept this who can." This passage has a long tradition of being read in support of the vocation of virginity or celibacy — of considering celibacy a higher calling than marriage (re: "it is better not to marry"). More recent scholarship has underscored the various roles and constructions of eunouchoi in Roman imperial and later Byzantine contexts, as well as the implications of Jesus' acknowledgment of people who complicate or exceed the sexual binary of male and female. See, for instance, Mathew Kuefler, *The Manly Eunuch: Masculinity, Gender Ambiguity, and Christian Ideology in Late Antiquity* (Chicago: University of Chicago Press, 2001); Kathryn Ringrose, *The Perfect Servant: Eunuchs and the Social Construction of Gender in Byzantium* (Chicago: University of Chicago Press, 2003); Walter Stevenson "Eunuchs and Early Christianity," in S. Tougher, ed., *Eunuchs in Antiquity and Beyond* (London: Classical Press of Wales and Duckworth, 2002). For contemporary theological explorations of this ancient category, particularly with regard to intersex people / people with disorders of sexual development (DSD), see Susannah Cornwall, *Sex and Uncertainty in the Body of Christ: Intersex Conditions and Christian Theology* (London: Equinox, 2010).

[72] As the paper, "A Biblical and Theological Framework for Marriage" also points out, in the Hebrew of Genesis 2:24 the verb is simply plural, whereas the Septuagint, which Jesus here quotes, supplies *hoi duo*, "the two."

[73] This is an instance where the Greek term *anthropos*, often translated as "human being," when paired with gyne, "woman" or "wife," becomes gender specific: "man." Further, unlike in English, in both Greek and Hebrew the terms for "man" and "woman" can also be translated as "husband" and "wife."

handiwork, becoming "one flesh" in new ways. Further, Jesus' citations signal the creative force unleashed when a couple shifts the balance of its relational identity from families of origin to one another. Here the verb *kollao* — to weld, to glue together, or perhaps, most accurately, "to cleave to" (as the King James Version translates it) — speaks to the complex dynamics of this creative shift. To cleave is to join at a deep level, both sexual and spiritual, to direct and channel one's deep desire. Yet to cleave is also to cut through or split, to part. The cleaving of marriage could be said to reform families by shifting their borders — often enlarging them through the inheritance of the spouse's family, but ultimately shifting the particular quality of earlier familial attachments.[74] Once it is vowed, once that cleaving has been liturgically enacted, to undo it is a very serious matter.[75] The cleaving of marriage has creative reverberations.

Complementarity considered

Jesus' juxtaposed reading of the Genesis creation accounts has contributed to a relatively recent thread that sees in Christian marriage the fulfillment of the created meaning of male and female. And although Jesus' comments on marriage do not address procreation (again, he declines to cite Genesis 1:28: "be fruitful and multiply, fill the earth and subdue it"), the above referenced passage (and its Markan parallel) has been paired with other key texts to ground the meaning and significance of marriage in binary sexual difference as well as in the human capacity to procreate. In this way, the unitive quality of marriage has at times been conflated with the procreative capacity that many, though not all, couples possess.[76] The question of how the vocation of marriage takes up and expresses the wider Christian call to growth and generativity will be addressed more fully below, in section 6. Here, however, the question is whether the vocation of Christian marriage must center on the binary sexual difference of male and female.

---

[74] The Task Force paper "Marriage as a Rite of Passage" discusses how, historically, betrothal practices allowed time for the new network of familial relationships to adjust and engage in their reconfiguration and growth.

[75] This is why our own conversations as a church about divorce took time to sort out, concluding that divorce and remarriage in the church are possible only under careful, canonically governed discernment. See Canon I.19 in *Constitution and Canons of the Episcopal Church* (2012), 60-61. See also the Task Force Paper on the history of the marriage canons.

[76] For example, Goldingay et al. read Jesus' citations of Genesis in Mark 10 (which are the same as those in Matthew 19) as implicitly including Genesis 1:28. The "divine intention of the union of male and female in one flesh ... entails the social, psychological, and physical union, including the fruitfulness of childbearing as part of the order of creation." John Goldingay, Grant LeMarquand, George Sumner, and Daniel Westberg, "Same-Sex Marriage and Anglican Theology: A View from the Traditionalists," *Anglican Theological Review 93*, no.1 (2001): 1-50. See also their discussion opposing the separation of the unitive from the procreative facets of Christian marriage, pp. 40-41.

Christian theology has a long tradition of reading marriage through the mystery of the relationship between Christ and the Church. Indeed, Christian "nuptial theology" tends to unfold the mystical interface of our Christology and our ecclesiology through the lens of marriage, dwelling in particular on the imagery of Ephesians 5, as well as on Christological readings of the Song of Songs. The task force paper exploring marriage within a wider theological arc treats the Ephesians passage at some length. The analogies between Christ and the Church, husband and wife, male and female have long been interpreted in ways that limit marriage to heterosexual couples and that instantiate an asymmetry between husband and wife. In recent decades, some Christian theologians have framed this line of thought as "sexual complementarity" or simply "complementarity."[77]

As Adrian Thatcher has noted, while this idea can be nuanced in different ways, including in egalitarian modes, complementarity is usually used to argue that "God has planned and ordained heterosexual marriage as the sole framework for legitimate, holy, sexual relations."[78] In different ways and with distinct emphases, this idea has emerged in some Roman Catholic and evangelical Christian writings.[79] It has also begun to appear in some Anglican contexts.[80] These contributions reveal how our conversation about marriage interfaces with and activates our broader understanding of the human person. Should the basic organization of Christian marriage privilege sexual difference — more specifically, a strictly dual understanding of sexual difference as male and female — over other sorts of human difference? Should marriage work to contain or channel human differences into a basic nuptial binary of male and female?

---

77 For a description of this term see, for instance, Adrian Thatcher's discussion in *God, Sex, and Gender: An Introduction* (Malden, Mass.: Wiley Blackwell, 2011), 185-86.
78 Thatcher, *God, Sex, and Gender,* 186. An exception to this is the argument by Deirdre Good, Willis Jenkins, Cynthia Kittredge, and Eugene Rogers, that "male-female complementarity" can be read as "typical but not exhaustive of [marriage's] witness." Good et al., "A Theology of Marriage Including Same-Sex Couples: A View from the Liberals," Anglican Theological Review 93, no. 1 (2011): 57. Another exception is Eugene Rogers, "Same-Sex Complementarity: A Theology of Marriage," Christian Century, May 11, 2011. http://www.christiancentury.org/article/2011-04/same-sex-complementarity.
79 See, for example, Pope John Paul II, *Man and Woman He Created Them: A Theology of the Body* (Boston: Pauline Books and Media, 2006); Wayne Grudem and John Piper, *Recovering Biblical Manhood and Womanhood: A Response to Evangelical Feminism* (Wheaton, IL: Crossway Books, 2006).
80 See, for example: House of Bishops of the General Synod of the Church of England, *Some Issues in Human Sexuality: A Guide to the Debate* (London: Church House Publishing, 2003), 10 (1.2.9); House of Bishops Working Group on Human Sexuality, *Report of the House of Bishops Working Group on Human Sexuality* (aka The Piling Report), section 117, pp. 33-34, and appendix 4, https://www.churchofengland.org/media/1891063/pilling_report_gs_1929_web.pdf. Goldingay et al., "Same-Sex Marriage and Anglican Theology: A View from the Traditionalists."

Mystery of new humanity

Here, from the fifth chapter of Ephesians, the mystery that characterizes Christ's relationship with the Church may offer a further way in which to understand the significance of difference in the union of marriage. After a call to "be subject to one another" in marriage (as also addressed in "A Biblical and Theological Framework for Marriage"), the author of Ephesians concludes with a quotation of Genesis 2:24, the same one cited by Jesus in Matthew 19: "For this reason a man will leave his father and mother and be joined to his wife, and the two will become one flesh." The letter then continues: "This is a great mystery, and I am applying it to Christ and the Church." The heart of marriage, that is, is a *mysterion*.

The concept of mystery expresses several key linked ideas in Ephesians. In its first chapter, the author uses the term to speak of the Good News itself: "With all wisdom and insight he has made known to us the mystery [*to mysterion*] of his will, according to his good pleasure that he set forth in Christ, as a plan for the fullness of time, to gather up all things in him, things in heaven and things on earth." In chapter three, the author proclaims that "this grace was given to me to bring to the Gentiles the news of the boundless riches of Christ, and to make everyone see what is the plan of the mystery hidden for ages in God who created all things; so that through the church the wisdom of God in its rich variety might now be made known to the rulers and authorities in the heavenly places" (Ephesians 3:8-10).

The content of the Ephesians' proclamation is "the boundless riches of Christ" and "the wisdom of God in its rich variety." This wisdom is instantiated in Jesus Christ who, in chapter two, is described as having broken down the dividing wall, "creating one new humanity [*kainon anthropon*] in place of the two" — that is, eradicating the divisions between Jews and Gentiles (2:14-16). Marriage, then, comes to reflect this mystery in chapter five as it symbolizes the relationship between Christ and the Church.

The mystery in which marriage participates, which it images forth or typifies, is of a new humanity, a union that simultaneously upholds and uplifts differences that extend beyond the sexual binary. Indeed, this mystery stretches across the rich and wise variety of creation itself. Read through this lens, marriage reflects in a distinctive manner the new humanity inaugurated by and in Christ. And in this way, once more, marriage evokes our baptism: the vocation of marriage in its own way reflects and activates the new Christic humanity into which we were baptized. We are said to have "put on Christ" in our baptism (Galatians 3:27), an act through which the Genesis-specified binary of "male and female," as well as that of Jew and Greek, slave and free, is in some sense "no longer." In "The Celebration and Blessing of a Marriage," Christ is said to have "adorned this manner of life by his presence and first miracle at a wedding in Cana of Galilee" (1979 BCP, 423).

The union of affinity and difference at the heart of marriage might be understood most fruitfully as a mystery at the heart of humanity and, indeed, of creation itself. In marriage, our vocation is not to erase our distinctions, even as we become "one flesh." Difference is neither eradicated nor "overcome" or transcended, but it is transformed. Our unique humanity is creatively activated, that the couple may be united one with another, becoming a new creation while simultaneously remaining two, distinct. This interplay of difference and unity in Christian marriage need not be limited to male and female, but it can be activated by all manner of human difference.

Indeed, as the Task Force paper "Marriage as a Rite of Passage" explains, the union of difference in Christian marriages can serve as a prophetic crucible in contexts of communal strife and division. Adrian Thatcher has further asserted that "it is helpful to see the author [of Ephesians] beginning a trajectory towards a real Christian theology of marriage, which for its completion needed further time ... Being 'subject to one another out of reverence for Christ' (Eph. 5:21) is starting to change everything."[81] Marriages of same-sex couples can also play an important role in dispelling any notion that one spouse could ever represent Christ, or the Church, more than the other. The "Celebration and Blessing of a Marriage" liturgy also signals the full equality of the couple as they carry out their role as "co-ministers."[82] Therefore, although the vocation of Christian marriage has historically been limited to heterosexual couples, the mystery it illumines arguably need not require this. Marriage's unambiguous and unambivalent embrace of the full spectrum of human difference, including that of sexual orientation, can enable it to image forth the rich variety of creation more fully than it has been able to in centuries past.

5. Ascesis and Stability

While love draws a married couple together, what binds and helps sustain their union over time is what might be called its disciplined ascetic quality. For Christian marriage is, as others have argued, a vowed vocation.[83] Its vows create a covenant that binds the two

---

81 Thatcher, *God, Sex, and Gender,* 108.
82 Thatcher, *God, Sex, and Gender,* 110, and *Marriage after Modernity,* 240.
83 Good et al., "A Theology of Marriage Including Same-Sex Couples: A View from the

spouses together, "as long as [they] both shall live." The spousal declaration in "The Celebration and Blessing of a Marriage" to "love, honor and keep" the beloved "in sickness and in health" and to be faithful to the beloved, "forsaking all others," is an askesis, a spiritual practice (1979 BCP, 424).[84] It shares this vowed quality with forms of religious life in which community members make lifelong professions.

The apostle Paul reads marriage through an ascetic lens. After commenting to the community at Corinth, "I wish that all were as I am" — that is, single and celibate — he speaks of marriage as a concession or indulgence and not as a command. Marriage here works as a tether for those who are not called to a life of celibate singleness (1 Corinthians 7:6-7). Even as Paul wishes that all were like him, he steps back and points to the more fundamental vocational issue: "But each has a particular gift [*idion charisma*] from God, one having one kind and another a different kind" (1 Corinthians 7:7). A few verses later, once more he underscores: "Let each of you lead the life that the Lord has assigned, to which God called you" (1 Corinthians 7:17). The particular graces or charisms gifted to each of us from God can come to their fullest fruition through the relationships and commitments we form. Christian marriage is one such pattern of life that binds the married couple to one another, to the church family in whose presence they make their vows, and to the wider Body of Christ, whose membership they now engage afresh through the lens of marriage.

The vowed quality of Christian marriage enables it to become a particular kind of relational vessel. Unique to each couple, these vessels of marriage create a sense of stability strong enough to allow the couple to support each other "for better for worse, for richer for poorer, in sickness and in health … until [they] are parted by death" (1979 BCP, 427). These vows are meant not simply to be limit-setting promises, but also a deep source of life. Here the Johannine quality of "abiding" can illumine the vitality of this form of vowed stability.

In the 15th chapter of the Gospel of John, Jesus unfolds the metaphor of the vine and the branches, declaring, "Abide [meinate] in me as

---

Liberals," 51, 62-63. "These vows mark marriage as an arduous form of training in virtue, by which the promises come true that God will heal human waywardness and teach us to love (Hos. 14:4; Jer. 3:22)."

84 Good et al. explain: "Our approach combines the two New Testament values of asceticism and household: marriage is a school for virtue, a household asceticism: 'for better for worse,' 'forsaking all others' (1979 BCP, 427, 424)." "A Theology of Marriage Including Same-Sex Couples," 58. Eugene Rogers also makes this point, arguing that we ought to understand "marriage as an ascetic discipline, a particular way of practicing love of neighbor. The vows do this: 'for better for worse, for richer for poorer, in sickness and in health, till death do us part.' Those ascetic vows — which Russian theologians compare to the vows of monastics — commit the couple to carry forward the solidarity of God and God's people. Marriage makes a school for virtue, where God prepares the couple for life with himself by binding them for life to each other." "Same-Sex Complementarity."

I abide in you. Just as the branch cannot bear fruit by itself unless it abides in the vine, neither can you unless you abide in me. I am the vine, you are the branches" (John 15:4-5a). The verb meino, "to abide" or "to remain," here becomes not simply a delimiting command, but a source of life. By abiding in the vine as a branch, one remains attached to that from which life emerges. To abide in John's Gospel is to dwell in divine love, to participate in it, to be transformed by it, to share it in community. "This is my commandment, that you love one another as I have loved you," Jesus continues, calling his disciples "friends." The vows that help establish the vessel of a Christian marriage abide in that same love.

6. Vocation of Growth and Generativity

These vows of stability that help support and bind a married couple to one another also enable the couple to serve as a means of grace-filled growth. "The decision to give my word about my future love can be part of converting my heart," writes Margaret Farley, "part of going out of myself truly to meet the one I love (not part of hardening my heart because of excessive fear of sanctions if I break the law that I give to my love)."[85] That conversion of heart can unfold through shared experience of vulnerability and trial as much as through joy and triumph. "Blessed are you, God of growth and discovery" intones a prayer from A New Zealand Prayerbook: "yours is the inspiration that has altered and changed our lives; yours is the power that has brought us to new dangers and opportunities. Set us, your new creation, to walk through this new world, watching and learning, loving and trusting, until your kingdom comes."[86] The lifelong commitment vowed in marriage emerges from a desire to "gather up our whole future and place it in affirmation of the one we love," even as we walk together through an unfolding future that remains unknown in fundamental ways. Our vows can ground and plant us even as love "grows into wholeness" over the course of a lifetime.[87]

Abiding in God and in one another, a Christian marriage responds to Christ's call in John 15 to "bear much fruit." Here the idea of fruitfulness is first and foremost a reflection of the broader call to growth as members of Christ's body.[88] As Paul urges in his letter to the

---

[85] Margaret Farley, "The Meaning of Commitment," in Kieran Scott and Michael Warren, eds., *Perspectives on Marriage: A Reader* (New York: Oxford University Press, 2007), 155.
[86] A concluding collect from the Eucharistic Liturgy of Thanksgiving for Creation and Redemption, in *A New Zealand Prayerbook* (The Anglican Church in Aotearoa, New Zealand, and Polynesia, 1988), 465.; http://anglicanprayerbook.nz/ 456.html.
[87] Farley, "The Meaning of Commitment," 155.
[88] Margaret Farley also explores an expansive notion of fruitfulness in *Just Love: A Framework for Christian Sexual Ethics* (New York: Continuum, 2006), 227-228, 290.

Romans, we are called to align ourselves with the New Covenant, "to bear fruit for God" (Romans 7:4). At the same time, our own birthing is most dramatically articulated not through biological gestation — the "be fruitful and multiply" enjoinder of Genesis 1:28 — but rather through adoption.

In his letter to the Romans, Paul declares: "[Y]ou have received a spirit of adoption. When we cry, 'Abba! Father!' it is that very Spirit bearing witness with our spirit that we are children of God, and if children, then heirs, heirs of God and joint heirs with Christ — if, in fact, we suffer with him so that we may also be glorified with him" (Romans 8:15b-17). Like the cry of a newborn, that distinctive parental exclamation — "Abba!" — signals a spiritual birth, a freshly forged, newly fruitful familiality. In the same letter, this transformative kinship is imaged as an engrafting: Gentile followers of Jesus could understand themselves as "wild olive branches ... engrafted contrary to nature [*para phusin enekentristhes*] into a cultivated olive tree" (Romans 11:24). Fruitfulness, for Christians, emerges through a creation that has been made new. We are not to be conformed to this world, Paul urges one chapter later, but rather "transformed by the renewing of our minds [*metamorphousthe te anakainosei*]" (Romans 12:2). Our lives are to be not static but metamorphic, constantly transformed into the likeness of the One through whom all things were made. Christian marriage becomes generative first and foremost through this context.

A gift of the Holy Spirit, fruitfulness is the result of the cleansing from sin and reconciliation to God gifted to us in baptism, the ongoing outgrowth of the lifelong process of conversion. Through its baptismal foundation, the vocation of Christian marriage can lead us deeper into the heart of the Paschal Mystery itself. "In [baptism] we are buried with Christ in his death. By it we share in his resurrection. Through it we are reborn by the Holy Spirit" (1979 BCP, 306). Once launched, that rebirth reverberates throughout our lives. "God gives the growth," Paul explains to the community at Corinth (1 Corinthians 3:6-7). As the letter to the Ephesians further urges: "[W]e must grow up in every way into him who is the head, into Christ, from whom the whole body, joined and knit together by every ligament with which it is equipped, as each part is working properly, promotes the body's growth in building itself up in love" (Ephesians 4:15-16).

As individual members of this body, Christians continually rediscover and live into the new humanity inaugurated in Christ. This humanity, referenced earlier, emerges from the dissolution of the walls that divide us from one another. It is pervaded by peace, grounded in the spirit of reconciliation that Christ bore into our midst (Ephesians 2:14-22). As we seek to live into the promises we make at our baptism (1979 BCP, 304-5), to embody this new humanity, to embrace the Paschal Mystery itself, we are caught up in the loving dynamic of a creation that in Christ, as Gregory of Nazianzus (c. 329-389) proclaimed, has been "rendered afresh."[89] Indeed, our individual growth also prompts the larger communal body to mirror more comprehensively the glory of the One through whom all things were made. When we are called to bear fruit that will last, this is first and foremost what is meant.

As one disciplined means of engaging this lifelong vocation to loving growth, Christian marriage is caught up in this trajectory of transformation. Its potential fruitfulness is always bound up with this metamorphic quality. Indeed, the story of the wedding at Cana, frequently referenced as a sign of Christ's support of Christian marriage and cited in the prologue to "The Celebration and Blessing of a Marriage" is at its heart a sign of transformation (1979 BCP, 423). In marriage, the divine power with which Christ "turned water into wine at the wedding feast of Cana" has the lifelong capacity to "transform [our] lives and make glad [our] hearts."[90] In Christ, transformation itself is revealed as a crucial quality of creation's givenness, the capacity for spiritual growth and fruitfulness. Rather than a sign of dissolution, transformation renders creation pregnant with untold possibility.

Christian marriage forms one important relational context for the transformative generativity that Christians are called to embody. Within the vocation of marriage, "being fruitful and multiplying" thus can indeed take the form of rearing children born to parents who conceive them through the shared sexuality of their marriage. Further, this common manner of child-bearing and rearing can celebrate the goodness of the biologically creative capacities with which many of us have been gifted. This form of parenthood can take place within marriage, and when it does it can indeed be very good. Yet parenthood need not always unfold in this manner.

Further, just as not all Christians are called to marriage, not all married couples are called to parenthood. To speak of parenting in this way is not to reduce it to "an optional 'project' for those so inclined or for those guided by social expectations" but rather to

---

[89] Gregory of Nazianzus, Oration 39, "On the Holy Lights": "What happened? And what is the great Mystery that involves us? Natures are made anew; God becomes human; the one who 'rides on the heaven of heavens in the sunrise' of his own proper glory and splendor, is glorified in the sunset of our ordinariness and lowliness, and the Son of God allows himself to become and to be called Son of [Humanity]," in Brian E. Daley, trans., *Gregory of Nazianzus* (London: Routledge, 2006), 134.

[90] From the Epiphany blessing, *The Book of Occasional Services* (New York: Church Publishing, 2003), 24.

identify it as a deeply relational vocation, a way of participating in the ongoing renewal of creation.[91] Those who discern a call to parenthood may not be able to have children, whether for biological, relational, or economic reasons. Ultimately, for those who do raise children within the context of marriage — regardless of whether parents and children are biologically related — parental procreativity is fundamentally adoptive.

Shaped as all vocations are by the adoptive charism of baptism, parenthood is a particular form of the call to carry forward the gift of God's active choice: "You did not choose me but I chose you. And I appointed you to go and bear fruit, fruit that will last" (John 15:16). At its most basic level, bearing that fruit through the vocation of parenthood prompts us to grow more deeply into our membership in Christ's body, to be agents of God's reconciliation, participants in the graced building of God's kingdom on earth as it is in heaven (2 Corinthians 5:18; 15:5; John 15:1-17). In various ways — for some, through marriage and for some, through parenthood, but for all through life-giving relationships with each other and with God — we are called to abide in that divine love, making known the fruit of Christ's saving embrace (Matthew 7:16-20).

Conclusion: Eschatological Communion with God and One Another

The vocation of Christian marriage is catalyzed by a love that unites two consenting adults in a holy bond, a sacred vessel in and through which they may grow throughout the course of their lives. Marriage is finite, temporal, and mortal. It is "until we are parted by death" and no longer. Yet in its characterization of the eternal union of Christ and the Church, marriage carries an eschatological dimension, extending beyond the border of created mortality. It exceeds the borders of individual souls, extending to all of creation, the ultimate renewal in which "Christ is all and in all" (Colossians 3:11). In all of this, marriage serves as a vessel not only of our love, of our union in difference, of discipline and ascesis, of generativity and fruitfulness, but also, ultimately, of our transformation, our re-creation. The vocation of Christian marriage finally serves as a vehicle for engaging our lifelong communal call to abide and grow in the love through which God brought forth creation and will finally draw it homeward into God's own heart.

---

91 Goldingay et al., "Same-Sex Marriage and Anglican Theology," 41.

Bibliography

The Book of Common Prayer. New York: Church Hymnal Corporation, 1979.

The Book of Occasional Services. New York: Church Publishing, 2003.

Breidenthal, Thomas. *Sacred Unions: A New Guide to Lifelong Commitment*. Cambridge, Mass.: Cowley Publications, 2006.

Clark, Elizabeth. *Reading Renunciation: Asceticism and Scripture in Early Christianity*. Princeton: Princeton University Press, 1999.

Coakley, Sarah. *God, Sexuality, and the Self: An Essay on the Trinity*. Cambridge: Cambridge University Press, 2013.

———. *Powers and Submissions: Spirituality, Philosophy and Gender*. Malden: Blackwell, 2003.

Cornwall, Susannah. *Sex and Uncertainty in the Body of Christ: Intersex Conditions and Christian Theology*. London: Equinox, 2010.

Daley, Brian E., trans. *Gregory of Nazianzus*. London: Routledge, 2006.

Farley, Margaret. *Just Love: A Framework for Christian Sexual Ethics*. New York: Continuum, 2006.

———. "The Meaning of Commitment." In Kieran Scott and Michael Warren, eds., *Perspectives on Marriage: A Reader*. New York: Oxford University Press, 2007.

Fatum, Lone. "Image of God and Glory of Man: Women in the Pauline Congregations." In Kari Elisabeth Borresen, ed., *The Image of God: Gender Models in Judaeo-Christian Tradition*. Minneapolis: Fortress, 1995.

Goldingay, John, Grant LeMarquand, George Sumner, and Daniel Westberg. "Same-Sex Marriage and Anglican Theology: A View from the Traditionalists." *Anglican Theological Review 93*, no.1. (2011): 1-50.

Good, Deirdre, Willis Jenkins, Cynthia Kittredge, and Eugene Rogers. "A Theology of Marriage Including Same-Sex Couples: A View from the Liberals." *Anglican Theological Review 93*, no. 1. (2011): 51-88.

Grudem, Wayne, and John Piper. *Recovering Biblical Manhood and Womanhood: A Response to Evangelical Feminism*. Wheaton: Crossway Books, 2006.

The House of Bishops of the General Synod of the Church of England, *Some Issues in Human Sexuality: A Guide to the Debate*. London: Church House Publishing, 2003.

The House of Bishops Working Group on Human Sexuality, *Report of the House of Bishops Working Group on Human Sexuality*. London: Church House Publishing, 2013. https://www.churchofengland.org/media/1891063/pilling_report_gs_1929_web.pdf.

Pope John Paul II. *Man and Woman He Created Them: A Theology of the Body*. Boston: Pauline Books and Media, 2006.

Kuefler, Mathew. *The Manly Eunuch: Masculinity, Gender Ambiguity, and Christian Ideology in Late Antiquity*. Chicago: University of Chicago Press, 2001.

Martin, Dale. *Sex and the Single Savior: Gender and Sexuality in Biblical Interpretation*. Louisville: Westminster John Knox, 2006.

The Primate's Theological Commission of the Anglican Church of Canada, *Report of the Primate's Theological Commission of the Anglican Church of Canada on the Blessing of Same-Sex Unions*; http://www.anglican.ca/primate/ptc/smr/

A New Zealand Prayerbook. The Anglican Church in Aotearoa, New Zealand, and Polynesia, 1988.

Ringrose, Kathryn. *The Perfect Servant: Eunuchs and the Social Construction of Gender in Byzantium*. Chicago: University of Chicago Press, 2003.

Rogers, Eugene. "Same-Sex Complementarity: A Theology of Marriage." Christian Century, May 11, 2011; http://www.christiancentury.org/article/2011-04/same-sex-complementarity

Runcorn, David. Appendix 4. In *Report of the House of Bishops Working Group on Human Sexuality*. London: Church House Publishing, 2013.

Schaff, Philip. *Nicene and Post-Nicene Fathers, First Series, Vol. 10. Chrysostom: Homilies on the Gospel of Saint Matthew*. Peabody, Mass.: Hendrickson Publishers, 1994.

Sheed, F.J., trans. Augustine Confessions, Books I-XIII. Indianapolis: Hackett Publishing Company, 1993.

Some Issues in *Human Sexuality: A Guide to the Debate*. London: Church House Publishing, 2003.

Stevenson, Walter. "Eunuchs and Early Christianity." In S. Tougher, ed., *Eunuchs in Antiquity and Beyond*. London: Classical Press of Wales and Duckworth, 2002.

Thatcher, Adrian. *God, Sex, and Gender: An Introduction*. Malden, Mass.; Oxford, UK: Wiley Blackwell, 2011.

———. *Marriage after Modernity*. Sheffield: Sheffield Academic, 1999.

Tolbert, Mary Ann. "Marriage and Friendship in the Christian New Testament: Ancient Resources for Contemporary Same-Sex Unions." In M. Jordan, M. Sweeney, and D. Mellott, eds., *Authorizing Marriage: Canon, Tradition, and Critique in the Blessing of Same-Sex Unions*. Princeton and Oxford: Princeton University Press, 2006.

To Set Our Hope on Christ: A Response to the Invitation of Windsor Report 135. New York: The Episcopal Church Center, 2005.

ESSAY 3:
A History of Christian Marriage

The history of Christian marriage is as complex and diverse as the history of Christianity, with the meaning of that word "marriage" having changed and morphed as generations of faithful Christians have sought to define for themselves the nature of a holy life lived out in the midst of daily life. In the same way, in varied contexts, societal and cultural understandings of marriage have interfaced and shaped our understandings of Christian marriage over the course of the last two millennia. To better understand our own contemporary understandings of Christian marriage, it is helpful to look at the historical development of marriage over the centuries.

Marriage:

- A mystical relationship preordained by cosmic forces?
- A blessed physical and spiritual union that mirrors for us a human experience akin to God's indissoluble steadfast love as it has found expression in the life of Christ?
- A legal relationship that protects property and inheritance?
- A social relationship that forms a basic fundamental unit of almost all human society?
- A less-than-optimal but necessary religious concession to the realities of the uncontrolled instincts and passions of earthly human creatures?
- An institutional social convention that restricts and restrains the boundaries of human relationship through social proscriptions and legal constraints on individuals' sexual expression and personal identity?
- A self-chosen, psychologically driven relationship that offers stability and intimacy for human growth and development?

When we discuss the history of marriage, of which of these are we speaking? And when we discuss the history of Christian marriage, of which of these are we speaking?

One might wonder why — when so many books have been written, and when the subject of marriage has so fully been examined at the historical, anthropological, social, economic, and spiritual levels — even include a history in our Task Force's study of marriage? The answer is partly because not only our definition of marriage, but even our understanding of what history is has changed in the 35 years since the 1979 Book of Common Prayer authorized its modern rite of marriage.

In an earlier era, we might have drawn one long, straight line from Adam and Eve to the marriage at Cana, to the various rites of the Book of Common Prayer over the centuries, to our contemporary rites for marriage. But now we see more clearly that there is no one line of history we can follow. There are many threads woven together and interwoven with one another, creating a rich and broad tapestry of understandings, viewpoints, and insights. Attending to these various strands and the ways in which they have cohered to create some sense of communally lived experience is the work of the contemporary historian — work that may benefit us greatly as we seek to understand the concept of marriage in our own historical era.

Marriage has meant numerous things in various geographic settings over the course of history, and even now when Episcopalians use the word "marriage," that word does not mean the same thing to all those who hear it. Part of the work of the Task Force on the Study of Marriage is to help us, as 21st-century Episcopalians spread across the globe, remember that when we speak of marriage, everyone is talking at once, meaning different things, viewing history through many contextual lenses. To understand what our moment in history has to say about the nature of Christian marriage, we benefit from an examination of the many things marriage has meant over the millennia.

This paper will explore the numerous ways in which the term "marriage" has been understood throughout the history of the Church. Perhaps it will also invite reflection on how our historical expressions of Christian marriage can enlighten our current discussions. It may even lead us beyond the boundaries of the ways in which marriage has been viewed in the past into new insights and new language, helping us develop the capacity to speak more articulately to contemporary Episcopal experiences and viewpoints.

IV. ESSAYS ON MARRIAGE

1. Jewish and Roman Marriage

Because early Christianity germinated and was formed out of its Roman, Jewish, and Hellenistic cultural context, it is helpful to step back and examine some of the roots of our Christian understandings of marriage in Judaism and in Roman Hellenistic culture. We begin our historical study of the topic with a discussion of our earliest recorded ritual text regarding marriage. Scripture and Jewish history are richly full of individuals who lived in family networks, households where they were bound together in sometimes-lifelong relationships — individuals such as Adam and Eve; Abraham and Sarah and Hagar; Jacob, Rachel, Leah, Zilpah, and Bilhah, whose lives and whose stories provide the pillars for all of Jewish history that follows.

However, it is not until deep in the intertestamental period that we see an extant example of a Jewish blessing prayer used as a part of the process of marriage. In the book of Tobit there are several blessing prayers — one put in the mouth of Sarah's father, Raguel, which seems to be a blessing at the time of the betrothal of Tobias and Sarah. A second blessing prayer is offered by Tobias and stands as a witness before God given in the wedding chamber and asking God's blessings and mercy on their life together.

> Blessed are you, O God of our ancestors,
> and blessed is your name in all generations for ever.
> Let the heavens and the whole creation bless you for ever.
> You made Adam, and for him you made his wife Eve
> as a helper and support.
> From the two of them the human race has sprung.
> You said, "It is not good that the man should be alone;
> let us make a helper for him like himself."
> I now am taking this kinswoman of mine,
> not because of lust,
> but with sincerity.
> Grant that she and I may find mercy
> and that we may grow old together.
> (NRSV Tobit: 8: 5b-7)

A third and final blessing is said by Raguel the morning after the couple's marriage, and it is in this blessing that we see a blessing on parents, children, and future generations. In this third prayer, marriage is clearly linked to procreation, continuity of family lines, and a hallowing of the future of a people.

What do we learn from Tobit? We see here that marriage was a process, a process that took some time, had several stages, and

involved multiple parties, not just the couple. We see that Sarah is
never asked to consent, but that her father and her new husband are
the actors. Nevertheless, we see that Tobias calls Sarah his beloved
— that true marriage is not about objectification of another human
being (lust), but about something else, a partnership that enriches
the present and protects the future of a people. Raguel asks blessings
upon both Tobias and Sarah through their union. Both are meant to
be blessed by marriage. We see that in this model of marriage, Sarah
is the helper to Tobias — not an equal, but a lifelong helper and
companion, not a possession. We also see that in this world there is
a clear link between marriage and procreation, the present and the
future.

Third-century Talmudic texts also shed light on what Jewish marriage
might have meant in the era in which Christian marriage was
beginning to be defined. Jewish marriage, by this time, involved a
two-step process of betrothal, where money was exchanged, contracts
were agreed to, or, in some less ideal (but perhaps quite common)
circumstances, cohabitation began. Blessings were given at the time of
betrothal, and further blessings were offered later (often a year later)
at the time of marriage. The second stage of marriage involved fasting,
confession, crowns, a veil for the bride (if a virgin), the formal signing
of a contract, music, dancing, and feasting. At the end of the meal, the
groom pronounced seven blessings, including the two below.

> O make these loved companions greatly to rejoice, even as
> of old thou didst gladden thy creature in the garden of Eden.
> Blessed art thou, O Lord, who makes bridegroom and bride
> to rejoice.

> Blessed art thou, O Lord our God, King of the universe, who
> hast created joy and gladness, bridegroom and bride, mirth
> and exaltation, pleasure and delight, love, brotherhood,
> peace, and fellowship. Soon may there be heard in the cities
> of Judah, and in the streets of Jerusalem, the voice of joy and
> gladness, the voice of the bridegroom and the voice of the
> bride, the jubilant voice of bridegrooms from their canopies,
> and of youths from their feasts of song. Blessed art thou, O
> Lord, who makes the bridegroom to rejoice with the bride.
> (Stevenson, Nuptial Blessing, 245)

In the seven marriage blessings of the Talmud, we see a picture of
marriage that is about love (a love that has most likely developed
during the time of the betrothal or perhaps as a result of having
known each other since childhood). Marriage is about joy and

gladness, love and delight, and fellowship. While a contract has been signed and a legal relationship established, there is, it seems from these blessings, something more — something deeply human, God-blessed, and God-blessing that is present in the character of marriage.

In conjunction with this rich and full image of blessing-filled life together, we must remember that Jewish laws of the time also allowed for divorce, and that some of the Jewish scholars of this era of first- and second-century Judaism were emphatic supporters of a man's right to divorce his wife on virtually any grounds, from an inability to bear children to such trivial grounds as burning a meal. While marriages may have begun with visions of belovedness, for many women this moment of joy and jubilation would eventually give way to a relationship of vulnerability and subservience to the man in the house who held legal power to sever the bonds earlier established in marriage. It is also important to remember that monogamy is not inherent in this particular model of marriage, and that polygamy was practiced by some who could afford to care for larger households. Contrary to our contemporary images of marriage, polygamy will continue to be part of the definition of marriage throughout much of the history of marriage and across numerous cultures.

At the same time that Christians from Jewish traditions were fashioning a view of marriage from the cultural vantage point of Judaism, Hellenistic Christians were developing an understanding of marriage based upon their cultural vantage point. In Hellenism even more than in Judaism, the central building block of society was the patriarchal family. Survival of this unit was possible only through the movement of women of childbearing ages from one household to another. The role of women in this setting was to ensure the line of their husbands and their fathers, the well ordering of a deeply patriarchal hierarchical society, and the inculcation of Roman patrilineal values from one generation to the next. Marriage provided the societal and legal vehicle to make this possible.

In contrast to the mutuality suggested by our Jewish blessing texts, Roman marriages were understood to be one-sided in their purpose. The Roman marriage changed the legal and familial status of a Roman woman, moving her from one household to another. The stages of Roman marriage in non-Christian settings were the arranging of the marriage by a marriage arranger, a local sacrifice to the gods on the morning of the marriage, the sealing of the marriage contract along with witnesses (with household gods present), and the consent of the father of the bride to this marriage. There was no mutuality. There was no change in the man's status. There was no direct consent by the woman, as there was no direct consent by the woman in Jewish rites.

While in loving households the daughter's desires would have been attended to, ultimately she could not decide her own fate. Fathers might — on occasion for their own interests or to provide safeguards for their daughters — arrange for a marriage that was sine manu and left these daughters under the father's authority rather than, as was the more typical practice, transferring authority for the woman from the father to the husband. Fathers, if the marriage was sine manu, also had the right to emancipate their daughters so that they became the owners of their own property and were able to function as independent agents in society. It is likely that many of the women described as supporting the work of the apostles in the New Testament operated through this kind of legal sanction.

Families in a Roman household comprised all those who were under the authority of the father. They might be wives, children, slaves, or indentured servants. One remained under the authority of the father one's whole life long, or perhaps until authority was transferred to a husband in marriage if one was a woman, or until emancipation by the father, if that was given. For much of Roman history, only free Roman citizens had the right to marry. This left much of Roman society outside the bounds of legal marriage, vulnerable to unwanted dissolution of any intimate sexual or parental relationship to which they might choose to commit over the course of their lives.

What can we learn about marriage from Roman society? We can learn that marriages can function in society as means to order that society and protect the authority and property of those in power, and that Western culture has a long heritage of refusing the legal privilege of marriage to those without freedom or without means and those living at the margins of society.

2. Christian Marriage in the Early Church

The early Church, through its several iterations, held various views of the nature of marriage. The first-century Christian eschatological worldview invites Christians to imagine a different kind of family from the paternalistic families of either Judaism or Rome. For these early Christians, family was found through identification with those with whom one formed spiritual bonds. Mothers and fathers were not created through either legal or genetic bonds. Mothers and fathers were those who had nurtured one in the faith and brought one from life outside the Christian community to life inside it.

Paul asserts that marriage was set aside for those who were not spiritually strong enough to maintain their chasteness in celibacy. The ideal was a celibate life spent devoting the whole of one's being to preparing for Christ's return. This new world order that is presented through Paul, the deutero-Pauline writers, the authors of the pastoral letters, and through the Gospel writers, stands in powerful, intentional, and direct contrast to the cultural mores of its day. Paul invites the Church into a way of life where none is viewed as property of another, none is objectified, and all live together in bonds of mutuality and mutual submission. One chooses as one's family members those who have chosen Christ, and the bonds that unite Christians as a family are as eternal, sacred, and nonseverable as the limbs of one's body are to one another.

While the early Church, in most communities, did not forbid marriage, the reality-forming values of the first-century Hellenistic world are turned on their heads by an approach to property, life, and family that defies the idolatry that frequently accompanied the patriarchal model of Hellenistic marriage. Marriage, in and of itself, is not seen as evil. Indeed, Christ's first miracle, according to John, was a blessing that took place at a marriage. But the attitudes and assumptions of first-century Hellenistic life that placed all authority in the hands of a human father rather than a heavenly father were found by the Church to be deeply suspect. Jesus' statements (Matthew 19:1-12, Mark 10:1-12) regarding marriage stress to his followers the priority of a life of devotion to God over any allegiance to societal or religious authorities or norms.

While Christians did engage in marriage, the ritual of marrying was not necessarily seen as a spiritual act unless it was entered into by two Christian persons who intended a relationship that would produce spiritual fruits. Not all Christians participated in Christian marriages. Christian women were strongly encouraged to bring their Christian values and ideals to their relationships, even when those relationships were with non-Christian husbands; and Christian husbands were encouraged to keep and convert their non-Christian wives. There is evidence that bishops of the patristic era questioned and contemplated the appropriateness of blessing marriages. If they happened to be in attendance at a marriage feast, they might be called upon to offer a blessing similar to what the father of the bride might offer at a non-Christian marriage feast.

But marriage rites were by nature in this time domestic rites with religious implications. Home and hearth, kin and community were aspects of life so fundamental that they were intricately related to human spirituality but less centrally focused on explicitly religious liturgical acts than what we will see in later moments of history when church and state become synonymous. While there is some patristic evidence that, in North Africa, Christian couples might have married in rites held within the faith community, there is no evidence to suggest this was common practice across the diverse geography of the early-church world or in the first generation of the Christian church.

As the Church moved deeper into the New Testament era, into the late first century and the second century, attitudes toward marriage changed in two directions. In both Hellenistic philosophy and in Christian understandings, there were strains of the tradition that grew even more deeply suspect of marriage and instead commended lives of abstinence, chastity, and singlehood as lifestyles more noble than marriage, even when the eschatological focus of Christianity had begun to wane. Because many human beings in the Mediterranean world were not eligible to participate in legal marriage because so many were slaves and not citizens, citizens and aristocrats in Roman society who were turning to Christianity as their religion wanted and needed their religion and their societal positions to come closer in line. Christianity was, in many settings, becoming less countercultural and more aligned with the practices and values of the empire, a necessary step if it was to grow beyond its first generation of followers.

The authors of the deutero-Pauline scriptural texts (scriptural texts likely written by followers of Paul after his death) and many of the early church fathers and mothers see the patrilineal ideals of Hellenism as not only appropriate to Christianity, but also as complementary to a now increasingly less apocalyptic and more present-focused vision of life in Christ. Many scholars believe that the Christian scriptural teachings about hierarchical understandings of marriage according to which the wife is subservient to the husband arise from this time period of the apostolic church.

It is also most likely that it was in this late-first-century Christian historical era that we see expressed for the first time the direct analogy that marriage represents the relationship between Christ and Christ's church, an analogy that would have easily grown out of familiarity with the several parables in the Gospels about brides and bridesmaids. This metaphor for marriage would have been understood by those hearing these letters for the first time as inherently hierarchical, and thereby in keeping with Roman sensibilities about the pater familias. At the same time, these passages continued to assert a Gospel message that was still countercultural to Hellenistic Roman worldviews since they assert a profound challenge to any repressive view of another as object or property.

Augustine, writing in the fourth and fifth centuries to an increasingly Christian culture, commends marriage and encourages those marrying to include the bishop in the arranging of marriages. Like many Christians of his day, his view of marriage is ambivalent, but he is clear in expressing the gifts marriage can offer to the Christian life. For Augustine, marriage was a sacred obligation, a sacramentum.

The reasons for marrying are threefold: fidelity, procreation, and the fulfilling of a sacred obligation. These values were deeply in keeping with the familial structure of Roman society, and still they invited those of Hellenistic backgrounds to contemplate marriage as not simply an act requiring a sacrifice to the gods, but as an act that (particularly for brides who were the sole subjects of marriage rites in Augustine's world) was in and of itself a means of giving one's life to God's service. One loved one's husband as the Church loved Christ. If one did not have the spiritual strength or the economic resources to commit one's self to a fully devout life of celibacy, one could still choose faithfulness and a contained concupiscence. This was the next best thing to celibacy, and a proper and fitting gift of one's self to God and to Christian society.

In the patristic period, the Eastern church was fashioning a somewhat different understanding of marriage. Here, too, celibacy was revered as the most holy state. However, for those who would marry, the nuptial blessings of marriage were given to both bride and groom. For both of them, the state of life and being was altered. As a central sign of this change of life status, and in recognition of the role marriage played in the spiritual life of the couple, crowns were placed on the heads of both bride and groom in marriage rites, signifying the high calling of Christ upon their lives and the eschatological nature of their life work. Bride and groom were expected to live lives worthy of this high calling given in Jesus Christ.

In its initial conversion of the western frontier to Roman Christianity, the church of the East held greater sway over the newly incubating Christian churches of Britain, Gaul, and Spain. This worldview allowed for an easier connection with Teutonic values than did the increasingly ascetic and aristocratically centered values of Rome. These Eastern sensibilities would continue to influence Gallican (of what is now Western Europe) and Visigothic (of what is now Spain and Portugal) views on marriage long after Europe had been thoroughly Romanized.

What does the late patristic era tell us about marriage that might inform our present-day understandings of marriage? We see in this period of history a widening of understandings of what it means to be human in a way that does not simply equate the human condition with procreative capacities. Celibacy becomes a virtue. We see, as we saw in the early church, alternative models for how to live the Christian life — models that offered women as well as men the means to imagine a life of faith lived beyond the personal and legal confines of Roman marriage.

We continue to see a deeply stratified and diverse Christianity in which marriage is not available to all who desire it. We hear explicitly a deep suspicion of the human body and human sexual instincts, a suspicion based in part on recognition of the physical and medical dangers inherent in sexual relationships and in pregnancy in that day. We see an already present tension between the concepts of marriage as a legal and societal act and Christian marriage as a blessed state of life given by God and blessed by the Church.

3. Marriage in the Medieval Church

For the Teutonic peoples who were coming to see themselves as a part of the Roman Empire and who lived away from the Mediterranean boundaries of the Western church, the world-renouncing spirituality of Rome was deeply problematic. Initially the concept of celibacy as a lifelong choice was abhorrent. Monogamy was a state reserved for those with the means only to procure one wife. In this setting, marriage was not essential, but an honoring of vows and promises was critical to the maintenance of the society.

As in the rest of the Christian church, betrothal was seen as essential to a proper marriage and formed a basic contract of commitment between two households. Marriage blessings were usually domestic in nature and often took place at feasts and at the marriage beds. For people who were still coming to grips with the notion of putting aside their gods of the home and hearth, the importance of domestic elements of blessing was critical. In these Teutonic cultures in these early centuries of Christian faith, the blessing was to be bestowed not just on the bride but on the groom as well, because it was only through their mutual familial partnerships that these tribal societies could continue.

As the centuries progressed into the period we now call the Middle Ages, Roman and Teutonic values became more deeply inculcated into one another, and the medieval church took on its new character. Celibacy took on great importance across the entire empire, as did the blessing offered by the now frequently celibate priest. Domestic life came to be seen as separate from and inferior to religious life. In eucharistic celebrations, the real bread of the hearth offered at the Eucharist gave way to "holy" bread formed in monastery kitchens and made by celibate holy hands. Coupling, birthing, and the raising of children continued, but these actions had even less to do with religious life lived in God than had been true in previous eras. By the medieval period, only priests could offer a marital blessing — not, as in earlier times, fathers or grooms.

The Church required monogamy in marriage, and linkages narrower than the seventh degree of relationship were considered incestuous, further reinforcing the chasm between the very few who could engage in blessed legal marriage and the vast majority who were forced to live, or were desirous of living, outside its boundaries. In a time of deeply concrete biblical literacy within the official church, those who entered into solemn marriage entered into an indissoluble state.

What marriage was, how it happened, and who was eligible to be married were matters of debate in this era of the Church. A marriage might involve a simple blessing by the priest at the doors of the church, a full nuptial mass within the church, or a blessing of the marriage bed. The consistent holdover from Roman law seems to have been the action that was still most associated with betrothal — namely, the consent to the relationship given by the groom and the agent who gave the bride.

Sacramentaries of the early medieval period resonate with a mishmash of the ideas of Augustine, the sensual sensibilities of Teutonic spirituality, and biblically based understandings of marriage. Marriage is given by God not just for the purpose of procreation but also for the exercise of fidelity, love, and mutual support. Throughout the next centuries in various parts of the Holy Roman Empire, different emphases in this amalgam of marriage paradigms take precedence, sometimes highlighting the mutuality of the relationship, often hearkening back to earlier Roman sensibilities according to which it is the bride who is given and whose status is changed. Nowhere is this return to Roman perspectives more clearly expressed than in the Gregorian Sacramentary's insertion into the marriage rite of the Ephesians' analogy of the relationship between groom and bride as parallel to the relationship between Christ and his church.

In the High Middle Ages, a time when making the right marriage became critical, when much of medieval life and culture were built around feudal codes, and when veneration of the Virgin Mary was becoming a core element of medieval piety, a new concept of chivalric romance began to be constructed. While the lives of most everyday men and women could not be compared in any way with the heroic stories of chivalric romance being produced at this time, a changed appreciation for the relationship between men and women seems to have entered into Western psychology.

Within the literate nobility, romance became a central theme in relationships between the sexes, and, as a result, a counter image to Eve the temptress was created, undoing much of the vilification of women that had entered life through Western philosophy and asceticism. Unfortunately, what also resulted was a different kind of objectification of women as noble, chaste, fragile, pure beings; and this romanticized view of the relationship between men and women in centuries to come helped shape the development of romantic expectations for all marriages and all sexual unions.

By the late medieval period, we see a deepening divide between all things sacred and profane, as well as a fully developed societal and legal authority invested in the officers of the Church. The continuing importance of the betrothal, with its emphasis upon consent and commitment, led to the necessity to make this consent an action done as a part of the marriage rite in the presence of the priest. This led to a diminishment of the role and efficacy of the whole communal betrothal process. While periods of betrothal, engagement, and courting clearly continued in society, cultural, social, and anthropological processes that had previously served as the building blocks of Christian society gave way in importance to brief formalized events now presided over by the priest and disconnected from the events of secular life.

The important part of a marriage rite — a rite that was becoming available to more individuals as the middle class began to burgeon in late medieval society — was now the consent given by the couples, and blessing given by the priest at the doors of the church, or followed by a full nuptial mass in the church with the nuptial blessing saved for the end of the mass.

As the scholastic church of the late medieval period was narrowing its understanding of how Christians were to understand sacrament, marriage (along with its counterpart, ordination) came to be seen as one of the seven sacraments of the Church. Both the man and the woman were now seen as entering into a sacramental act, and now both the man and woman were expected to voice their consent. Vows were exchanged — vows that in most circumstances (but not all) required the woman to swear her obedience to her husband. A life-transforming process that had formerly been left in the hands of families and communities who sought God's blessing on it was now authoritatively placed in the hands of the official, priest-led church, with clearly structured expectations and obligations prescribed and demanded by the Church and the assurance of clear, spiritual benefit to be derived from formal marriage with its sacramental nuptial blessing.

What can we learn with regard to marriage from this late medieval period of history in the Church? In this period, we see that in the process of further sacralizing the nature of Christian marriage in a culture that was growing less enamored with celibate life as the ideal, there was also an unintentional desacralizing of the deeply human elements of marriage. Entering into marriage came to be associated with participating in a particular religious ceremony presided over by a priest, rather than participating in a communal multistage process presided over by the couple and their families and blessed by God in the midst of celebration and feasting.

The question of who is worthy of marriage and entitled to the sacraments of the Church has continued to be an issue even until our present day. The strict focus that developed around the actions of an official in validating and legitimizing marriage, as opposed to the witness of a whole community, further intensified the needs of the disenfranchised to gain this right and privilege for themselves. The nature of human sexuality and its inherent goodness in human life once again found expression in parts of the Church and society in this era, with evolving views of manhood and womanhood helping to shape future iterations of life in marriage.

It is difficult to overstress the critical role that property acquisition played in changing mores around marriage. In an earlier day when few held property or wealth of their own, communal understanding and consensus could form the framework of family life. In Roman times, the family included anyone under the authority of the *pater familias.* In the early medieval period, local chieftains decided and defined the nature of family, claiming for themselves significant numbers of the women and children of a village in their family and leaving others to define their place at the margins of society.

In the late medieval period, as more and more individuals gained their personal and economic freedom and became the holders of land and property, the need for formal marriage and legal marriage was accentuated. Questions regarding who was married, how public their marriage was, the legitimacy of offspring, and rights to inheritance became paramount. It was this new landed and propertied world that created a pervasive demand for unambiguous legal marriage that was previously unprecedented in the West. In the late medieval period, for perhaps the first time in the history of the West, a sizeable percentage of Christians had the opportunity and the necessity to pursue officially recognized lifelong marital partnerships.

4. The Reformation and Marriage

The primary changes to the understanding of marriage that arose from the Reformation were theological rather than practical. The rejection of the primacy of the celibate life was a core tenet of Reformation thinking, and with that rejection came a new emphasis upon marriage. Marriage was seen as the natural and original means of ordering human life. Established by God in creation, marriage was expected of all Christian people. In an adaptation of Augustine's teachings on marriage, Luther identified the three goals of marriage as procreation, a remedy for concupiscence, and companionship. However, this marital companionship no longer grew out of a sacramental understanding of marriage. Indeed, for Luther there were only two sacraments — Baptism and Eucharist.

Martin Bucer was the lone reformer who asserted that companionship was the primary purpose of Christian marriage. This companionship articulated by the reformers was based on a patriarchal model of life in keeping with ancient understandings of woman as the helper to man. Because marriage was no longer seen as a sacrament and Christ seems to allow for the possibility of divorce in the Gospels, divorce took on a prominent place in the Protestant history of marriage. Cranmer's 1549 rite of marriage names the service "Solemnization of Matrimony," indicating both its solemn importance to society and that it was not to be understood in that time as a sacrament. Rings were still exchanged, but were no longer blessed. The vows — the contract elements of marriage — were said in the nave of the church, and the blessing prayers for the couple were said at the altar, with the possibility of communion.

Protestant reformers saw the family as the central building block of the Christian life. They saw the act of marrying as a solemn act and a solemn obligation. They used marriage ceremonies as occasions to teach the entire community the Church's expectations regarding life lived in marriage — expectations that made procreation and child-rearing the vocational center for all women, and which called all women to take vows of obedience to their husbands.

In contrast to some earlier periods of history, marital fidelity was an expressed expectation of both members of the marriage and not just of the woman. Familial and communal feasts and celebrations that had historically accompanied and been a part of marriage were severely criticized in some reform communities. If the medieval period had strongly urged that marriages take place in churches and be presided over by priests, most reformers absolutely required church marriages with pastors and witnesses present. While the theological principle of the priesthood of all believers was being espoused by reformers, they were simultaneously unwilling to allow the authority of local believers to govern the establishment of daily life, seeing church officials as the necessary religious and legal agents of society in the establishment of marriages.

At roughly the same time, the Council of Trent (1545-1563) was reaffirming that for Roman Catholics, marriage was a divinely given sacrament and therefore indissoluble. A new, formal definition of marriage appeared which required that all marriages be publicly announced with banns and vows before a priest and two witnesses. Most of the cultural activities associated with marriage continued: the celebrations, the dancing, and the feasting. But the Church had now made it clear that these activities, while encouraged by the Council for cultural reasons, did not validate a marriage. Only the church could validate a marriage. At this point it even became possible to validate marriages retroactively by gathering all children born prior to the marriage under the marriage canopy to legitimize them when a couple chose to receive the full sacrament of marriage.

In 1653, during the Puritan period of the English Commonwealth, the nature of marriage was once again reshaped by theological constraints. In this radical, Puritan setting, marriage became a simple vow between a man and a woman using a prescribed Puritan form from the Westminster Directory. The vow was made before a justice of the peace, and there were no prayers and no ordained minister involved, making it absolutely clear that marriage was not to be understood as a sacramental act, thereby allowing considerably more latitude in arguing for the potential dissolubility of a marriage. Puritans saw marriage as an event with significant spiritual and religious implications. And yet, this form of marriage ceremony, carried out in a manner that was totally divorced from church life, opened the way in later historical periods for a returned view of marriage as a legal, social, and cultural event rather than a religious one.

This period of history tells us that Christian marriage, even when understood as both a legal and a religious act, has not held the same meaning for all Christians across the Church, nor has there been any form of consensus regarding the dissolubility of marriage. The divide between Catholic and Protestant understandings of marriage continued in the Reformation era to shape the Christian churches and especially Anglican dialogues about marriage. This was especially true within the New World, as The Episcopal Church continued to hold Old World sensibilities regarding marriage in creative balance with Protestant and Enlightenment worldviews.

Perhaps the only consistent elements within early modern Christian marriage practices were that marriages created legal contracts that protected the property rights of those with material goods; and that family and culture played a central role in how marriages were recognized and celebrated, even when the Church offered little opportunity for ritual celebrations to occur. The church and the state could control what took place in official settings; what happened outside those settings was less readily controllable.

5. Marriage in the New World

American understandings of marriage were diverse from the founding of the United States. Puritan values regarding marriage as a central building block of society were continued among white Protestant Americans; and the sacramental, unbreakable bonds of marriage continued to be upheld by Roman Catholic Christians of the New World.

A core stricture that entered into Roman Catholic Spanish marriage practices and then quickly became a part of Latin-American marriage practices was the principle of "equality" — not equality as a source of mutual companionship between the genders, but social, racial, and economic equality between the two parties marrying. While those who were black or of mixed race were initially exempted from this law, the Real Pragmática made it illegal for españoles (white individuals) to marry across social or economic boundaries, thereby assuring protection of property rights within the white landed aristocracy and preventing the possibility of intentional mixed marriages.

In addition, this act was unprecedented in Catholic practice in requiring parental permission for any marriage to take place, taking the power of choice away from the groom as well as the bride. Once the marriage had been attained, the understanding within society and within the Church was that the patriarchal role of head of household required obedience of the woman in her relationship with her husband and afforded him the privilege of "correction" of her through corporal and other forms of punishment. While fidelity was a stated goal of marriage, as it had been in previous eras, the deep concern with fidelity was still placed upon the wife, while husbands were forgiven for straying. Particularly in aristocratic families, honor and female sexual purity took on an important role in Christian marriage practices of the New World.

In colonial Latin America, in response to the pervasive ethnic, cultural, legal, and economic oppression that restricted the day-to-day existences of the vast majority, marriage was often viewed as an unavailable or an undesirable option for couples seeking to spend their lives together — it was often viewed with skepticism and cynicism regarding its value and its purposes. The Church played such a controlling role in marriage that many sought freedom of relationship outside the bonds of the Church.

As a result, illegitimate children were a pervasive reality of early modern Hispanic life, despite the real constraints and limits that illegitimacy placed upon the inheritance rights of these children. However, illegitimacy was understood as considerably more deleterious to the lives of the elite than it was to the lives of slaves, mixed-race individuals, natives, and others whose rights to freedom, property, and autonomy had always been, at best, fragile.

Seventeenth-century confessional manuals that were used by priests of the New World define marriage as contractual in nature, with expectations that husbands would support their wives, and wives would be obedient to their husbands unless the husband's demands were deemed unreasonable, irrational, and unjust by civil authorities. Beginning in the 17th century, we also see pastoral language of equality and reciprocity that imagines marriage in the ideal as a mystical union. This ideal was rarely experienced in real life by women who married.

It is not until the 1928 Book of Common Prayer, with its Anglo-Catholic influences, that this language of mystical union enters into the Anglican rites of the Church. These evolving understandings of marriage, with the tension between the civil and the religious aspects of marriage and the tension between marriage as contract and marriage as spiritual union, continued to hold sway over the next several centuries in the development of our understanding of the nature of Christian marriage.

Methodist influences on marriage rites highlighted the high level of respect due to the institution of marriage. In the 1784 Sunday Service of the Methodists in North America, John Wesley removed the giving away of the bride from the ceremony, and, as was most often already the case in practice, also removed the option of communion at the ceremony. The giving-away ceremony came and went from Methodist and Episcopal rites over the course of the next hundred years.

Those who were brought to the United States and the Caribbean as slaves were not eligible for any form of legal or Christian marriage, although particularly pious slaveholders did on occasion create for their slaves domestic rites with some semblance to Christian marriage — rites over which the slaveholder presided and which held no legal sway. Instead, slaves were the property of their owners and were subject to even greater vulnerabilities in their sexual and parenting relationships than had earlier been the lot of slaves in ancient and medieval societies. The Reformation valuation of marriage as a God-given duty, privilege, and responsibility did not hold for those members of society who were identified by their owners and oppressors as subhuman and incapable of consent.

Despite the lack of legal or societal support for their marriages, black slaves in the Americas developed their own rites of marriage and established their own highly valued networks of family and kinship. Slave marriages held no legal authority, and those who had united themselves to each other in such relationships often experienced the severing of those relationships through slave sales. For the purpose of producing more slaves, at times slaves were "married" to one another by their masters, against their will and in direct violation of any already existing, unofficial, self-chosen "slave marriage." Following the emancipation of the American slaves, all black Americans were allowed to marry, as long as they married a member of their own race. Biracial marriage continued to be illegal in parts of the United States into the second half of the 20th century.

Across the Americas, Native Americans were denied legal marriage rights. Miscegenation laws making it illegal for a person of another race to marry a Native American abounded, and often Native Americans were treated similarly to slaves, subject to the whims and desires of their overlords. Coming out of cultures with a variety of different understandings of what constituted both family and marriage, Native Americans continued throughout the 17th, 18th, and 19th centuries to develop their own network of kin, even while the religious and political authorities around them sought to coerce them into relationship definitions alien to their own cultural identity and values systems.

Asian Americans entering the Americas in the eighteenth and nineteenth centuries found a world largely hostile to their own values of family and kin. Immigration quotas allowed for the immigration of very few families, with almost no Asian women being allowed to immigrate. As a result, men built same-sex communities for support and protection. Often these immigrants left behind spouses in their

Asian homelands and endured long absences from spouse and kin, so that they could offer financial support to extended networks still in Asia. In the early 20th century, single men who had immigrated from Japan and Korea, and who were not legally allowed to marry white women, sought "picture brides" from their homelands. These picture-bride marriages were performed by proxy in Asia, afterward allowing these Asian wives who had often never even met their new husbands to immigrate to the Americas as immigration restrictions were relaxed somewhat.

Indian and Filipino men living in the western United States often married Latino women, creating families of blended ethnicity. In some Asian cultures, arranged marriages continued to be the norm. Chinese cultures, with their deep Confucian valuation of family, kin, and ancestors, began to thrive when doors were open for the migration of whole families. One significant commonality among most Asian-American and Latino families of this era was the primary role of the husband to serve as breadwinner, and the role of the wife to respond in support and obedience to her husband.

This portion of history helps illuminate for the Church the numerous ways in which marriage law was used to oppress, and the numerous ways in which subjugated people continued to find means to establish intimate bonds of familial relationship, despite the impediments to volitional marriage. In communities of deep suffering, these self-chosen bonds played a critical role in helping to sustain the spirits and the life energies of those living in the midst of oppression and subjugation. Once again, we see the ways in which relationality, kin networks, and culture trump any legal or political restrictions imposed upon the deeply human relationship of marriage.

Episcopalians who have remained in their homelands and not confronted the particular challenges to marriage definition and practice that have been such a critical part of the immigrant experience have continued to fashion cultural and ritual practices of marriage in accord with the deep traditions of their communities, while at times finding themselves addressing the encroaching westernization of marriage practices that has influenced marriage traditions across the world. Aligning local cultural and social sensibilities with the language and symbolism of a very Western marriage rite, as found in the 1979 Book of Common Prayer, has offered its own particular challenges for these indigenous communities.

6. The Victorian Concept of Marriage

In the 17th century, the 1662 Book of Common Prayer asserted that the purposes of marriage were procreation, a remedy against sin and fornication, and mutual society (help and comfort), indicating little change in understanding since the Reformation period. But with the Victorian era (1837-1901), new patterns of practice regarding marriage began to appear in British and American society. As a result of industrialization and changed upper-class familial practices, a greater separation between home and work developed. Working-class women postponed marriage as they spent their early adulthood in paid factory labor. Lower-class rural families married early and produced children to help provide the family the labor force needed for a subsistence life.

Expanding economic prosperity allowed couples to marry earlier if they had the financial means to do so, and greater maternal health led to increases in birth rates. The expanding use of birth control among women in their later childbearing years allowed working women to return to the work force or to revenue-producing activities, and prevented dependent children from further taxing the resources of the family as older sons and daughters were able to leave and begin their own lives.

In the Victorian era, the home-workplace split led to a reconfiguration of familial identity that made the husband in the household the sole breadwinner and defined the many and necessary tasks of the wife as homemaking. Prosperous families prided themselves on their ability to function with one breadwinner, and children in this setting came to be seen less as essential contributors to the economy of the family and more as precious innocents who needed to be nurtured and formed in the faith by their ever-present mothers. Married women continued to perform significant tasks in support of the financial and personal well-being of the family, but their work was no longer seen as part of an economic partnership with their spouses, as it had been in a more agriculturally focused era.

Societal expectations, particularly for middle- and upper-class married women, were that wives were loving, genteel nurturers, caring for young children and providing spiritual and emotional support to the entire family, while husbands, as heads of the household, provided economic leadership and the public face of the family. Some families that could afford to redefine the boundaries of family life functioned as nuclear families with a husband, wife, and children living together in separate homes from their kin, unraveling long-standing traditions of extended family and multigenerational households and thereby developing the model of the modern family.

By the late Victorian era, with its neo-Gothic influences in society and religion, many of the romantic notions born in the age of chivalry were finding their way into popular culture and helping to shape a growingly romantic image of women as fragile flowers, men as their champions, and marriage as an idealized activity laced with passion and gallantry. The marriage of Queen Victoria to Prince Albert in 1840 provided Anglicans across the globe with a new romantic model for the ideal marriage ceremony. An elaborate ritual, a long white dress, a horse-drawn carriage, and sacred vows said before a priest came to be seen as the desirable way in which to marry.

In Anglo-Catholic segments of the Church, the term "sacrament" was again being used to explain the nature of the rite. The diversity of understandings regarding who was acting in marriage, under whose authority they were acting, and what role the Church was playing in this rite was significant. Many, of course, did not have the resources to allow for such elaborate celebrations of their marriages and made do with the legal requirements imposed by the state, coupled with whatever familial and cultural festivities were possible.

By the end of the Victorian era, we also see changes in the relationship between men and women impacting understandings of marital roles. These new paradigms for women and men neatly sliced up human life between the public and economic world of men and the private spiritual and domestic world of women. This public-private split had the effect of confining women's activity to a degree that was in some ways unprecedented. Women who in the past had found their identities through participation in familial businesses and farms, through celibate lifestyles, and through economic partnerships (albeit unequal partnerships) with their husbands were now confined to the roles of mothering and homemaking. In working-class families where such clearly delineated roles were most often not possible, families were left with a sense of failure and shame.

The response to that narrowing of roles that arose by the late 19th century was a new call for rights and freedoms for women, including the right to vote. Women began to organize on behalf of themselves, the poor, exploited laborers, and children. The tension between women's public selves in these arenas and in their private domestic roles would in the next century lead to dramatic changes in the nature of marriage and family life, including Christian marriage.

7. Twentieth-Century Episcopal Marriage

Women's suffrage became law in the United States in 1920, signaling the radical changes in women's roles and the nature of Christian marriage that were already afoot. The 1920s were an era of sexual and economic liberation for women, with many women rejecting the traditional boundaries of marriage that called for obedience to husbands and instead promoting sexual and marital relationships that were peer-based. In response to social and theological changes taking place in the Church, the Form of Solemnization of Matrimony in the 1928 Book of Common Prayer removed the vow for the wife to obey her husband. Otherwise, the rite looked surprisingly similar to Cranmer's first marriage rite, despite the nearly 400 years of history and radical changes in marital, familial, and social customs and mores that had transpired.

U.S. marriages were to take place only within the confines of state law. An exhortation regarding the nature of marriage was still read. Vows were still exchanged. Rings could be given, and blessing prayers were still said by a priest. By the mid-20th century, all Christian persons were fit candidates for Christian marriage so long as there were no legal impediments that would prevent the marriage; however, miscegenation laws continued to make it illegal for persons to marry one another across racial lines. What was also changing was the prioritization of the reasons for marriage. The vision of companionship that Bucer had already promoted in the 16th century was now coming to play a central role in the understanding of the nature of marriage, but now more as companionship among equals rather than according to the hierarchical model of relationship expressed by the medieval and reform churches.

In response to changing cultural patterns, the 1967 General Convention of The Episcopal Church called for a study of issues closely related to sexuality, including contraception, abortion, divorce and remarriage, and homosexuality. Slow in materializing, the first clear response to that call was seen in a 1976 General Convention resolution stating that "homosexual persons are children of God who have a full and equal claim with all other persons upon the love, acceptance, and pastoral concern and care of the Church."

The second half of the 20th century brought the fruits of the Liturgical Renewal Movement to all the rites of the Church, including the "Celebration and Blessing of a Marriage" — language that would not have been used for such a rite since the Reformation. The new introduction to marriage in the 1979 Book of Common Prayer lists as the first intention of marriage the couple's mutual joy. This is followed by reference to the help and comfort given one another in prosperity and adversity (language, we have seen, that has been a part of the Church's understanding of marriage for hundreds of years).

Last in the priority is the procreation of children. After centuries of traditional ritual language that only in small degrees reflected the enormous, although gradual, changes taking place in the nature of Christian marriage, here was a rite for a new generation of Christians. Or was it? Quickly following its promulgation, there arose voices in the Church that questioned the wisdom of including the reference to Ephesians 5 in the introduction to the marriage rite and the inclusion of the Ephesians 5 reading in the list of options for the epistle in the service. Questions also arose about the advisedness of offering an option for the giving away or presentation of the bride. What did these rites say about the nature of Christian marriage and how Christian marriage related to understandings of largely egalitarian romantic marriage in the broader society?

Modern liturgical reformers have had fewer difficulties letting go of earlier reform sensibilities about the nature of the marriage rite. They describe marriage as a solemn and public covenant between a man and a woman — language that would have been in keeping with Protestant sensibilities regarding marriage. Requirements for this service are that at least one person be baptized, that there be at least two witnesses, and that the marriage conform to the laws of the state and the canons of the Church.

But there are also significant changes from the Cranmerian rites of the 16th century. Twentieth-century liturgical reformers added a clear blessing of the rings given in marriage, a pronouncement by the priest that the couple is husband and wife, and a specific prayer that is identified as the nuptial blessing and only to be performed by a priest or a bishop. Taken as a whole, this rite says more about the changes that have taken place in The Episcopal Church's understanding of itself and the role of priests (of who can bless and under what circumstances) than it does about its understanding of the nature of Christian marriage since the Reformation era.

In response to dramatic social and cultural changes, the 1991 General Convention further addressed the issue of human sexual relations by adopting a resolution designed to shore up established views of human sexuality and marriage. That resolution stated that "the teaching of The Episcopal Church is that physical sexual expression is appropriate only within the lifelong monogamous union of husband and wife." The resolution also recognized "the discontinuity between this teaching and the experience of many members" of The Episcopal Church.

By examining 20th-century issues related to marriage, we see that questions that have been a part of the pattern of the development of marriage continue to arise in the modern era. The Church affirms the significance of mutual joy as a central purpose of marriage, even as it expands its own definition of mutuality. The Church continues to ponder the question of divorce. It continues to struggle with the question of who may marry whom, and with the relationship between legal marriage and spiritual marriage. It continues to converse with the voices of culture and society that are so central to any people's understanding of what marriage is. These same questions help shape our work in present-day discussions of marriage.

8. Twenty-First-Century Christian Marriage

Industrialized society has continued to change at breakneck speed over the 35 years since the ratification of the 1979 Book of Common Prayer. Women have been recognized as full partners in the workforce, even if they are not yet paid accordingly. Men and women expect to share the responsibility of childrearing. As the life expectancy of married persons has risen significantly, divorce rates have skyrocketed since the Victorian era to a new plateau, where, for the last 30-plus years, almost half of all marriages are expected to end in divorce. Sexual relationships before marriage are largely seen as normative, and sexual relations in general are understood to be a true gift and pleasure of human life. Cultural norms have changed so that increasingly greater numbers of people decide to cohabitate before marriage, including older persons who, for financial reasons, are not economically able to make a decision to marry.

Birth control is readily accessible, and growing numbers of individuals choose to have children outside of marriage. Technological medical resources help couples to conceive outside the boundaries of heterosexual conjugal sexual relations, and those same technologies help bring to term the children that are produced, sometimes resulting in ambiguous answers to the question of who are the child's real parents. Only a minority of cultural settings in The Episcopal Church support the notion of marriage as anything besides a partnership between equals. Those who reject marriage often do so because they fear that current cultural mores around marriage have not progressed far enough, and that the institution of marriage can be stifling and restricting, potentially depriving one or both members of the marriage of full opportunities to participate in contemporary society.

Another radical change in the nature of our understanding of marriage has come in the last several decades as gay, lesbian, bisexual, and transgender people have taken on greater visibility in our society and have worked to gain a voice, a presence, and legal rights within both the broader culture and the Church. The question of same-sex union has inevitably led The Episcopal Church into a discussion of whether culturally, legally, morally, and spiritually same-sex marriage fits our current definitions of Christian marriage. As states across the United States and nations around the world move to legalize same-sex marriage and to allow for adoption of children by same-sex couples, the imperative to develop a theologically sound and culturally sensitive response to the question of the sanctity of a same-sex marriage has heightened.

In response to a directive from the 2009 General Convention of The Episcopal Church, the Standing Commission on Liturgy and Music (SCLM) developed and collected theological and liturgical resources addressing the issue of love and commitment in same-sex partnerships. It is in large part as a result of the conversations begun in that setting that the current Task Force on the Study of Marriage has been asked to develop resources that will help the Church more fully explore the historical, theological, practical, and canonical issues surrounding Christian marriage.

Hearkening back to earlier chapters in the Church's history, the SCLM framed core Christian values identified within our marriage traditions and expressed those in language fitting to our contemporary context. The "'I Will Bless You, and You Will Be a Blessing'" document provided the following expectations for all persons desirous of living in a Christian marriage: that relationships "be characterized by fidelity, monogamy, mutual affection and respect, careful, honest communication, and the holy love which enables those in such relationships to see in each other the image of God." It is our hope that this brief historical overview of marriage will offer members of the Church a road map that allows us all to see the historical continuity between this definition and the unique elements of this definition that have come to our understanding of Christian marriage over the course of the last hundred years.

Words are not static representations of some concretized unmoving reality. They are fluid, symbolic vehicles for naming that which we know to be true in our own time, our own day. "Marriage," "mutuality," "faithfulness," "companionship," "love": when understood within the context of history, these words have meant different things in different times. How we define marriage in our own day can be guided and informed by the many definitions we have encountered in history. But like all aspects of our faith life, the call from God ultimately is to come to experience and understand the Christian life in our time, our places, and our widely divergent historical, spiritual, psychological, and sociological contexts. That work is left to the Church. All that we of the Task Force on the Study of Marriage can even hope to do is to shine a light on the many meanings and purposes of marriage that have been part and parcel of the Christian life and faith.

Discussion Questions Related to the History of Marriage

1. Reading through the entire history of marriage, draw a diagram that compares and contrasts the concepts of marriage that are held by the wealthy and powerful as compared to those held by the landless, propertyless, and powerless in a society. Is it possible that marriage means different things to people, even within the same historical and cultural time frame?

2. Much of history tells us that marriage is a process, not an event. One of the central features of almost all marriage practices is the presence of betrothal rites. In earlier periods of history, betrothals lasted longer and were more formalized. Many of the elements that have been subsumed into our contemporary marriage rite began as parts of Jewish, Roman, or medieval rites of betrothal. What benefit does betrothal offer a couple and the communities in which the couple participates? How might contemporary betrothal practices be augmented to further support the process of marriage?

3. Who writes laws that prohibit individuals from marrying each other, and, from a historical perspective, what have been the primary motivations for these laws?

4. Since the beginning of time, men and women have entered into sexual and domestic relationships for the betterment of their own lives and their societies. Sometimes those unions have been defined by a shared communal ethic. At other times definitions have been primarily legal. Occasionally marriages have been described as primarily spiritual unions. Are all legal marriages spiritual unions? Is legal marriage required to validate a spiritual union? How central to a marriage is the public nature of it — whether it is witnessed to and affirmed by extended family networks and social relationships?

5. When you look with a long lens at the history of marriage, has it evolved or simply changed? Are contemporary Episcopal

understandings of marriage, and particularly of the necessity and significance of mutuality in marriage, more evolved understandings of the human condition than what was understood at earlier points in history?

6. How, if at all, does this discussion of the history of marriage inform your own views regarding the wisdom of the Church allowing same-sex marriage?

7. If almost 50 percent of marriages are currently ending in divorce, is that good or bad? What might the 21st century Episcopal Church do to make Christian marriage a more viable and robust institution in the coming decades?

Bibliography

Antonio, David William. *An Inculturation Model of the Catholic Marriage Ritual*. Collegeville, Minn.: Liturgical Press, 2002.

Astell, Ann W., ed. *Lay Sanctity, Medieval and Modern: A Search for Models*. Notre Dame, Ind.: University of Notre Dame Press, 2000.

Bell, Catherine. *Ritual: Perspectives and Dimensions*. New York: Oxford University Press, 1997.

Breidenthal, Thomas. *Christian Households: The Sanctification of Nearness*. Cambridge, Mass.: Cowley Publications, 1997.

Brown, Peter. *The Body and Society: Men, Women, and Sexual Renunciation in Early Christianity*. New York: Columbia University Press, 1988.

Browning, Don S., Bonnie J. Miller-McLemore, Pamela D. Couture, K. Brynolf Lyon, and Robert M. Franklin. *From Culture Wars to Common Ground: Religion and the American Family Debate*. Louisville: Westminster John Knox Press, 1997.

Burris, Virginia, ed. *A People's History of Christianity, Volume 2: Late Ancient Christianity*. Minneapolis: Fortress Press, 2010.

Chakkalakai, Tess. *Novel Bondage: Slavery, Marriage, and Freedom in Nineteenth-Century America*. Urbana: University of Illinois Press, 2011.

Chryssavgis, John. "The Sacrament of Marriage: An Orthodox Perspective." *Studia Liturgica* 19, no. 1 (1989): 17-27.

De Vos, Susan. "Nuptiality in Latin America: The View of a Sociologist and Family Demographer," Center for Demography and Ecology University of Wisconsin-Madison Working Paper No. 98-21. Madison: University of Wisconsin, http://www.ssc.wisc.edu/cde/cdewp/98-21.pdf.

Gregorio, Robert. "The Bond Made Holy: A History of Christian Marriage." *Liturgy* 4, no. 2 (Spring 1984): 37-43.

Grimes, Ronald. *Deeply Into the Bone: Re-inventing Rite of Passage*. Berkeley, University of California Press, 2000.

———. "The Need for Ritual Practice." Liturgy 4, no. 2 (Spring 1984): 9-13.

Gudzie, Tad. "New Models for Celebrating Marriage." Paper presented at the Canadian Liturgical Society, May 1983.

Harcus, A. R., and Haywards Heath. "Betrothal and Marriage." Expository Times 109, no. 3 (D 1997): 73-75.

Isasi-Diaz, Ada Maria. *Mujerista Theology*. Maryknoll, N.Y.: Orbis, 2001.

Kasper, Walter. *Theology of Christian Marriage*. Translated by David Smith. New York: Seabury Press, 1980.

Kreider, Alan. *The Change of Conversion and the Origin of Christendom*. Eugene, Ore.: Wipf and Stock Publishers, 1999.

Lavrin, Asunción, ed. *Sexuality and Marriage in Colonial Latin America*. Lincoln: University of Nebraska Press, 1989.

Lee, Shelley Sang-Hee. *A New History of Asian America*. New York: Routledge, Taylor, and Francis, 2014.

Lewittes, Mendell. *Jewish Marriage: Rabbinic Law, Legend, and Custom*. Northvale, N.J.: Jason Aronson, 1994.

Luecke, David L. *Marriage Types: Identifiers and Handbook*. Columbia, Md.: Relationship Institute, 1986.

Mannion, M. Francis. "The Four Elements of Love." *Liturgy* 4, no. 2 (Spring 1984): 15-21.

Martinez, German. *Worship: Wedding to Marriage*. Washington, D.C.: Pastoral Press, 1993.

Matrimort, Aime George, ed. *The Church at Prayer: An Introduction to the Liturgy New Edition, Volume 3: The Sacraments*. Collegeville, Minn.: Liturgical Press, 1984.

McCann, Carole, and Seung-Kyung Kim. *Feminist Theology Reader, Third Edition*. Hoboken, N.J.: Taylor and Francis, 2013.

Meeks, Wayne. *The First Urban Christians: The Social World of the Apostle Paul.* New Haven: Yale University Press, 1983.

Meyendorff, John. *Marriage: An Orthodox Perspective.* [Tuckahoe, N.Y.]: St. Vladimir's Seminary Press, 1970.

Meyers, Ruth. "'I Will Bless You, and You Will Be a Blessing': Liturgy and Theology for Blessing Same-Sex Couples in the Episcopal Church (USA)." Presentation given to Oxford liturgists, October 2013.

Milavec, Aaron. *The Didache: Text, Translation, Analysis, and Commentary.* Collegeville, Minn.: Liturgical Press, 2003.

Nilsson, Nils-Henrik. "Marriage Rites in the Swedish Cultural Context." LWF Studies 1 (1999): 195-216.

Olson, David H., David G. Fournier, and Joan M. Druckman. *Prepare Enrich Counselor's Manual.* Minneapolis: Life Innovations, 1994.

Osiek, Carolyn, and David Balch. *Families in the New Testament World: Households and House Churches.* Louisville: Westminster John Knox Press, 1997.

Ostdiek, Gilbert, OFM. "Human Situations in Need of Ritualization." *New Theology Review* 3, no. 2 (May 1990): 36-50.

Price, Charles, and Louis Weil. *Liturgy for Living.* New York: Seabury Press, 1979.

Ruether, Rosemary Radford. *Christianity and the Making of the Modern Family: Ruling Ideologies, Diverse Realities.* Boston: Beacon, 2000.

Russell, James C. *The Germanization of Early Medieval Christianity: A Sociohistorical Approach to Religious Transformation.* New York: Oxford University Press, 1994.

Satlow, Michael. *Jewish Marriage in Antiquity.* Princeton: Princeton University Press, 2001.

Sedgwick, Timothy F. *Sacramental Ethics: Paschal Identity and the Christian Life.* Philadelphia: Fortress Press, 1987.

Stevenson, Kenneth W. *Nuptial Blessing: A Study of Christian Marriage Rites.* London: Alcuin Club / SPCK, 1982.

―――. *Worship: Wonderful and Sacred Mystery.* Washington, D.C.: Pastoral Press, 1992.

―――, and Mark Searle. *Documents of the Marriage Liturgy.* Collegeville, Minn.: Liturgical Press, 1992.

Sullivan, Andrew, ed. *Same-Sex Marriage: Pro and Con—A Reader.* New York: Vintage Books, 1997.

Swidler, Arlene. "Marriage in the World Religions." *Journal of Ecumenical Studies* 22, no. 1 (Winter 1985): 1-119.

Thatcher, Adrian. *Marriage and Modernity: Christian Marriage in Post Modern Times*. Washington Square, N.Y.: New York University Press, 1999.

Turner, Victor. *The Ritual Process: Structure and Anti-Structure*. New York: Aldine de Gruyter, 1995.

van Gennep, Arnold. *The Rites of Passage*. Translated by Monika B. Vizedom and Gebrielle L. Caffee. Chicago: University of Chicago Press, 1960.

Ward, Hannah, and Jennifer Wild. *Human Resources: Worship Resources for an Age of Change*. New York: Mowbray, 1995.

Westerhoff, John. *Will Our Children Have Faith?* New York: Seabury Press, 1976.

———, and Gwen Kennedy Neville. *Learning Through Liturgy*. New York: Seabury Press, 1978.

ESSAY 4:
Marriage as a Rite of Passage

The catechism of the 1979 Book of Common Prayer describes the rite of marriage as a sacramental rite which "evolved in the Church under the guidance of the Holy Spirit." It goes on to say that "[a]lthough they are means of grace, they are not necessary for all persons in the same way that Baptism and Eucharist are" (860). This is, in part, why we describe marriages as sacramental rites rather than as sacraments.

While marriage may provide deep and rich spiritual blessings to the lives of those who are called to this state, not all marry, nor do we believe God ever intended for all to marry. From our Christian perspective, we understand the marriage covenant, like the covenant to a life of celibacy, to have a special, graced place in our lives. We pray that the Holy Spirit is at work in our daily lives through our ongoing participation in the life that proceeds out of the sacramental rite of marriage. We hold this rite in high esteem, and as Christian people we work diligently to uphold both the dignity and the integrity of the rite and of the graced life to which it calls us.

The rite of marriage carries with it a special weight and has at times been described as the one liturgical rite in the lives of laypersons where they may be invited to have a central role in its planning and administration. No one who understands our Christian theology regarding God's sacramental presence in the world would dare diminish its significance to the life of those Christians who have been called to this sacred vocation.

There is, however, an overarching, almost universal phenomenon that applies not only to Christians entering into marriage, but to all persons of all religions who choose to engage in their cultures' marriage rites. What are these rites about? What do they do? How important are they to their participants, and are they purely for the sake of the two people being joined to one another?

1. Marriage as a Rite of Passage

Marriage rites are omnipresent in human societies across history, cultures, and geography. How marriages take place, what their purposes are, how they are interpreted, and who officiates varies across time and space. In the early 20th century, a French anthropologist, Arnold van Gennep, began to look at rituals from a scientific perspective to try to ascertain their purposes beyond those already articulated from a religious perspective. The work he first produced has helped inform our understandings of human rituals throughout the modern era.

Van Gennep came to identify a certain type of ritual activity as "rites of passage." By this he meant that these formal ritual actions were used to help individuals or communities transition from one life state to a new one. They provided a ritual passage that enabled the members of a society to navigate the complicated and often perplexing waters from pregnancy to parenting, from uninitiated to initiated, from childhood to adolescence, from adolescence to full adulthood, from singlehood to married life, from follower to leader, and from life to death. Marriage fits within this category that he labels rites of passage — along with initiation rites (including Baptism and Confirmation), ordinations, quinceañeras, monastic rites of profession, adoption rites, marriage-anniversary celebrations, burial rites, and a host of other, less-formalized rites practiced in our journey from birth to death.

There are, of course, other forms of ritual that serve other purposes; that help remedy sin or a rupture in the relationship with the divine; that call upon the divine for assistance, that return people to health and wholeness; and that create a pathway for communion with the divine. Van Gennep asserted that, somewhat differently from these other forms of ritual, rites of passage served core sociological, cultural, psychological, and political purposes within a society. They help to keep society intact. They serve the needs of not only the individual but, just as important, they serve the greater good by making ways forward that mediate against chaos, confusion, and anomie within particular communities during specific moments of transition and change.

2. Liminality in Rites of Passage

As van Gennep examined rites of passage across cultures, he began to notice a generalized pattern to those rites. He identified a pattern that began with an event of separation from one's old identity, followed by a transition time that allowed for changes in role and status, followed by an event of reincorporation into the community with one's new identity and status.

Victor Turner built on the work of van Gennep. He further fleshed out his own sense of what was happening during a rite of passage, and how that rite reshaped the community in which it took place. Turner paid particular attention to the period of transition leading up to the rite that finalized the change in status of the person or the community. What he witnessed in his anthropological research was a kind of liminality that was particularly at work in this transition time. Individuals during this period were "betwixt and between," neither fish nor fowl. This period of liminality often both allowed for and required a kind of suspension of former rules and categories in relation to the person in transition. Because of this, there was a sense of graced time which created an experience which Turner described as "communitas."

Communitas is about more than just everyday communal relationships. It is a shared ethos and experiential context that allows for greater freedom, greater intimacy, and higher levels of care and bonding than might normally be part of the fabric of everyday life in society. During periods of communitas, trust is built. Relationships are forged, and bonds of affection are created. This period of communitas, this liminal period in the life of an individual, creates a kind of elasticity of identity that encourages and allows for greater adaptivity, creativity, and spontaneity.

If people are to reinvent themselves, there must be room to allow for trial and error and evolution. One does not come to sport a new identity overnight — not successfully. As the community makes room for this kind of liminality, these forays into communitas provide a rich and full societal environment for intimacy, creativity, and adaptive change. The whole of society benefits from its participation in individuals' rites of passage that are taking place.

Turner's studies of this period of liminality led him to believe that its significance to the change of status process was so central that he renamed van Gennep's three stages of rites of passage as the pre-liminal, the liminal, and the post-liminal stages. He also revised van Gennep's work (and the work of others who were exploring ritual) to assert that while at times rituals become the vehicles for societal stabilization and support of the status quo, at other times they become the means to overturn the status quo and create greater systemic change in the society. Sometimes what is called for is a loosening of power, an overturning of tradition, or an adaptive process of redefining the nature of life in community. All of these goals could be met, Turner believed, through ritual processes, particularly rites of passage rituals.

Turner's observations affirm that marriage rites can move individuals from one family constellation to a new one, can unite two previously unconnected families, can create avenues for dealing with important social and economic status changes within two families, can cement new political alliances and power dynamics among its participants, and can serve the greater good by promoting a culture of trust and relationship, even among those who might previously have been strangers to one another within the community.

As Christians we might posit that all of this is work the Holy Spirit might find immensely rewarding and might choose to participate in, whether the individuals taking part call themselves Christian or not. Anthropologists, of course, would have no need to affirm divine providence over this work and would assert that it is simply the natural, evolved cultural adaptation of a society to the need for growth, flexibility, and movement within human society.

3. Betrothal and Marriage

For much of the history of marriage in many parts of the world, the process of marrying has been just that: a process. While this is still true in many parts of the world, it is less true in modern, westernized societies. Often the event of separation that has marked the movement out of the pre-liminal stage into the liminal stage has been some form of betrothal rite in which promises are made and preparations are begun that will, in time, lead to a final rite of marriage. Often there have been small rites along the way that are a significant part of this liminal period. Perhaps there is a feast to announce the betrothal. At times there has been an exchange of gifts or tokens as signs of the promises being entered into. Public acknowledgements of intent have been expected.

During the period of betrothal, there have often been opportunities for the two families represented in the marriage to communicate with one another and begin to build bonds. There might be discussions and even negotiations about material goods to be transferred from one family to the other as a result of the marriage. During this period, couples have often been allowed an opportunity to come to know each other better, and sometimes a new degree of intimacy between the two who are to marry is allowed or even encouraged.

Communities have seen a marriage as taking place through a series of rites that culminate in one final ritual action that moves the couple, their families, and the communities in which they are embedded into a new understanding of the identities of the married persons and new bonds of relationship within society. An entire network of relationships is altered through a marriage, and betrothal practices have allowed time for all those within that network to grasp and apprehend this new configuration of relationships.

The ritual studies scholar Ronald Grimes has written about the ways in which contemporary society has compromised the fabric of North American and other westernized rites of passage to a degree that is potentially detrimental. The movement out of singlehood into marriage requires comprehensive transformations for the individuals involved and the families of which they are a part. Virtually every aspect of one's life is changed through the act of marrying; economic, political, legal, emotional, psychological, social, and spiritual changes are expected of those who marry. In a different period in history, couples took months or even years to make those changes.

Now, in our contemporary society, marrying is seen as a single act on a given day at a prescribed time. That rite may occur either through a legal action completed by signing a license and appearing before a representative of the state or through a religious action that requires a legal component to be fully recognized as marriage. Whichever form a marriage takes, there is currently nothing in the process that requires a period of liminality greater than the state's prescribed requirements about how long before the wedding one must obtain the license or the religious community's expectations about how far in advance one must announce one's wedding and participate in the required premarital counseling (if any is required).

By asking individuals to believe that a marriage can take place through a ritual action that might be as brief as ten minutes with virtually no period of preparation, some ritual scholars believe we have truncated our ritual processes to such a degree that the rites may no longer be able to do what they are designed to and claim to do. A legal contract can be signed in a few brief moments. But individuals, societies, and the Church believe that marriage is meant to be far more than a simple legal contract.

4. Creating a Liminal Space in a Contemporary Context

Those desiring to marry in The Episcopal Church have worked and continue to work with rubrical and canonical expectations that have to some degree been instituted to mediate against the danger of people marrying before any public preparatory liminal period has occurred. The publishing of banns originated at a time when some within society were engaging in secret marriages — marriages that were not public and did not represent usual patterns of public recognition by all in the society of the nature of the relationship. This situation left the secret spouse in an extremely vulnerable position. This private, secret marriage status made it easier to "put away" a spouse who might prove a financial, political, or social liability. The publishing of banns militated against bigamy, against marriages by those who had taken vows of celibacy, and against marriages that would not be supported by the extended families or the legal and social communities that might, by the very definition of marriage, be expected to affirm and respect this relationship.

In the 20th century, in large part in response to changing patterns of marriage and divorce in contemporary North American society, the Church added a canonical requirement for premarital counseling prior to marriage in an Episcopal rite administered by an ordained Episcopal minister. This premarital counseling requirement set up and made use of a period of liminality in which the couple could explore the depth of change that marriage would bring to their individual and shared lives. Effective premarital counseling is meant to foster the development of "communitas." It calls for attention not just to the ritual preparations for the rite of marriage, but also to preparations for all that it will mean to live in the hoped-for, lifelong state of holy matrimony.

When premarital counseling is abridged into a brief discussion of the ritual details of the wedding itself, it ceases to fulfill either its spiritual or societal purposes. While premarital counseling is not the only way to facilitate the forming of a marriage, it is at least an expression of the Church's deep conviction that the intentional development of a relationship that can support the state of holy matrimony is both necessary and helpful to a Christian marriage.

One hears, at times, of premarital counseling paradigms that focus almost exclusively on helping the couple explore the spiritual aspects of their marriage. In this counseling there is often a great deal of attention given to the sacramental element of a marriage, the nature of marriage as a lifelong covenant, the theological meanings of marriage, and the couple's decision to participate in some religious community as an ongoing part of their Christian marriage. While all of these are deeply worthwhile conversations, it is also important to remember the nonreligious aspects of life lived as a married couple. Economic stewardship, parenting, the roles and expectations of daily life, extended familial relationships, sexuality, and intimacy are all significant aspects to holy matrimony.

They all also have a secular parallel. Even when couples seeking to be married in the Church do not grasp the theological significance of these aspects of their marriage, their social, economic, and political significance continues to be paramount. Therefore, it behooves those preparing couples for marriage to attend actively to the larger picture of what marriage means for those who are deeply faithful Christian persons who will build their whole marriage on a spiritual frame — and for those for whom the spiritual component of marriage is viewed as simply one aspect among many.

One cultural shift we are witnessing in much of contemporary western society is a movement toward cohabitation as a stepping-stone to marriage. At a time when former models of marriage that created space for a liminal period have eroded, couples appear to be building their own liminal period betwixt and between singlehood and full entrance into a societally sanctioned lifelong partnership. Demographic evidence suggests that for those who choose lifelong partnerships, marriage is still most often the hoped-for status; however, cohabitation seems to be serving as a middle ground for those not yet able to take on the full weight of marriage expectations.

Seen from an anthropological point of view, we can view this move toward temporary cohabitation and "capstone marriages" as a potential correction to precisely the set of concerns raised by Ronald Grimes and others. Many seem to be viewing marriage as something that can and should be eased into rather than jumped into. Anthropological research affirms the wisdom of this basic intuition. Whether cohabitation is the best means possible for creating this liminal period is certainly a subject worthy of debate. But the need for a transition time between singlehood and marriage is readily evident. How this liminal time is optimally used by the couple, the families, and the greater community (including the faith community) is another question worthy of further discussion.

5. Marriage as a Prophetic Act

While the history of marriage document in the work of the Task Force highlights the ways in which legal marriage has often been a means to maintaining existing power structures and supporting the status quo, it is important for contemporary Christians also to heed Victor Turner's assertion that marriage can, at times, be a ritual that subverts the status quo and invites the larger society to reconsider its own assumptions about how the world should be.

In an age when political tensions are high among those of different Abrahamic faith traditions, contemporary societies are also seeing unprecedented levels of interfaith marriages between Christians, Muslims, and Jews. These marriages can become both the signs of and the means to stronger bonds of mutual love and support among these groups. At a time when racial tensions run high across much of our society, we are also witnessing unprecedented levels of interracial marriage. Each of these marriages invites the societies around it to explore visions and strategies for living that enable solidarity and mutual support rather than public strife and rupture.

Marriages can cross class lines, political affiliations, ethnicities, and a host of other societal and cultural divides that have become established between peoples. These marriages can serve as grassroots training grounds for learning a new way to be and live together — a way that celebrates love, openness, communication, partnership, mutuality, community, and shalom. Marriage rites among diverse couples can become occasions for celebrating all that unites us in our humanity rather than all that divides us in our differentness. They become important public attestations to a different way of being — a way of being that speaks to the core of the Gospel message but is not always witnessed to publicly in our larger society or even in our sometimes-segregated church communities.

When marrying couples have prepared themselves for marriage; have worked with families and friends to create new bonds of relationship; have already publicly lived into vows of mutual support and fidelity; have expressed to those around them the commitment they are making to a lifelong union that will not be undone by prosperity or adversity, then these couples have made their rituals into subversive acts — prophetic acts that challenge the values of the society around them and call that society to a richer, fuller, more robust way of living human life.

The language of Episcopal marriage rites promotes this fuller vision of humanity; however, words alone are not enough. It is vital that marriage vows be entered into with integrity, with awareness, and with a truthfulness that will not ultimately call the rite into question. Instead, the couple and the enacted rite will call into question the choices of a society that does not actively protect and support this vision. Effective intentional ritual action has this capacity. It can become a means to political, social, economic, and societal justice by allowing all those who participate in the words and gestures of that ritual to see the world as it can be. But this can only take place when the rite is perceived in its execution as being wholly guileless and completely truthful in its message and its intent.

One of the very important questions the Church faces in an age when almost 50 percent of marriages end in divorce is, how do we prepare couples to be ready to enter into just such deeply truthful and culturally challenging rites? How do we imbue our marriage rites with Christic integrity, so that the truths they can proclaim can be heard and received by those present for these rituals? Are betrothal periods — periods of marriage formation comparable to baptismal formation — necessary and essential for this to take place? And how do we undergird and support processes of marriage formation that truly prepare couples not just for wedding ceremonies, but for married life as well?

There are no easy answers to any of these questions, and assuredly the answers we come to will vary across our cultural landscapes. Exploring these questions seems important and life-giving work for our Episcopal religious community. If we perceive marriage rites as substantial, life-giving sacramental acts that have the potential to call us deeper into the heart of God, into spiritual renewal and greater life transformation, then it is incumbent upon us to turn our hearts and minds to these questions for our own sake, and for the sake of the world.

Bibliography

Antonio, David William. *An Inculturation Model of the Catholic Marriage Ritual.* Collegeville, Minn.: Liturgical Press, 2002.

Bell, Catherine. *Ritual: Perspectives and Dimensions.* New York: Oxford University Press, 1997.

Chapungco, Anscar J. *Worship: Progress and Tradition.* Beltsville, Md.: Pastoral Press, 1995.

Collins, Mary. "Ritual Symbols and the Ritual Process: The Work of Victor W. Turner." *In Worship: Renewal to Practice,* 59-72. Washington, D.C.: Pastoral Press, 1987.

Grimes, Ronald. *Deeply Into the Bone: Re-inventing Rites of Passage.* Berkeley: University of California Press, 2000.

———. "The Need for Ritual Practice." *Liturgy* 4, no. 2 (Spring 1984): 9-13.

Harcus, A.R., and Haywards Heath. "Betrothal and Marriage." *Expository Times* 109, no. 3 (December 1997): 73-75.

Isasi-Diaz, Ada Maria. *Mujerista Theology.* Maryknoll, N.Y.: Orbis, 2001.

Saliers, Don. *Worship Come to Its Senses.* Nashville: Abingdon Press, 1996.

Stuhlman, Byron David. *Occasions of Grace: An Historical and Theological Study of the Pastoral Offices and Episcopal Services in the Book of Common Prayer.* New York: Church Publishing, 1995.

Swidler, Arlene. "Marriage in the World Religions." *Journal of Ecumenical Studies* 22, no. 1 (Winter 1985): 1-119.

Turner, Victor. *The Ritual Process: Structure and Anti-Structure.* New York: Aldine de Gruyter, 1995.

van Gennep, Arnold. *The Rites of Passage.* Translated by Monika B. Vizedom and Gebrielle L. Caffee. Chicago: University of Chicago Press, 1960.

ESSAY 5:
The Marriage Canon:
History and Critique

1. Overview

Resolution 2012-A050 directs the called-for Task Force to explore the biblical, theological, historical, liturgical, and canonical dimensions of marriage; and to consult with the Standing Commission on Constitution and Canons and the Standing Commission on Liturgy and Music to address the pastoral need for priests to officiate at the civil marriage of a same-sex couple in states that authorize such. Additionally, Resolution 2012-D091, calling for specific amendments to Canon I.18 intended to allow same-sex marriage, was referred to the Task Force for study. These issues cross biblical and theological dimensions that are explored more thoroughly elsewhere in this report. This section of the report surveys the history of the Episcopal canons addressing marriage and then explores current issues presented to this Church in Canon I.18, including the current description of marriage as applying only to couples comprising one man and one woman.

2. History

Canonical history in The Episcopal Church is consistent in one respect: canons follow practice. That is, the Church changes and evolves its practice and then amends the canons to reflect the current practice.[92] Sometimes this happens relatively quickly — for example, in the case of the ordination of women; sometimes this happens slowly — for example, in the case of the Church's practices regarding divorce and remarriage. In either case, a review of the journals of General Convention and of *The Annotated Constitution and Canons* (White & Dykman, eds., 1979) shows that oftentimes the discussion has taken

---
[92] There are other instances when amending the canons was intended to change the practice. A recent example is the serial revisions of Title IV between 1994 and 2009.

place over a number of years before the amendment passes General Convention. The marriage canon has followed this norm.

It should be noted that the term "Holy Matrimony" may appear to be used interchangeably with marriage. Holy Matrimony is not defined but in usage refers to the sacramental rite of the Church, and some prefer its use in the context of the Church's relationship to weddings and marriage. The connotation of "Holy Matrimony" is something more than marriage as defined by civil law. That "something more" is expressed in covenant language: the exchange of vows in the presence of a priest and at least two witnesses and blessed in the Name of God. Yet the marriage rite in the Book of Common Prayer 1979 is entitled, "The Celebration and Blessing of a Marriage." And both civil and church law talks of "solemnizing" marriage. Even if Holy Matrimony is understood as "something more," that understanding is more aspirational than real, as marriage in the Church is no guarantee of success of the relationship.

The canons addressing marriage or Holy Matrimony first addressed not the making of the marriage but its dissolution. The first mention of marriage in the canons[93] of The Episcopal Church appears in the Convention of 1808. The House of Deputies referred a communication to the House of Bishops, then consisting of the two bishops in attendance, White and Claggett, making a request. The communication asked the bishops to consider adopting the English canon regarding marriage and inserting it into future editions of the prayer book.

The bishops responded by deferring the matter to consideration and action by a future convention, pointing to the absence of some of their members, as well as absences among the deputies. The 1808 convention instead passed a joint resolution stating "the sense of this Church" regarding the remarriage of the divorced, declaring, "it is inconsistent with the law of God, and the Ministers of this Church, therefore, shall not unite in matrimony any person who is divorced, unless it be on account of the other party having been guilty of adultery" (White & Dykman, 398).

This joint resolution of 1808 remained the only statement of the General Convention on the subject of marriage until 1868 when the first canon was enacted as Canon II.13:

> No minister of this Church shall solemnize Matrimony in any case where there is a divorced wife or husband of either party still living; but this Canon shall not be held to apply to

---

[93] The Constitution of The Episcopal Church has not historically addressed marriage. The discussion here is confined to the canons.

the innocent party in a divorce for the cause of adultery, or to parties once divorced seeking to be united again.

The new canon restated what the joint resolution of 1808 had put forward: remarriage of a divorced person is allowed only when the divorce occurs because of the adultery of one of the partners and then only of the innocent partner. It also adds a clarifying statement that allows a divorced couple to reunite and remarry in the church. This statement regarding divorce and remarriage relied on what is commonly called "the Matthean exception," referring to Matthew 5:32: "But I say to you that anyone who divorces his wife, except on the ground of unchastity, causes her to commit adultery; and whoever marries a divorced woman commits adultery." Allowing this exception to the general prohibition of remarriage of a divorced person while the other partner lived was an Episcopal Church step away from the Church of England's blanket ban on remarriage of divorced persons (White & Dykman, 398-99).

The 1877 convention repealed Canon II.13 as it was enacted in 1868 and enacted a new version entitled "Of Marriage and Divorce":

- Section 1 declared unlawful any marriage "otherwise than as God's Word doth allow";
- Section 2 prohibited ministers from knowingly solemnizing, after due inquiry, the marriage of any divorced person whose spouse is alive, if divorced for cause arising after marriage, and retains the exception for the innocent spouse or divorced spouses seeking to reunite;
- Section 3 prevented reception of a person not married according to the Word of God and the discipline of this Church into Baptism, Confirmation, or Holy Communion without the "godly judgment" of the bishop. But no minister could refuse the sacraments to a penitent person in imminent danger of death;
- Section 4 required referral of the facts of any case arising under section 2 to the bishop of the diocese or missionary jurisdiction in which the case arose, or, in the absence of such a bishop, to a bishop designated by the Standing Committee. The bishop was empowered to make inquiry into the matter as he found expedient and then deliver a judgment. No guidelines are given to serve as the basis for entering judgment;
- Section 5 applies the new canon only prospectively as to any penalties that may attach. (White & Dykman, 400-1)

The House of Bishops had concurred with the amendments in 1874 but the House of Deputies deferred consideration until the next convention in 1877. The 1868 amendments applied only to clergy, while the 1877 revision added penalties for laity by excluding from the sacraments those who married outside the Church.

Divorce rates remained low in the 1800s because secular law and social norms made divorce difficult. Spouses had to prove fault in some manner to obtain a divorce. Women, alone or with children, had few options for economic survival — a deterrent to seeking divorce. Divorce statistics were not even recorded prior to 1867. Less than 10 percent of marriages ended in divorce between 1867 and 1900. Nonetheless, the Church wrestled with how it should respond to its members who divorced. The idea of divorce ran counter to church values and ideas about marriage, but it played out in how the Church responded to its divorced members. The Church's response came in the language of punishment: of clergy for knowingly officiating at the marriage of a person who was divorced from a living spouse, and of laity who divorced and remarried.

The convention of 1883 appointed a joint committee of bishops and deputies "to consider the duty of the Church in relation to the whole subject of Marriage, including the impediments to the contract thereof, the manner of its solemnization, and the conditions of its dissolution, and to report to the next General Convention" (White & Dykman, 402). In their report to the 1886 convention, the committee contrasted the traditional view held by the Church with the prevailing secular sentiment seeking easier separation. The cause was identified as the ease with which first marriages were contracted, noting that children as young as 12 could marry without parental consent and without witnesses. The committee's response was a proposed canon that featured:

- Setting 18 as the minimum age to marry without parental consent;
- Requiring solemnization to occur in the presence of at least two witnesses personally acquainted with both parties;
- Requiring clergy to keep a register of marriages recording certain facts, and signed by the parties, at least two witnesses, and the minister;
- Setting the law of the Church concerning divorce as that contained in Matthew 5:32 and 19:9, Mark 10:11-12, and Luke 16:18;
- Prohibiting divorce except for adultery or fornication, with

the unfaithful spouse prohibited from marrying again during the lifetime of the innocent spouse;
- Subjecting clergy who violate the canon to ecclesiastical trial and admonition for a first offense and suspension or deposition for repeat offenses;
- Barring spouses from receiving Holy Communion for violating the canon except upon repentance and after separation from the new spouse.

The House of Deputies declined to concur in the adoption of the proposed canon which was referred to the next conventions of 1889, 1892, 1895, and 1901 with similar results. (White & Dykman, 402-3).

The convention of 1904 took up the proposal to revise the marriage canon and passed Canon 38, "Of Solemnization of Matrimony," by a narrow majority after four days of debate in the House of Deputies meeting as a committee of the whole. Canon 38 set the following requirements:

- Section 1 required ministers to observe the law of the state governing the civil contract of marriage in the place where the marriage was performed.
- Section 2 required the presence of at least two witnesses to the solemnization and the recording in the proper register of the name, age, and residence of each party, signed by the parties, the minister, and at least two witnesses.
- Section 3 prohibited the minister, knowingly and after due inquiry, from officiating at the marriage of any person who was divorced from a living spouse, except the innocent party to a divorce for adultery. It added the new requirements in the latter case of a one-year waiting period and presentation of the divorce decree and record with "satisfactory evidence touching on the facts of the case" to the ecclesiastical authority, along with evidence that the opposing spouse was personally served or appeared in court. The ecclesiastical authority, after taking legal advice on the evidence, declared in writing that in his judgment, the case of the applicant conformed to the requirements of the canon. It further allowed any minister as a matter of discretion to decline to solemnize any marriage.
- Section 4 authorized any minister to refuse the ordinances of Holy Baptism, Confirmation, or Holy Communion to anyone who has been married "otherwise than as the Word of God and discipline of this Church allow" until the case

was presented to the ecclesiastical authority for his godly judgment. But no minister was to refuse the sacraments to a penitent person in danger of death.

As adopted, the canon represented a compromise — one that had eluded the General Convention for 15 years — between those who would prohibit remarriage of persons divorced from a still-living former spouse, and those who advocated the limited adultery exception, previously enacted in 1868, for the so-called innocent spouse in a divorce for adultery (White & Dykman, 403-4).

Efforts to drop the adultery exception continued without success in the conventions of 1910 and 1913, when the question was referred to a joint committee on marriage. The committee's report to the 1916 convention argued for the exercise of discretion in excluding persons from the sacraments, recognizing that a subsequent marriage may have been entered into in good faith and in ignorance of the Church's law or while not subject to the Church's discipline, or may result in the break-up of a family. This discretion would lie with the minister of the congregation and the bishop of the diocese. The proposed canonical amendments failed in 1916 and 1919.

A number of changes in American social and economic structures from 1850 to 1920 kept the Church's discussions of the role of divorce and remarriage going. The Industrial Revolution drew men and women from rural community to the cities, from kinship community to a community of peers, and began to redefine the roles of men and women. Women organized to advocate for their civil rights in 1848 after the all-male Liberty Party added suffrage for women to its national platform. A month later, the Seneca Falls Convention met and adopted a "Declaration of Sentiments" demanding rights for women so that they could protect their homes and families.

Among the rights sought were equal treatment before the law; participation in the government of both State and Church; the right to own, inherit, and dispose of their property; and fair treatment in divorce. The Women's Christian Temperance Union (WCTU) organized in 1874, seeking to ban alcohol, and later tobacco and other drugs, in order to protect the home. Women protested their lack of civil rights and sought the rights that would treat them as adults in the eyes of the law, as opposed to the legal protections that kept them dependent on their fathers, husbands, and sons. Unable to vote, women — especially married women — lacked legal rights to retain custody of children and control of their own property in a divorce; legal protection against rape and other assaults, including domestic violence; and access to the economy to become self-supporting when they were widowed or divorced.

The institutions of that time were controlled by white men. Legislatures were all male. Women faced juries of men in civil and criminal cases. The Church reflected its times: only men could be ordained as clergy, and only men could serve on vestries and as deputies to General Convention. The WCTU obtained passage of Prohibition with the 18th Amendment to the federal constitution in 1920, subsequently repealed in 1933 in response to the uneven application of the law across economic class and in the face of widespread and open disregard for a law with a raft of unintended consequences. In short, Prohibition was unworkable. But women obtained the right to vote in 1920 with ratification of the 19th Amendment.

Women's roles in society continued to change with the Depression and World War II. Divorce rates increased in the early 20th century, doubling from 8 percent in 1900 to 16 percent in 1930. Divorce continued to be fault-based divorce codes, which required proof of abuse, adultery, or abandonment. Divorce rates dropped slightly during the Great Depression, in part because couples could not afford the economic consequences of divorce on top of unemployment. As the unemployment rate dropped, divorce rates began to rise gradually. By 1940, 20 percent of marriages ended in divorce. Fertility rates increased immediately following World War I, but then resumed a 50-year decline that was slowed only by the unreliability of available birth control (Coontz, 211).

The General Convention of 1922 amended section 3 of Canon 38, making it unlawful for any member of the Church to enter into a marriage when either of the parties was divorced from a living husband or wife. The convention of 1925 considered and rejected an amendment to section 3 of Canon 38 that restricted remarriage to cases where the bishop, acting with legal advice, found on the record that the divorce was granted for cause arising before marriage, essentially annulling the marriage, allowing remarriage of either party. The House of Bishops considered a separate amendment that allowed remarriage of either party of any divorce, abolishing the Matthean exception. The proposal failed, and the Matthean exception survived.

The Joint Commission on Marriage and Divorce presented an extensive revision of the marriage canon that was adopted in 1931. Compared with the previous limited measures to regulate the solemnization of marriage by the Church, the new Canon 41, "Of the Solemnization of Holy Matrimony," enacted far more detailed regulation of church marriage:

- Section 1 for the first time stated an affirmative duty that clergy instruct their congregations, both publicly and privately, on the nature and responsibilities of Holy Matrimony, and the mutual love and forbearance required.

- Section 2 retained the 1904 admonition that ministers conform to the laws of the state governing civil marriage, and added a parallel admonition to conform to the laws of the Church regarding the solemnization of Holy Matrimony.

- Section 3 expanded to five the list of conditions that the minister must discern before solemnizing a marriage. Among the new conditions were verifying that the parties had a right to contract a marriage under church law; instructing the parties on "the nature of Holy Matrimony, its responsibilities, and the means of grace which God has provided through His Church"; and requiring the parties to give the minister at least three days' notice of their intent to marry. Requirements for at least two witnesses and entry into the parish register were retained.

- Section 4 added a new requirement that the parties to an imperiled marriage must present the matter to the minister who has "the duty ... to labor that the parties may be reconciled."

- Section 5 retained the 1904 process and expectations for the remarriage of the divorced.

- Section 6 added new provisions and conditions for the annulment or dissolution of a marriage by reason of the presence of one of the listed impediments to the marriage: relationship by blood within the prohibited degree (consanguinity within first cousins); absence of free consent; mistake as to the identity of either party; mental deficiency affecting exercise of intelligent choice; insanity of either party; failure of a party to reach puberty; undisclosed impotence, venereal disease, or facts making the marriage bigamous. Section 6 added a role for the ecclesiastical court in the exercise of judgments on annulment or dissolution petitions as an alternative to presentation to the bishop. A further provision stated that no judgment was to be construed as addressing the legitimacy of children or the civil validity of the relationship.

- Section 7 retained the 1904 provision for excluding from the sacraments persons not married "according to the word of God and discipline of this Church" and the process for review by the bishop. Section 7 added an additional process for admitting persons married by civil authority or "otherwise than as this Church provides" to the sacraments. The process involved judgment by the bishop or ecclesiastical court.

Two of the 1931 proposals were subject to debate and amendment. The Joint Commission's proposal did not include continuing recognition of the Matthean exception that was added back by the convention. The second major change, removing the right of determining nullity of a marriage from the local clergy to the bishop or ecclesiastical court, has an unclear basis, but a best guess is that clergy were thought to be too lenient with their congregants. Requiring the bishop to make the determination opened the door to more uniform results and more objective consideration. One additional significant change was the omission of the section 3 clause that permitted any minister in his own discretion to decline to solemnize any marriage (White & Dykman, 406-8).

The 1934 convention modified the three days' notice requirement to allow the minister to waive "for weighty cause" when one of the parties was a member of the minister's congregation or was well known to the minister — facts which had to be reported immediately to the ecclesiastical authority (White & Dykman, 408).

The report of the Joint Commission on Marriage and Divorce to the 1937 General Convention lamented that the Church's views on divorce and marriage were increasingly ignored by the Church as well as by the public at large. To remedy this concern, the commission made observations about the points of tension, noting that "[a]lmost everyone agrees that the present Canon is inadequate, but there is a wide difference of opinion as to the course that should be followed" (Joint Commission on Marriage and Divorce, quoted in White & Dykman, 409). The report went on to identify three issues:

- Some are slow to make changes, foreseeing difficulties and dangers and hence voting for the status quo.
- Others want to prohibit remarriage or the blessing of a remarriage of divorced persons, a strategy that has failed.
- Still others want to adopt annulment as done in the Eastern Orthodox and Roman churches, observing that "[t]o most Anglicans and Protestants this seems nothing but divorce

under another name. In either case it 'puts asunder' those whom, to all appearances and understanding 'God hath joined together.' "

The commission proposed only two minor changes to the impediments section of the canon, which were adopted, adding "[l]ack of free and legal consent of either party" and "[i]mpotence or sexual perversion of either party undisclosed to the other" (White & Dykman, 410 [emphasis added]). Sexual perversion would include homosexuality.

The commission proposed more extensive revisions of the marriage canon in 1940 and 1943 without success, receiving unfavorable action in the House of Deputies in a vote by orders. The 1943 convention passed successfully a reorganization of canons related to marriage by transferring section 7 (1931), governing the access of divorced persons to the sacraments, to Canon 15, "Of Regulations Respecting the Laity." Section 4, the duty to seek counseling; section 5, the Matthean exception to the prohibition of remarriage after divorce; and section 6, annulment, dissolution, and the impediments to marriage, became a new Canon 17, "Of Regulations Respecting Holy Matrimony and the Impediments Thereto." And sections 1-3, telling ministers their duties and obligations in solemnizing marriage, became the new Canon 16, "Of the Solemnization of Holy Matrimony."

After almost 80 years of struggle, the 1946 convention eliminated the prohibition of the remarriage of divorced persons, including the Matthean exception. Applying solely to active members in good standing, the revised and renumbered Canon 18, "Of the Regulations Respecting Holy Matrimony," allowed a person whose marriage was annulled or dissolved by a civil court to petition the bishop or ecclesiastical authority of the diocese of canonical residence for a judgment of status or permission to be married by a minister of this Church. A one-year waiting period after issuance of the civil judgment was required, and petition had to be made at least 30 days before the planned date of marriage.

In considering such a petition, the bishop was required to be "satisfied that the parties intend a true Christian marriage," and, if so finding, refer the petition to his council of advisers or the court if the diocese has established one. The bishop or ecclesiastical authority was to base the judgment on, and conform with, the doctrine of the Church, "that marriage is a physical, spiritual, and mystical union of a man and a woman created by their mutual consent of heart, mind and will thereto and is a Holy Estate instituted of God and is in intention lifelong."

Canon 18 references the list of conditions in Canon 17 as forming the basis for the judgment of the ecclesiastical authority. The result of the judgment is that no marriage bond recognized by the Church was established and may be so declared by the proper authority. However, the judgment was held not to say anything about the legitimacy of children or the civil viability of the former relationship. Judgments were to be rendered in writing and kept as a permanent record of the diocese. Any person granted such a judgment could then be married by a minister of the Church (White & Dykman, 416-18). Essentially, the convention accepted remarriage of divorced members as determined by civil law.

Controversy lingered over a perceived ambiguity in Canon 18, Section 2(b), whether the impediments listed in Canon 17, section 2(b), "are shown to exist or to have existed which manifestly establish that no marriage bond [existed]." Some bishops were only willing to consider granting petitions to remarry if the marriage impediment arose before the marriage, a concept of contract law known as nullity ab initio, meaning that some defect occurred in the formation of the marriage contract.

Others were willing to recognize that for causes arising after marriage, the marriage bond dissolved. A special committee of the House of Bishops reported to the 1949 convention on this split of opinion by taking the middle way opposing further clarification, stating: "But as a matter of fact there is no ambiguity here. The Canon recognized two points of view as legitimate; one, that if one or more impediments existed before the marriage, no marital bond was created; the other, that if one of the impediments arises after marriage, the marital bond is broken." The bishops could have it both ways (White & Dykman, 419, quoting the 1949 journal, 439).

The 1946 revision changed the requirement that both parties have received Holy Baptism to requiring that only one party be baptized. The change addressed a disagreement in interpretation that had arisen. Some clergy felt that the nature of Holy Matrimony implied its availability only to baptized persons. This interpretation pushed unbaptized parties to seek instruction and Holy Baptism before being married in the Church, as some clergy refused to solemnize the marriage otherwise. This view is rejected by requiring at least one party to have been baptized (White & Dykman, 414).

The 1949 convention nonetheless made two changes:
- Removed the referral by the bishop to his council of advisers or to a court formed for that purpose;

- Added the requirement that, if the remarriage was to be solemnized in a different jurisdiction than where the judgment is granted, the bishop or ecclesiastical authority of the second jurisdiction had to give approval as well.

These changes left the granting of permission to remarry to the bishop or ecclesiastical authority, without requiring consultation with attorneys, psychologists, a council of advice, or an ecclesiastical court, as had been required in prior times.

Proposals to return to the principle of nullity ab initio (1958) and to shorten the one-year waiting period (1970) were defeated.

From 1945 to 1947, a distinct spike in divorce rates was evident in the aftermath of World War II, reaching 43 percent when compared to the number of marriages in 1946. There may have been many reasons for this rise: hasty marriages immediately before deployment to the war, newfound independence among wives on the home front, and inability to undertake the burden of sustaining marriages to returning war veterans who were injured physically or psychologically as a result of their service. Divorce rates leveled off in the 1950s and 1960s, averaging about 24 percent over the two decades.

As General Convention prepared to convene in 1973, bishops and deputies submitted from 30 to 40 resolutions calling for amending or repealing the canons on Holy Matrimony. Both houses appointed special committees that met jointly during the first week of the convention, came to agreement on major issues, and drew up proposed amendments to the canons which were adopted by considerable majorities without significant floor changes.

Canon I.16, "Of Regulations Respecting the Laity," was amended to repeal Section 7 addressing a minister's withholding of the sacraments from a person "married otherwise than as the word of God and discipline of this Church allow."

Canon I.17, "Of the Solemnization of Holy Matrimony," was repealed, and a new canon was adopted in its place.

- Section 1 was retained, requiring clergy to conform to state law governing civil marriage and the laws of this Church governing Holy Matrimony.
- Sections 2 and 3 required clergy to meet the conditions and follow the procedures in solemnizing any marriage. The list of impediments to marriage was eliminated in an effort to move clergy from a legalistic evaluation of the marriage to a

more pastoral approach emphasizing the nature of Christian marriage. The clergy were required to instruct and ascertain the understanding of the parties that marriage is a physical and spiritual union entered into in the community of faith by mutual consent of heart, mind, and will intending to be a lifelong commitment. Further, the parties must satisfy the minister that they are entering into marriage without fraud, coercion, mistaken identity, or mental reservation. Section 3 procedures requiring 30 days' notice to the minister, presence of at least two witnesses, and recording the marriage in the proper register were retained, as was the requirement that the couple sign the "Declaration of Intent" contained in section 3(d), which was first introduced into the canon in 1949. The Declaration of Intent was connected to the required instruction, but it sounded, in fact, more like a confessional statement expressed as the couple's "understanding" of Christian marriage.

- Section 4 retained the clergy's discretion to decline to perform any marriage.

Canon I.18, "Of Regulations Respecting Holy Matrimony: Concerning Preservation of Marriage, Dissolution of Marriage, and Remarriage," was repealed and a new canon adopted:

- Section 1 addressed the duty of the parties and the minister to attempt reconciliation in the face of imperiled marriage unity before filing legal action.
- Section 2 allowed a party who wished to remarry after receiving a civil decree of annulment or dissolution to petition the bishop or ecclesiastical authority for a judgment of nullity or termination. The requirements for this permission were streamlined from earlier versions. Reliance on a civil decree of annulment or dissolution continued.
- Section 3 set out procedures for the minister to follow in preparation for solemnizing the marriage of a party who was previously married to a living spouse. As revised, section 3 made clear that divorced persons could remarry in the Church, and set out the simplified procedures for ministers to follow and obtain the bishop's consent.
- Section 4 makes Canon I.17 applicable to all remarriages (White & Dykman, 413-15).

No-fault divorce arrived in the 1970s as states changed their laws to move away from the necessity of proving a grievous wrong to the marriage, and toward recognition that marital relationships simply do not work out or meet the expectations of both parties. In the 1980s, equitable distribution of marital property became the law, reducing the battles between divorcing spouses over property as a means of punishing the other or reducing an offending spouse to abject poverty. Divorce rates jumped from 33 percent in 1970 to 50 percent in 1985 as these two legal trends took hold nationwide. Divorce rates continue to run to about 50 percent of marriages in 2014.

The 1973 rewrites of Canons I.16, I.17 and I.18, renumbered as Canons I.17, I.18 and I.19 in 1985, settled the canons on marriage and remarriage for the next 30 years. There have been a few relatively minor changes adopted subsequently:

- In 1979, Canon I.18.3 (now I.19.3) was amended to clarify which bishop would be consulted when a member of the clergy canonically resident in one diocese was licensed to perform a remarriage in another diocese. The canon required consulting with, and reporting to, the minister's bishop.

- In 2000, Canon I.19.1 was amended to clarify the duty of clergy when consulted by the parties to an imperiled marriage. The prior canon emphasized reconciliation as the purpose of the consultation. Some clergy apparently took this charge literally, encouraging women in abusive relationships to work matters out without regard to the physical safety of the woman and/or children. Societal, legal, and law enforcement norms regarding domestic violence, spousal abuse, and child abuse changed significantly during the 1980s and 1990s. The amendment changed the charge to reconcile if possible, and imposed an additional duty on the clergy to "act first to protect and promote the physical and emotional safety of those involved and only then, if possible, to labor that the parties be reconciled."

- In 2000, General Convention further amended Canon I.19.3 to add reporting to the bishop of the diocese where the member of the clergy is canonically resident or the bishop where the member of the clergy is licensed to officiate, and to report to that bishop on the remarriage.

Even though the marriage canons did not change dramatically, discussion of issues related to marriage continued in General Convention in parallel with secular society. These discussions occurred under the umbrella of human sexuality and across interim bodies of the General Convention, debating what the Church should say and do about premarital sex and adultery; infertility and emerging technologies to allow infertile couples to conceive and bear children and surrogacy; abortion and birth control; couples cohabiting without marriage; marriage across religious denominations; interracial marriage; and full inclusion of gay and lesbian, later widened to include bisexual and transgender persons (LGBT), in community.

Calls continue for revision of the canons to permit same-sex marriage or some form of recognition for same-sex relationships; to remove clergy from acting as agents of the state in solemnizing marriage; to allow blessings for same-sex couples, for heterosexual couples who choose not to marry for financial reasons, and for immigrants living illegally in the United States. These issues will be considered further in the critique of the present canons.

3. Critique of the Current Marriage Canon (Canon I.18)

This section will review current marriage-canon-related issues that have come under discussion in the Church in recent years; discuss whether and how the canon might address those issues; and suggest how the canon might be revised to resolve the issues.

Canon I.18, "Of the Solemnization of Holy Matrimony," commonly known as the Marriage Canon, outlines the current regulations of this Church regarding marriage. Its companion Canons I.17, "Of Regulations Respecting the Laity," and Canon I.19, "Of Regulations Respecting Holy Matrimony: Concerning Preservation of Marriage, Dissolution of Marriage and Remarriage," also address regulations related to Holy Matrimony and marriage.

As the historical review shows, the marriage canons are regulatory in nature. The marriage canons reflect the current thinking about how marriage occurs in the Church and, with the exception of Canon I.17, apply to clergy only, describing the duties and responsibilities of clergy who officiate at the solemnization of marriage. To the extent that the rules require the clergy to assure that the couple seeking to marry complies with certain duties, the laity is also regulated. But it is clergy who are subject to Title IV discipline, should the member of the clergy fail to conform to the marriage canons.

Canon I.18.1: Should the Church move away from clergy acting as agents of the state in solemnizing marriage?

> Sec. 1. Every Member of the Clergy of this Church shall conform to the laws of the State governing the creation of the civil status of marriage, and also to the laws of this Church governing the solemnization of Holy Matrimony.

Canon I.18.1 sets out the requirement that the clergy conform to both civil law and church law when solemnizing Holy Matrimony. Generally, state law requires a license issued to the couple, signed by the officiant, and returned to the recording agency for registration, subject to penalties for the officiant who fails to file the license; consent of the couple, freely, seriously, and plainly expressed in the presence of the other; in the presence of a designated officiant; and with a declaration or pronouncement by the officiant that the couple are married according to state law.

Officiants are designated government officials such as magistrates, justices of the peace, and judges; and ordained ministers of any religious denomination or ministers authorized by a church. This provision sets up a dual role for the clergy officiating at Holy Matrimony, reflected in the pronouncement in the BCP Marriage Rite, "I pronounce that they are husband and wife, in the Name of the Father, and of the Son, and of the Holy Spirit." In that dual role, the clergy sign and file the civil marriage license, record the marriage in the church register, and pronounce and bless the marriage. While the state-law qualifications to obtain a marriage license may overlap with the canon-law qualifications to marry, each also has its separate requirements that will be addressed in the discussion of Canon 1.18.2 and I.18.3.

Some clergy have expressed increasing discomfort with that dual role on behalf of both state and church. Some express reluctance to act as agents of the state, reflecting the culture of separation of church and state in the United States. Some recognize that Episcopal clergy in some European and Latin-American dioceses function within the model where a separate civil ceremony is later blessed in a church setting, such as in some European and Latin-American dioceses.

Indeed, the Book of Common Prayer contains a separate rite, "The Blessing of a Civil Marriage," for this purpose. A few have taken a stand on the prohibition of same-sex marriage, declaring that they would not officiate at any marriage until they could marry every couple who desired to commit themselves in marriage. Some clergy, and a greater number of laity, recognize the symbolism and emotional attachment to signing the civil marriage license within the marriage liturgy and, in some places, on the altar itself.

Remarkably, despite the raising of this concern, no legislative proposals to change the model in this Church have come before General Convention since 1994. Resolution 1994-D102 proposed to strike the phrase, "to the laws of the State governing the creation of the civil status of marriage and also" and was referred to the Standing

Committee on Constitution and Canons for further study. The 1997 Blue Book Report from Constitution and Canons made no mention of their consideration of this change and made no recommendation to amend the canons to eliminate conformity with state law.

The Task Force on the Study of Marriage recommends the following amendment of Canon I.18.1, retaining the dual conformity to state law and church canons, along with three additional changes:

~~CANON 18: Of the Solemnization of Holy Matrimony~~
Canon 18: Of the Celebration and Blessing of Marriage

> Sec. 1. Every Member of the Clergy of this Church shall conform to the laws of the State governing the creation of the civil status of marriage, and also to ~~the laws of this Church governing~~ *these canons concerning the solemnization of marriage* ~~Holy Matrimony~~. *Members of the Clergy may solemnize a marriage using any of the liturgical forms authorized by this Church.*

First, the canon is renamed to reflect and connect to the title of the marriage liturgy in the Book of Common Prayer, and "Holy Matrimony" is changed to "Marriage" accordingly. Second, the wording, "the laws of this Church governing" marriage is clarified by making specific reference to the canons. And, third, the last sentence is returned to section 1, having been moved in 1973 from section 1 to section 3 setting out the Declaration of Intent. This sentence gives recognition to the current situation in which General Convention has authorized a number of liturgical forms that are not yet incorporated into the Book of Common Prayer.

Amending the Book of Common Prayer remains the third rail in The Episcopal Church, reflecting the residual bitterness of the battles over adoption and reception of the 1979 version.

Canon I.18.2: What criteria should the clergy evaluate before solemnizing a marriage? Should the canon restrict marriage to one man and one woman? Should the canon recognize same-sex marriage, and under what conditions (for example, where authorized by state law)?

> Sec. 2. Before solemnizing a marriage the Member of the Clergy shall have ascertained:
>
> > (a) That both parties have the right to contract a marriage according to the laws of the State.
> >
> > (b) That both parties understand that Holy Matrimony

is a physical and spiritual union of a man and a woman, entered into within the community of faith, by mutual consent of heart, mind, and will, and with intent that it be lifelong.

(c) That both parties freely and knowingly consent to such marriage, without fraud, coercion, mistake as to identity of a partner, or mental reservation.

(d) That at least one of the parties has received Holy Baptism.

(e) That both parties have been instructed as to the nature, meaning, and purpose of Holy Matrimony by the Member of the Clergy, or that they have both received such instruction from persons known by the Member of the Clergy to be competent and responsible.

As recently as the 2012 General Convention, a proposed amendment to Canon I.18.2 (b) changed "a man and a woman" to "two persons" (Resolution 2012-D091); the amendment was referred to the Task Force for consideration. Reflecting the theological views presented elsewhere in this report, the Task Force has come to the position of recommending recognition of same-sex marriage in this Church.

Appearing initially in 1946 in what was then Canon 18 (now Canon I.19) regulating remarriage after divorce, the Bishop or Ecclesiastical Authority was directed to apply the following standard to decisions to grant an application for remarriage:

> The Bishop or Ecclesiastical Authority shall take care that his or its judgment is based upon and conforms to the doctrine of this Church, that marriage is a physical, spiritual, and mystical union of a man and a woman created by their mutual consent of heart, mind and will thereto, and is a Holy Estate instituted of God and is in intention lifelong; …

The phrase, "a physical and spiritual union of a man and a woman" was moved to then Canon 17 (now Canon I.18) in 1973, at a time when the concept of same-sex marriage arose for the first time. Baker v. Nelson,[94] decided in the Minnesota Supreme Court in 1971 and turned down for review by the Supreme Court of the United States in 1972, was the first known attempt to establish a constitutional right to marriage for a same-sex couple.

It may be better understood as a description of the then-current understanding of marriage — one which has undergone considerable revision in subsequent years. Indeed, General Convention began three

---

[94] Baker v. Nelson 291 Minn. 310, 191 N. W. 2d 385 (1971), appeal denied 409 U.S. 810 (1972).

years later to affirm the pastoral needs and concerns of homosexual persons. (Resolution 1976-A069). General Convention 1997 called for continued study of the theological aspects of committed same-sex relationships (Resolution 1997-C003).

In 2000, General Convention recognized the presence of "other lifelong committed relationships, characterized by fidelity, monogamy, mutual affection and respect, careful, honest communication, and the holy love which enables those in such relationships to see in each other the image of God" (Resolution 2000-D039). In 2012, after much study and call for a new liturgy to bless same-sex relationships, General Convention authorized the liturgy, "The Witnessing and Blessing of a Lifelong Covenant," for provisional use under the direction of diocesan bishops. This Church has reached a point, as has civil society, where same-sex relationships are no longer "other" and have become "equal" and should be recognized as such.

The proposed revision retains the requirement of subsection (a) that clergy ascertain that the couple may contract the marriage under state law. Although state law is rapidly changing, it is not yet uniform regarding the legalization of same-sex marriage. That recognition is expected to accelerate in the face of the Supreme Court of the United States' decision to deny review to the Court of Appeals decisions in three circuits, letting stand decisions ruling state bans on same-sex marriage unconstitutional. The legal landscape will remain in flux as the various lawsuits currently on file in the remaining states that have not yet recognized same-sex civil marriage are addressed and resolved.

While the apparent trend is toward striking down state bans, opportunities to uphold the ban remain viable as the grounds on which the bans are challenged are varied and not yet clearly resolved. Consequently, opportunities for this Church to recognize same-sex marriage will continue to depend on state law, which continues to vary from state to state. That should not deter General Convention from addressing how the Church extends a generous pastoral response to its LGBT members who wish to have their loving, committed relationships recognized and blessed by this Church where same-sex marriage is legal.

Subsection (b) is deleted in the proposed revision. The current wording does not reflect the understandings of marriage expressed in the marriage liturgy, which makes no mention of "a physical and spiritual union of a man and a woman" but instead speaks of "[t]he union of husband and wife in heart, body and mind" but not in spirit. Like the Declaration of Intent, it sounds like a creedal statement that the couple is asked to affirm rather than the aspirational statement it is. Deleting subsection (b) also removes the temptation to read "a man and a woman" as a definition of marriage rather than a description.

Subsections (c), (d) and (e) are relocated to section 3 with minor rewording.

Canon I.18.3: What procedures should be required? Should the Declaration of Intent be retained? How should the Declaration of Intent be modified to recognize same-sex marriage?

> Sec. 3. No Member of the Clergy of this Church shall solemnize any marriage unless the following procedures are complied with:
>
>> (a) The intention of the parties to contract marriage shall have been signified to the Member of the Clergy at least thirty days before the service of solemnization; Provided, that for weighty cause, this requirement may be dispensed with if one of the parties is a member of the Congregation of the Member of the Clergy, or can furnish satisfactory evidence of responsibility. In case the thirty days' notice is waived, the Member of the Clergy shall report such action in writing to the Bishop immediately.
>>
>> (b) There shall be present at least two witnesses to the solemnization of marriage.
>>
>> (c) The Member of the Clergy shall record in the proper register the date and place of the marriage, the names of the parties and their parents, the age of the parties, their residences, and their Church status; the witnesses and the Member of the Clergy shall sign the record.
>>
>> (d) The Member of the Clergy shall have required that the parties sign the following declaration:
>>
>> (e) "We, A. B. and C. D., desiring to receive the blessing of Holy Matrimony in the Church, do solemnly declare that we hold marriage to be a lifelong union of husband and wife as it is set forth in the Book of Common Prayer.
>>
>> (f) "We believe that the union of husband and wife, in heart, body, and mind, is intended by God for their mutual joy; for the help and comfort given one another in prosperity and adversity; and, when it is God's will, for the procreation of children and their nurture in the knowledge and love of the Lord.

(g) "And we do engage ourselves, so far as in us lies, to make our utmost effort to establish this relationship and to seek God's help thereto."

Section 3 sets out specific procedures for clergy to follow when requested to officiate at a marriage. Subsection (a) sets a notice requirement: the couple must make the request known at least 30 days in advance, but it allows for waiver at the discretion of the member of the clergy. Waiver is permitted for a member of the congregation. Waiver may also be considered when a party can provide satisfactory evidence of a good reason to waive the waiting time. Deployment in the military and pregnancy are two such situations to have received waivers, at least in the past. Marriage after childbirth is more common today. Issuance of a waiver may lie within the member of the clergy's discretion but must be reported to the bishop immediately.

The proposed revision retains Section 3(a) renumbered Section 2. Both parties must be involved in the presentation of a case for waiving the 30 days' notice requirement, and the additional language, "shortening the time," is inserted, suggesting that marriage upon demand is not sanctioned.

Subsection (b) requires that the ceremony occur in the presence of at least two witnesses. State law frequently requires the presence of at least two witnesses who sign the civil marriage license.

Subsection (c) spells out the information to be entered into the church registry. Subsections (b) and (c) are combined as Section 4 in the proposed revision.

Subsections (d)-(f) spell out the Declaration of Intent, which the member of the clergy must have the couple sign before proceeding with the marriage. The prescribed declaration is a series of statements to which the couple must assent: marriage is lifelong; a union of heart, body, and mind, intended by God for mutual joy, for help and comfort in prosperity and adversity, and for the procreation and nurture of children when God so wills; and pledges the couple's utmost efforts to establish the relationship with God's help. Traditionally, the prescribed declaration is signed as part of the required pre-marriage counseling.

The proposed revision of Canon I.18 deletes the declaration from the canon. The language of the declaration rings as a creedal statement, a statement of belief that may not be accurate. The couple is required to declare their belief in a set of statements about marriage; but the intentions of marriage are properly about performance, not belief. Since baptism is required for only one partner to the marriage, the declaration may force a false compliance on a nonbeliever or a person who holds to a tradition with a different theology of marriage or no theology at all.

An unbaptized nonbeliever or an atheist may marry in church for the sake of a spouse, but that person ought not to be placed in the situation of affirming a belief about whether marriage is "intended by God." Again it is the performance of the content of the vows that is the proper focus of the couple's intention. The marriage liturgy itself includes the Declaration of Consent, as well as the vows, and the wording in the proposed canonical revision points to these as the operative texts.

In lieu of the declaration, the proposed revision expands the essentials of the required pre-marriage counseling, basing the counseling upon the vows the couple will pledge to each other and on an assessment by the member of the clergy that the couple understands the duties and responsibilities of marriage. Also added is recognition that the community plays a role in supporting the marriage, a recognition that is also reinforced in the liturgy.

The proposed revision adds a new section 5, giving recognition that in the civil jurisdictions of some dioceses of The Episcopal Church, the civil ceremony and the church blessing are undertaken separately. While the requirement that clergy conform to the civil law of their jurisdictions may already encompass this situation, especially since there is a liturgy for the blessing of a civil marriage, explicit recognition of the different context is desirable.

Canon I.18.4: Shall clergy continue to have sole discretion to decline to solemnize any marriage?

Finally, the proposed revision retains section 4:

> Sec. 4. It shall be within the discretion of any Member of the Clergy of this Church to decline to solemnize any marriage.

Bishops and clergy alike have called for retaining this discretionary authority. The clause in the context of heterosexual marriage allows the clergy to make a subjective decision regarding the particular couple seeking marriage. Clergy have expressed a desire to retain the ability to refuse marriage without repercussions in appropriate cases.

Some support for retention is the belief that in this transition time there should be a "conscience clause" to accommodate those for whom same-sex marriage violates their personal beliefs. The clause in the context of same-sex marriage would permit continued discrimination against a class of church members. Such discrimination appears to be prohibited by Canon I.17.5:

> Sec. 5. No one shall be denied rights, status or access to an equal place in the life, worship, and governance of this Church because of race, color, ethnic origin, national origin, marital status, sex, sexual orientation, gender identity and expression, disabilities or age, except as otherwise specified by Canons.

A similar conscience clause was enacted in conjunction with the ordination of women with unsatisfactory results. The unrealized intent that gradually all bishops would come on board and ordain women did not occur. Rather it contributed to a division in this Church that caused some clergy and laity to feel devalued, and eventually they left. In the context of the decision to allow women clergy to serve as bishops in the Church of England, accommodation of those who, for reasons of theological belief and conscience would not accept or recognize women bishops, has been a central point of contention.

Similar results might occur in the context of same-sex marriage over the long term. Assuming that the conscience can change or can be changed through legislation is misplaced. Similar battles continue in the civil context as well, where legislators are introducing exceptions to permit government officials to refuse to perform same-sex marriages without losing their jobs. So far, the civil judiciary has rejected such exceptions to a fundamental right to marry.

While recognizing the potentially discriminatory aspects of the call for retaining section 4, the Task Force on the Study of Marriage nonetheless supports retaining the discretion of clergy in deciding whether to marry a particular couple. A better approach is to amend Canon I.17.5 to delete the last phrase, "except as otherwise specified by Canons," thus banning discrimination against the enumerated classes altogether.

Bibliography

Constitution and Canons of the Episcopal Church (Church Publishing Inc., 2012).

Coontz, Stephanie. *Marriage: A History* (SJ Coontz Company, 2005).

Jones, Audrey M., "Historical Divorce Rate Statistics" on website Love to Know Divorce, http://divorce.lovetoknow.com/Historical_Divorce_Rate_Statistics.

National Conference of State Legislatures, http://www.ncsl.org/research/human-services/same-sex-marriagelaws.aspx#2.

White, Edwin A. and Jackson A. Dykman, eds. *Annotated Constitution and Canons for the Government of the Protestant Episcopal Church* (Church Publishing, 1979).

Women's Christian Temperance Union website, Early History, http://www.wctu.org/earlyhistory.html.

ESSAY 6:
Agents of the State: A Question for Discernment

Over the last decade, as Episcopalians have discussed our theology of marriage and the place of marriage in the life of the Church, the role of clergy as agents of the state in solemnizing civil marriages has come under consideration. Increasingly, the question has emerged, "Should we be in the marriage business?" Usually when this question is raised, the question is not whether we should perform Christian marriages in our churches.[95] Rather, the question is whether in these celebrations clergy should also legally solemnize civil marriages as agents of the state. That is, should clergy sign marriage licenses and return them to the town clerk? In the United States this is the action that renders a couple legally married in the eyes of the state, regardless of the vows they make in church.[96]

1. Invisible/Visible

In the life of many congregations, this interface with civil marriage may be nearly invisible. The signing of the marriage license may take place off to the side, perhaps in a sacristy. Many people may not realize that clergy routinely perform double duty when they officiate at marriages, acting as agents of both church and state. In contrast, in states with marriage equality and in which congregations have permission to officiate at same-sex weddings, the signing of the marriage license may well take a place of honor. And indeed, due to this new attention to the role of clergy in signing marriage licenses, some may be newly aware of this double duty.

---

[95] One exception to this argument can be seen in "Familiar Idolatry and the Christian Case against Marriage," by Dale Martin, in *Sex and the Single Savior: Gender and Sexuality in Biblical Interpretation* (Louisville: Westminster John Knox, 2006), 122: "I am deeply ambivalent about pursuing same-sex marriage as a solution to the injustices of homophobia. I believe that both the state and the church should get out of the marriage business."
[96] V. Gene Robinson, *God Believes in Love: Straight Talk about Gay Marriage* (New York: Vintage, 2013), 141.

2. Strategic Disengagement

Some congregations have sought to pause or eliminate this double duty, however. In dioceses where same-sex and different-sex couples might experience legal or ecclesial discrepancies in access to marriage, some congregations have taken up a new policy. They require the marriages of all couples to be solemnized by a civil official before being blessed in the course of the church liturgy. Here the concern is to treat all couples equally, regardless of sexual orientation.[97] Such congregations are emulating, in their own way, some European countries (for example, France), where couples have historically married first at a courthouse or mayor's office and then later joined their communities at their places of worship.[98]

Some have further argued from a position of support for same-sex couples that even where marriage equality is legal and there are no discrepancies of access between civil and ecclesial marriage, clergy in The Episcopal Church still should no longer legally solemnize any marriages. At the same time, others are beginning to urge a similar practice of strategic disengagement to critique the expansion of marriage to include same-sex couples.[99] Here the concern is to stand apart from understandings of marriage that are not strictly heterosexual. Both of these perspectives express concern about how serving as agents of the state may compromise their ability to bear authentic witness to their understandings of Christian marriage, and perhaps even of the gospel itself.

3. Pastoral Concerns

Not surprisingly, Episcopalians have varieties of responses to these practices of strategic disengagement. While many proponents of marriage equality prefer having a civil official sign the marriage license, other proponents have wondered why the Church might question its role as an agent of the state in marriage at a time when more dioceses may be prepared to extend that practice to same-sex couples. People of various perspectives have further wondered about the pastoral impact that might be felt by couples and families across the Church if we were to require all couples to engage a civil official as well as a clergyperson as part of "how we do marriage." It may well be that in France, such duality of practice is widespread, this line of reasoning explains, but in the United States a shift to this model could simply feel alienating in our congregations.

---

97 Robinson describes such a scenario on pp. 144-45.
98 Robinson, 144.
99 See, for example, the Reverend Ephraim Radnor and the Reverend Christopher Seitz, "The Marriage Pledge," http://www.firstthings.com/marriage-pledge.

4. Whether and/or How

On this question, therefore, it seems clear that we have some discernment in which to engage as a church. Having approached Christian marriage through a vocational lens in the paper "Christian Marriage as Vocation," the question arises as to whether and/or how the Church may be called to serve as an agent of the state in this arena. In *God Believes in Love*, Bishop V. Gene Robinson describes a fictional scenario in which a church has discerned a call not to have its priest serve as an agent of the state.[100]

Yet how exactly did this congregation embody this distinction? In Robinson's example, the congregation's senior warden serves as an agent of the state for all marriages at the parish. The warden signs the marriage license of all couples in the doorway at the back of the Church, embodying quite literally the border of the civil and ecclesial spheres. While wardens are not clergy, they are members of their parishes. Therefore, although the distinction between church and state is indeed much clearer here than it is when a clergyperson signs the marriage license, the parish as a community is still making a conscious decision to interface with civil marriage in a particular (in this case, spatial) manner. The community might have asked all couples to have their marriage licenses signed someplace outside the Church altogether, for instance. A congregation might choose a path of greater church-state linkage or separation, and it might do so in a number of different ways. Thus the discernment is not only whether a parish might or might not decide to participate in civil marriage, but potentially how.

5. Implications for Discernment: Unjust Structures

Our discernment process should also consider the ways in which our participation in civil marriage may contribute to the status of privilege accorded to marriage in the civil as well as ecclesial spheres. The paper, "Christian Marriage as Vocation" points out that marriage is both a profound vocation in its own right as well as a manner of life to which some (but not all) are called. Our canons further specify that equal access to a "place in the life, worship and governance of this Church" cannot be denied on the basis of marital status (Canon 1.17.5).

Yet a further question to consider is how the Church's participation in civil marriage may contribute to marriage in the civil sphere more broadly. In what ways might that participation interface with our call

---

100 Robinson, 144-45.

to help transform unjust structures in that sphere?[101] Our discernment process might consider, for instance, how health insurance and tax benefits are linked to civil marriage, how unevenly civil marriages are recognized by the states at present, and how profoundly that lack of recognition can impact the daily lives and basic needs of those who remain unrecognized. It is one thing for the Church to embrace the widespread discernment of vocations to Christian marriage, but how we interface with its civil recognition is a distinct matter.

6. Implications for Discernment: Ecclesiology and Mission

How we discern our call to interface with civil marriage down the road clearly emerges in important ways from our theology of marriage. Yet further theological considerations should also prompt our reflection. While our canons currently prohibit the solemnization of marriages that are not considered legal according to the laws of the state (Canon I.18.2), the two Task Force papers on biblical and theological dimensions of marriage suggest that our theology of Christian marriage does not emerge from marriage's civil status.

Discernment related to this question — of whether and/or how to serve as agents of the state — should arguably flow more fundamentally from our ecclesiology and understanding of mission. How might our theological understanding of the Church, and particularly of its vocation at its interfaces with the civil sphere, inform this discernment? This solemnization question challenges us to clarify how we are called to be agents of the Good News at the borders of the ecclesial and civil. Does our service as agents of the state enable us to be better agents of reconciliation and transformation in the world than we otherwise would be? Does it make us complicit in the furthering of injustices in that world? What if our participation catches us up in both? If that is the case, how might we discern not simply the lesser of two evils but instead the expansion of the greater good?

Whatever we ultimately discern, the clear mandate from our baptism to respect the dignity of every human being (1979 BCP, 305) calls us both now and in the long run to be consistent in our practice, regardless of the sex, sexual orientation, or gender identity and expression of the prospective spouses, just as we already should

---

101 "To seek to transform unjust structures of society, to challenge violence of every kind and to pursue peace and reconciliation" is the fourth of the Five Marks of Mission which were adopted as strategic priorities at the 76th General Convention (D027) and reaffirmed at the 77th General Convention (A007). For more on the Five Marks of Mission, see http://www.anglicancommunion.org/ministry/mission/fivemarks.cfm

be with respect to their race, color, ethnic origin, national origin, disability, or age (Canon I.17.5). Should the General Convention decide in the future, for example, to limit the scope of the Church's engagement in marriage to its theological, liturgical, and pastoral facets and to canonically decouple Christian marriage from its legal, civil counterpart, we should engage this process with consistency across the demographic particularities of our communities. All of this calls for careful conversation, reflection, and prayer.

Works Cited

Martin, Dale. *Sex and the Single Savior: Gender and Sexuality in Biblical Interpretation.* Louisville: Westminster John Knox, 2006.

"Mission – The Five Marks of Mission" at http://www.anglicancommunion.org/ministry/mission/fivemarks.cfm.

Radnor, Ephraim, and Christopher Seitz. "The Marriage Pledge." http://www.firstthings.com/marriage-pledge.

Robinson, V. Gene. *God Believes in Love: Straight Talk about Gay Marriage.* New York: Vintage, 2013.

ESSAY 7:
Changing Trends and Norms in Marriages

Executive Summary

From the moment it is published, a report entitled, "Changing Trends and Norms in Marriages" will necessarily be challenged to stay abreast of society's rapidly evolving views, laws, and practices. We also recognize that further research and data gathering from non-U.S. Episcopal Church dioceses and from our ecumenical and Anglican partners is needed.

Our executive summary, therefore, offers a synthesis of some of the emerging trends and norms we have discerned, and suggests questions that our Church might consider. Much has changed in terms of how people approach marriage, and when and how they decide to make such a commitment. Educational differences, economic issues, age, race, and ethnicity are among the myriad of factors impacting marriage in North America and Western Europe, as well as in Latin-American and Asian countries. Yet, the Task Force on the Study of Marriage also noted some trends that transcend all variables:

- The age at which people enter into a first marriage is rising.
- The rates at which people are marrying are significantly declining.
- Student debt and job insecurity are prevalent reasons cited for delaying marriage.
- For women, delayed marriage can often bring an "income advantage" as they pursue their careers.
- Delayed marriage, especially among less-educated adults, has a significant economic impact especially for children raised in households with unmarried partners or with single parents.

- For those young adults, raising children in cohabitating and serial partnerships is becoming the new norm.
- Forty-eight percent of all first births are to unmarried women.
- Cohabitation prior to marriage has increased by nearly 900 percent over the last 50 years.
- Acceptance of same-sex marriage is growing, though not in all racial or ethnic communities.
- As of late 2014, 64 percent of Americans live in states where same-sex couples may marry.
- As of late 2014, 64.3 percent of Episcopalians in 64 U.S. dioceses live in states or jurisdictions where same-sex marriage is legal.

The rate at which people are marrying has been declining precipitously. The option — especially for young adults to enjoy what they consider the benefits of marriage through cohabitation and extended relationships while remaining single — is increasingly appealing to them. Research consulted by the Task Force reveals, however, that most teenagers report that having a "good" marriage "one day" is still their desire. That same data, however, illustrate that the median age at which both women and men enter into their first marriage is rising.

Researchers have identified this declining trend in marriage alongside the ever-shrinking middle class as the "Marriage Gap," with noted disadvantages for young adults with less education. Interestingly, we note that the decision to delay marriage does not necessarily mean postponing entrance into parenthood. This has caused the coining of another term by researchers known as the "Great Crossover." The result is that almost half of all new births now are to unmarried women.

Data are clear that unmarried couples break up more frequently, often leaving young mothers to be responsible for raising their children alone. This contributes to, or begins a cycle of, poverty that can exist for generations. This reality underscores the need for educational, economic, and family policies that do not complicate and unnecessarily stress an already fragile situation for parents and children.

The evidence is irrefutable that a high school education alone is no longer enough to lift individuals out of poverty. At the same time, burdensome student debt can not only prevent a mother, for example, from emerging from poverty, but may also contribute to a delay in marriage. Mass incarceration, particularly of a disproportionate number of young black men, is still another factor contributing to decisions by couples to delay marriage.

The Task Force attempted to better understand the role one's race and ethnicity might play in terms of deciding whether to marry or not. Among the interesting data uncovered was that African-American teens are less likely to date or participate in serious romantic relationships than are teens from other racial or ethnic groups. In the wider Hispanic and Latino community, familial relationships are considered even more essential to community life than the marriage itself, and divorce rates among Hispanic men and Latina women are lower by comparison with the general population.

The clan system found in many tribes in the Native-American community is actively engaged in child-rearing, with elders in particular playing important roles. Asian Americans have the highest percentage of marriage and the lowest divorce rate. A high value on marriage where the extended family is an integral component is an aspect of Asian culture.

Additionally, there has been a seismic shift in cultural acceptance of same-gender marriage in the United States, especially within the last decade. However, this shift in increasing acceptance of marriage between same-sex couples is by no means limited to the United States. Indeed, governments and citizens in countries from every continent have embraced marriage equality and have actually outpaced the United States in making this shift.

Virtually every religious tradition has been engaged in discussing what these shifting norms mean for their believers and followers theologically and liturgically. Recent decisions, especially by the Presbyterian Church USA and the Evangelical Lutheran Churches in America, have garnered much attention. Even more recently, and as this report was being prepared, bishops in the Roman Catholic Church were wrestling with an expressed desire by Pope Francis to embrace members of the faith that had been excluded due to cohabitation, divorce, and childbearing outside of marriage. A desire not to judge others due to sexual orientation was also recently expressed by the pope. We cite these as significant examples of religious institutions' recognizing and responding to changing norms for and among the faithful.

The Task Force on the Study of Marriage invites you to read the full extent of our research in the pages that follow and to consider the following questions and others that may come to mind as you review this section of our report:

- How might the Church engage the significant justice issues related to marriage that so impact educational and economic opportunities?
- What changes to family law, the tax codes, student loans, and other public policies might address the changing norms around marriage?
- What resources can the Church bring to help alleviate stress and strain on individuals desiring marriage but unable to make such a commitment due to economic and other factors?
- What can the Church contribute to the conversation that would be helpful for young people as they make decisions about cohabitation versus marriage?
- How could the Church lead an effort to bring about alternatives to the mass incarceration of large numbers of young black men that has such dire consequences for marriage and family life in the African-American community?
- What would be the best way for the Church to learn from and share the "best practices" around marriage offered by different racial and ethnic groups?
- What changes might The Episcopal Church make to our liturgies for marriage to better embrace the emerging realities of delayed marriage, childbearing prior to marriage, marriage with blended families, and same-sex marriage?
- What guidelines and pastoral resources might we develop for our clergy that they might better respond and prepare couples for lifelong covenants of mutual joy, respect, and fidelity?

1. The State of Our Unions

On the one hand, our culture seems to be fixated on marriage, from the extravagant $50 billion spent annually on weddings, to our active debate on same-sex marriage. On the other hand, societal norms and trends concerning marriage are in flux. Divorce rates have declined since the mid-1980s — a positive trend. Yet, another significant trend is emerging. The rates at which people are marrying are significantly declining, especially among those whose highest level of education achievement is a high school diploma. For those young adults, raising children in cohabitating and serial partnerships is becoming the new norm. For example, by age 25, 44 percent of women have given birth, while only 38 percent have married. Overall, 48 percent of first births were to unmarried partners.

Why should we care? Marriage is not merely a private matter; it is also a complex social institution. Stable marriages better the chances for stable families, generally ensuring greater prosperity for individuals and families as a whole. Marriage contributes to the stability of neighborhoods and school systems, and helps families and individuals weather difficult economic times. Indeed, researchers are finding that the disappearance of the middle class in the United States directly correlates in many communities with the decline in marriage.

The 1979 Book of Common Prayer emphasizes that marriage is both a private matter for the couple and a public covenant. The underlying assumption in our prayer book is that the very private love of the couple entering into marriage has public and sacramental value to the community as a whole — they are to "make their life together a sign of Christ's love to this sinful and broken world, that [their] unity may overcome estrangement, forgiveness heal guilt, and joy conquer despair" ("The Celebration and Blessing of a Marriage," 429).

What follows in this section of our report are some of the changing trends and norms in marriage in the United States, Canada, and much of Western Europe. This report is based on several studies that are noted at the end of this document. Information about current trends and norms in countries outside the United States where dioceses of The Episcopal Church are located is less available; however, in conversation with bishops from those dioceses, we can identify some of the realities on the ground. Some are similar to those found in the research related to North American and Western European countries, and some are not. Our report highlights some of those findings, even as we continue to do additional research.

In the United States, annual surveys continue to report that teens plan to marry "one day" and that having a "good" marriage is "extremely important" to them. At the same time, the median age for a first marriage has risen sharply — now 27 for women and 29 for men. Researchers link this phenomenon to the rapid rise in rates of cohabitation and to a dramatic increase in the number of children born outside of marriage. A growing number of couples, both young and old, now live together with no plans eventually to marry.

Additionally, as the historian Barbara Dafoe Whitehead has recently written, "Four decades ago, moderately educated Americans led the kind of family lives that looked much like the family lives of the more highly educated." She continues: "Today, they are less likely to achieve a stable marriage, or even form one in the first place." The plight of this demographic in our society — that is, those who still aspire to marriage but increasingly are unable to achieve it — may be the silent social and economic issue of our times.

The decline of marriage in America is trending directly alongside the decline of the imperiled middle class and is seen to help foster a society of winners and losers. Pew researchers have referred to this as the "Marriage Gap," a phenomenon increasingly aligned with the growing income gap. Marriage remains the norm for adults with a college education and a good income but is now markedly less prevalent among those on the lower rungs of the socioeconomic ladder.

2. The Rising Age of Marriage — Costs and Benefits

With the exception of the three decades following World War II, people in the United States and other Western nations have been notable for their leisurely approach to settling down. In 1900, the median age of marriage for women in the United States was 23, and for men, about 26.

As noted above, the age at which men and women marry is now at historic heights and is still climbing. A report from a University of Virginia study of marriage entitled, "Knot Yet" explored the positive and negative consequences of delayed marriage for twenty-something women and men, their children, and the nation as a whole. Their findings are recapped below:

Benefits

- Women enjoy an annual income premium if they wait until age 30 or later to marry.
- Delayed marriage has helped bring down the divorce rate in the United States since the early 1980s, because people who marry in their late teens or early twenties are more likely to divorce than couples who marry later.

Costs

- Though couples are postponing marriage into their late 20s and beyond, they are not putting off childbearing at the same pace. Known as the "Great Crossover," this phenomenon has resulted in a historic new trend in which, by age 25, 44 percent of women have had a child, while only 38 percent have married. Overall, 48 percent of all first births are to unmarried women.

- Twenty-somethings who are unmarried report a higher rate of substance abuse than their married counterparts, and report lower levels of satisfaction with their lives than do married twenty-somethings.
- Evidence shows that there is an earning advantage known as the "marriage premium," especially for men. Studies are lacking that examine racial-ethnic groups separately to account for discrimination factors.

Marriage delayed is the centerpiece of two different potential life paths for members of the next generation — paths that significantly depend on whether or not the person who delays marriage is college-educated. The University of Virginia marriage research project indicates that the Great Crossover is part of a "sad and ironic cycle" — both a generator of, and a response to, the economic troubles enveloping Middle America. Young couples with children may defer or stay clear of marriage because a parent does not have a decent-paying job. But unmarried couples break up more often, leaving mothers raising children alone, and reinforcing generational cycles of family instability and poverty.

Of particular interest to the Task Force on the Study of Marriage were the conclusions drawn by the researchers involved in the University of Virginia study. Their recommendations focused on three crucial areas: educational and economic policy, family policy, and relationship culture. These recommendations might be of value as our Church tries to better understand our mission to support and sustain living-giving relationships. We cite three interesting examples below:

1. Even when marriage is not immediately on the horizon, we can assist young adults to see their romantic relationships as opportunities to grow in love and commitment.

2. Parents and peers (and we would add faith communities) should encourage today's twenty-somethings to develop their plans for parenthood and marriage to align with plans for their sexual behavior.

3. Student debt and job insecurity cause large percentages of twenty-somethings to delay or avoid marriage (though not childbearing). What can our Church do to support educational policies and reform that foster relationship and family stability?

3. Explaining the Marriage Delay Phenomenon

Again with a primary focus on data from the United States, in the 1970s, a man (the assumption then being that men were the primary source of family income) with a high school diploma could count on finding a good blue-collar job that paid a living wage at an establishment where he could continue to work until he retired with a comfortable pension. By their late teens or early 20s, the men of this era were ready to support families. Now this world is all but gone. Today young adults without a high school education have little hope for a stable job. Since the Great Recession, the same can be said for those who have completed high school. Marriage for these young adults is delayed until they feel they can find jobs that will provide them with a middle-class lifestyle. Lack of economic opportunity, financial insecurity, and student debt all contribute to the delayed-marriage phenomenon. And one must not forget the impact that the mass incarceration of young black men has had on all aspects of the African-American community, delayed marriage being only one of the many serious consequences.

Another reason for putting off marriage is more personal, especially for women. Today women expect, and are expected, to become economically independent. In addition to the self-fulfillment aspects of a career for women, earning potential is seen as a hedge against poverty should their marriage end. Indeed, a recent poll of high school seniors — those on the cusp of adulthood — found that nearly half did not expect to remain married to the same person for a lifetime, a stunning statistic in its own right. Women also place a high value on a career that brings income and personal meaning — an accomplishment that requires years of education and on-the-job experience.

While earlier generations looked at marriage as their entry point into adulthood and a crucial vehicle for defining themselves as mature individuals, today young men and women expect to achieve individual and autonomous identities before they become bound as a couple. The psychologist and researcher Jeffrey Jensen Arnett calls it "emerging adulthood," an extended time of exploration and of trying out various possibilities in love and work. In this new environment, marriage is transformed from a "cornerstone" to a "capstone" of adult identity.

Ninety percent of young adults believe that they must be completely financially independent, have finished their education, have substantially paid off student loans, and be stable in their careers before they marry. Twenty-five to thirty-five percent believe they should be able to pay for their own weddings and have purchased a home before tying the knot.

Also helping to redefine marriage is what many sociologists call the "soul mate ideal." As women have become more economically equal and empowered, marriage for them has been drained of its primary economic incentive. Young adults are now more inclined to focus on marriage for its potential for deep emotional and sexual connections.

4. The Desire to Marry

Some might see the decline or delay of marriage as proof that young people think marriage is obsolete. However, the large majority of young adults in the United States and many Western countries say that they hope to marry "someday." Eighty percent of young adult men and women rate marriage as an "important" part of their life plans. Increasingly, and by dramatic percentages as compared to just 20 years ago, young adults see cohabitation as a necessary step toward marriage. They believe cohabitation as temporary emotional and sexual coupling to be an essential part of emerging adulthood.

There continues to be disagreement among researchers as to whether or not cohabitating couples are more likely to divorce (studied as the "cohabitation effect"). What is less disputed is what scholars call the "inertia hypothesis," asserting that cohabitation creates inertia in relationships, pushing marriage indefinitely into the future. Also noted is that cohabitating couples create financial and property entanglements that cause them to slide into marriage rather than to make active decisions about the future of the relationship.

Pew researchers find that for those who have never wed, marriage remains a life goal. About six in ten men and women would eventually like to get married. The same study showed that a trip to the altar is not so appealing for those who have been married before. Among divorced or separated adults, only 29 percent say they would like to marry again, with women more likely than men to say they do not want to enter into another marriage.

5. Cohabitation Trends and Consequences

Cohabitation has increased by nearly 900 percent over the last 50 years. More and more, couples are testing the waters before diving into marriage. U.S. Census data from 2012 show that 7.8 million couples are living together without having walked down the aisle, as compared to 2.9 million in 1996. And two-thirds of couples married in 2012 shared a home together for more than two years before they married.

Studies show that cohabitation is also more common among those who are less religious than their peers, among those who have been divorced, and among those who have experienced parental divorce, fatherlessness, or high levels of marital discord during childhood. A growing percentage of cohabiting-couple households — now more than 40 percent — include children.

As noted above, cohabitation prior to marriage is often hotly debated; research is unclear as to whether living together might make a couple more likely to divorce. The true variable seems to be the age at which the couple says "I do," according to a 2013 study from the nonpartisan Council on Contemporary Families. Among the strongest predicators of divorce was the age of the two people when they entered the marriage.

Some of the current and prevalent trends for cohabitation, marriage, and the definition of family are as follows:

- The percentage of the population who are married is rapidly shrinking; in 1960, 72 percent of the adult population was married; by 2008, that percentage was 52 percent.
- Americans have an expansive definition of what constitutes "family"; only 29 percent say that the decline in so-called traditional families is a "bad thing."
- Fifty-seven percent of Americans are accepting of cohabitation prior to marriage.
- There is widespread acceptance for premarital sex; 95 percent of all Americans have had a sexual encounter outside of marriage.
- Rates of premarital cohabitation are exploding. In 1960, just 5 percent of people lived together prior to marriage. Today that figure is 60 percent and climbing; 64 percent of cohabiting couples thought of this living arrangement as a necessary step toward marriage.
- Eighty-six percent see no problem with interracial marriage.
- Fifty-seven percent say it is okay for both gay couples and unmarried adults to raise children.
- Seventy-seven percent believe that it is easier for a married person than for a single person to raise a family.

IV. ESSAYS ON MARRIAGE

- There is a strong belief that "to get ahead in a career," it is better to be single.

6. Race, Gender, and Ethnic Differences

Falling marriage rates and the rising average age for first marriages are consistent across nearly all racial/ethnic groups who reside in the United States, Canada, and Western Europe. Below we recount some of the different ways in which marriage is perceived by major ethnic and racial groups in the United States:

Marriage and divorce in the African-American community

During the last several decades, the rates of marriage in the black community have declined, while the rates of divorce, separation, cohabitation, births to single moms, and children residing in female-headed households have increased. Notable trends include the following:

- In 2006, Gallup's annual "Minority Rights and Relations" survey found that 69 percent of black persons said that it is very important to marry when a man and woman plan to spend the rest of their lives together as a couple.
- African-American teens are less likely to date or to participate in serious romantic relationships than are teens from other racial/ethnic groups.
- Eighty-eight percent of African-American teens view marriage as "important"; however, only 72 percent feel well prepared for marriage.
- Churchgoing, African-American, married mothers are 31 percent more likely to report that they have excellent relationships with their husbands.
- Only 45 percent of African-American households include a married couple, compared to 80 percent of white households and 70 percent of Hispanic households (U.S. Census). Fifty percent of black persons said that it is very important to marry when a man and woman have a child together.
- African Americans are significantly less likely than other racial/ethnic groups ever to marry; are less likely to remarry; are more likely to divorce, separate, cohabit, and to bear and rear children out of wedlock (and in mother-only households).

- There is a marriage gap in the African-American community based on educational attainment. Only 28 percent of black individuals with no education are married compared to 55 percent of black persons with a college education.
- Black women divorce at a rate nearly double that of either white or Hispanic women.

Marriage and divorce in the Hispanic and Latino community

Marriage in the Hispanic culture is often seen in a familial context extending beyond the nucleus of the married couple. Familial relationships are even more essential to community life and identity than is the marital relationship. Being a good parent to children, and involving extended family members or close friends as trusted sources of support, are common beliefs and practices upheld by the Hispanic/Latino community, both in the United States and in Latin-American countries.

- Sixty-seven percent of Hispanic households in the United States consist of a married couple; 44 percent consist of a married couple with children under the age of 18.
- When compared to the population at large, Hispanics have higher rates of never marrying. More than one-third of Hispanic men (38 percent) and 30 percent of Hispanic women have never married.
- Thirty-five percent of all low-income married couples are Hispanic; 40 percent of all low-income married parents with children under age 6 are Hispanic.
- Researchers have found that, compared to the overall population, the divorce rates among Hispanic men and women are lower. In the general population, approximately 9 percent of men were divorced, and approximately 11 percent of women were divorced. In comparison, Hispanic men have a divorce rate of 6 percent; Hispanic women have a divorce rate of 9 percent.
- When compared to marriages involving two white non-Hispanic individuals, marriages between a Hispanic individual and a non-Hispanic individual have a similar or lower likelihood of divorce.
- Educational attainment has a positive association to divorce rates for Hispanics. Hispanics with less than a high school education are far less likely than white individuals to divorce. In contrast, Hispanics with post-high school

education are more likely than white individuals to divorce. Hispanics are slightly less likely to cohabit than white persons.

- Bishops of The Episcopal Church in Latin-American countries report that the principal concern is with high teenage pregnancy rates. In the Dominican Republic, for example, 35 percent of the young mothers giving birth are unmarried teenagers. This trend is also prevalent throughout Central America, with higher percentages reported in rural areas, again pointing to poverty and education as influential factors.

The percentage of university-educated women is increasing across Latin America and is matched by rising rates of divorce. As is true in the United States and many industrialized nations, women in Latin America delay marriage to pursue career goals and tend to be disinclined to stay in unsatisfying relationships for financial security.

Marriage and divorce in the Native-American community

- When it comes to defining marriage or family, there is much variety among Native-American tribes. Many tribes have a clan system that is actively involved in child-rearing and have elders who engage in family life.
- A higher share of Native-American births is to never-married mothers (58.4 percent compared to 33.2 percent for the United States as a whole).
- Native Americans face many challenges to forming and sustaining healthy marriages. One of the greatest challenges is poverty. The proportion of Native Americans living below the poverty line is more than twice the national average. Native-American children are twice as likely to live in poverty as their non-Native counterparts. They are almost twice as likely to live in a home in which neither parent is employed.
- Native Americans are less likely than those in any other racial or ethnic group to report that they had been involved in a marriage-preparation class.
- Approximately 39 percent of the American Indian or Alaska Native population is currently married (excluding couples who are separated). The same percentage has never been married, and approximately 13 percent are divorced.
- More than half (56 percent) of Native Americans are married to individuals from other racial or ethnic groups.

Marriage and divorce in the Asian-American community

As evidenced by their high rates of marriage, Asian-American cultures generally place great value on marriage. Marriage is considered the means to building families, and families are fundamentally important to Asians. In most Asian cultures, a marital relationship is not solely a relationship between spouses, but involves the extended family as well.

- Many followers of traditional Asian cultures value interconnectedness, in contrast to the Western value of independence. This difference can result in a marriage that is considered healthy by Eastern standards and unhealthy or codependent by Western culture.

- Romantic attachment is the primary goal in the selection of a marital partner in contemporary U.S. society. This provides a dilemma for recent immigrants whose cultural values may consider other factors as more important — for example, financial situation, family status, or ensuring the continuity of family lineage. In some Asian groups, traditional family members want to screen and make the final selection of marriage partners for their adult children.

- As a group, Asian Americans have the highest percentage of marriages (65 percent versus 61 percent for white Americans) and the lowest percentage of divorce (4 percent versus 10.5 percent for white individuals).

- Studies have shown that, in contrast to U.S. families as a whole, Asian-American families tend to have lower divorce rates and to have fewer households headed by single women.

- Asian Americans have a high rate of intermarriage (that is, marriage to someone from another racial or ethnic group).

- The low rates of divorce and separation among Asian-American groups may help to account for the relatively low proportion of such families with incomes below the poverty level.

- Divorce and separation rates among native-born Asians differ little from rates of native-born white persons. However, foreign-born Asian women are less likely to be divorced or separated compared to their American-born counterparts.

Marriage and divorce in other cultures and communities

In conversation with the bishop of Taiwan, we found much similarity with many of the above trends in that diocese of The Episcopal Church. In particular, emerging trends in Taiwan include the delay of marriage for economic reasons, the increased pursuit of higher education among women, and the realities of their place in the workforce. Some indication of increased cohabitation prior to marriage is also noted.

In conversation with the bishop of Haiti, we heard that there is a definite "slowdown" in the rate of marriage among young adults, and an increasing rate of divorce among those who do marry. The common trend noted is that many young people subscribe to a "new vision of love" where pleasure and freedom are the norm, and they do not need to get married for those. An increasing number of young adults in Haiti are living together but are not married. While the practice is increasing, even outside urban centers, many people still do not approve of these "free unions." The bishop did not note a delay in marriage for those who want to be married, but rather an increase in the number of those choosing not to marry at all. There is no legal provision for same-sex union in Haiti presently. A large part of the population is against this, believing that marriage is the union of one man and one woman.

7. Same-Sex Marriage

As of mid-year 2014, a majority of Americans, 53 percent, favor allowing gay and lesbian couples to marry legally. Religious groups fall on both sides of the same-sex marriage debate: more than 8 in 10 Jewish Americans, roughly two-thirds of religiously unaffiliated Americans, 62 percent of mainline Protestants, 58 percent of white Roman Catholics, and 56 percent of Hispanic Catholics favor marriage equality for same-sex couples. By contrast, nearly 7 in 10 white evangelical Protestants and 59 percent of black Protestants oppose same-sex marriage. Hispanic Protestants are roughly split on the issue. Majorities of Americans perceive three religious groups to be unfriendly to LGBT people: the Roman Catholic Church, the Mormon Church (LDS), and evangelical Christian churches.

By generation, there is a more than 30-point gap: 7 in 10 young adults (ages 18-29) favor marriage equality, compared to 38 percent of seniors (age 65+). The gap is also geographic: 60 percent of Americans residing in the Northeast and 58 percent of those residing in the West support allowing gay and lesbian couples to marry legally. A slight majority of Midwesterners, 51 percent, support same-sex marriage, while those residing in the southern United States are split between those who support it (48 percent) and those opposed (48 percent), with a small percentage still undecided.

8. Marriage Equality

In the United States, the changing opinions around same-sex marriage seem to have begun in the mid-1990s when, by legislation or by referendum, states began banning same-sex marriage, culminating with the federal Defense of Marriage Act (DOMA) in 1996 (Wisconsin banned same-sex marriage in 1979). Massachusetts's Goodridge Decision from the Supreme Judicial Court came down (4-3) in favor of marriage equality in November 2003. The court's response to the legislature's attempt to substitute civil unions was rejected in a decision released in 2004. The first marriage licenses were issued May 17, 2004. Decisions in support of marriage equality in other states followed. In June 2013, the Supreme Court of the United States, in a 5-4 decision, overturned DOMA, ruling that the federal law deprives same-sex couples of liberty without due process guaranteed by the 5th Amendment to the Constitution.

As of November 15, 2014, 33 states and the District of Columbia now allow same-sex marriage. Five states have same-sex marriage bans that have been overturned and where appeals are in process. The other states remain in some form of limbo, awaiting the outcome of appellate rulings or lawsuits. It is expected that the Supreme Court of the United States will hear one of the appeals on its 2014-2015 docket calendar. As of late 2014, 64 percent of Americans live in states where same-sex couples may marry.

More broadly, many nations have approved freedom for same-sex couples to marry. They include the Netherlands, Belgium, Spain, Norway, Sweden, Portugal, Iceland, Denmark, Brazil, South Africa, France, New Zealand, the United Kingdom, Luxembourg, Canada, and Argentina. Nations that offer some spousal rights and protections to same-sex couples include Andorra, Austria, Australia, Columbia, Uruguay, Ecuador, Mexico, Venezuela, Croatia, Czech Republic, Slovenia, and Switzerland. Same-sex marriage has been constitutionally or legislatively banned in Honduras, El Salvador, the Dominican Republic, and Bolivia. In 81 countries around the world, including much of Africa and Asia, sexual activity by lesbian, gay, bisexual, and transgender persons remains a crime, in some cases punishable by death.

According to the Office for Congregational Development, 64.3 percent of Episcopalians (1,200,622) in 64 U.S. dioceses live in states or jurisdictions where same-sex marriage is legal, although that should not be construed to suggest that all Episcopalians living in those states support same-sex marriage.

9. A Word about Our Consultation with Others

In Resolution A050, the Task Force on the Study of Marriage was asked to consult with ecumenical partners and others from around the Anglican Communion. With our budgetary and time limitations, we were able only to go so far. With the help of our church-wide staff, we gathered some resources from ecumenical partners, including the Evangelical Lutheran Church in America (ELCA), the Presbyterian Church USA, the Unitarian Universalist Association, the United Church of Christ, the Orthodox Church in America, and the U.S. Conference of Catholic Bishops (USCCB). Most of this information came to the Task Force as we were approaching publication deadlines, but it provides some useful material for the continuing work that we believe is needed in our study of changing norms and trends.

From the ELCA we received its "Social Statement on Human Sexuality: Gift and Trust," approved by their 2009 church-wide Assembly. We also received documents related to ELCA's consideration of same-sex relationships. However, no action with regard to this subject has been taken. ELCA remains very interested in our work.

From the Presbyterian Church USA we received two documents: 1) the official publication of their six-week study on marriage that includes biblical and confessional resources; and 2) an unofficial piece — a 2014 book by the theologian Mark Achtemeier entitled, *The Bible's Yes to Same-Sex Marriage: An Evangelical's Change of Heart.*

From the USCCB we received the most current document (2009) from its Marriage and Family Committee: "Life and Love in the Divine Plan."

Our ecumenical office provided us with the 2013 Orthodox Church in America Synodal "Affirmation of the Mystery of Marriage."

The ecumenical office also provided us with a curriculum about sexuality education and marriage adopted by the United Church of Christ and the Unitarian Universalist Association and entitled, "Our Whole Lives."

In 2012, the Pew Research Center published a paper entitled, "Religious Groups' Official Positions on Same-Sex Marriage" [http://www.pewforum.org/2012/12/07/religious-groups-official-positions-on-same-sex-marriage/], which provides a useful summary.

Members of the Task Force also participated in the consultation on same-sex marriage convened by the Standing Commission on Liturgy and Music. This consultation included participants from many U.S. dioceses where civil same-sex marriage is legal, as well as several ecumenical participants and participants from other parts of the Anglican Communion. A fuller report on that consultation is included in the Blue Book report of the Standing Commission on Liturgy and Music.

From the perspective of the work of the Task Force on the Study of Marriage, this consultation provide a unique opportunity to engage in face-to-face conversation about the subject of marriage and, in particular, the topic of same-sex marriage. What we heard from Episcopal, ecumenical, and Anglican-Communion participants was an appreciation for the work of The Episcopal Church and encouragement to continue the effort toward full marriage equality for all. Our ecumenical and Anglican-Communion partners were particularly interested in staying connected to our work and in the many shared resources from their own context.

10. A Word about the Need to Continue Our Work

As noted in this report, much of the data we were able to study focused on the contextual realities in the United States and other Western countries. We were also limited in our capacity fully to research the resources of our ecumenical and Anglican-Communion partners, although we did manage to collect some important resources and information that will be useful in deepening our understanding of and engagement with these partners. Clearly, there is a need to gather more data related to the non-U.S. dioceses of The Episcopal Church, and we have asked the bishops from those dioceses to assist us in that work. Likewise, we need to continue our efforts with our ecumenical and Anglican-Communion partners. Additional resources (human and financial) will be needed to accomplish this.

Selected Bibliography

Arnett, Jeffrey. "Emerging Adulthood: A Theory of Development." American Psychological Associates, 2000.

Cohen, Philip N. "Racial-Ethnic and Gender Differences in Returns to Cohabitation and Marriage." United States Bureau of the Census.

Gallup Annual Minority Rights and Relations Survey, July 2006.

Jamison, Tyler. "Major Changes and Trends in Relationships." University of Missouri, 2014.

National Marriage Project (NMP). "Knot Yet," a 2013 study produced by the NMP, a nonpartisan, nonsectarian, interdisciplinary initiative located at the University of Virginia. The project's mission is to provide research and analysis on the health of marriage in North America.

Pew Research Center Social and Demographic Trends. "The Decline of Marriage and the Rise of New Families." November 2010.

Pew Research Center's Social and Demographic Trends. "Love and Marriage." February 2013.

Public Religion Research Institute. "Gay and Lesbian Issues." June 2014.

United States Department of Labor. "Marriage and Divorce Patterns by Gender, Race, and Educational Attainment." October 2013.

V. Dearly Beloved: A Toolkit for the Study of Marriage

prepared by the
Task Force on the Study of Marriage 2012-2015

V. DEARLY BELOVED: A TOOLKIT FOR THE STUDY OF MARRIAGE

Contents

Introduction
    Purpose of this toolkit
    Who should use this toolkit
    How to use this toolkit
    The role of the bishop and the diocese
    The role of the clergy and laity
    Publicizing your forums or event

FORMAT 1 — CARRY-ON CONVERSATIONS
    Facilitator Guides
    Handout Sheets
    Our Experience of Grace in Relationship
    Historical Considerations and Questions
    Changing Norms in Contemporary Context
    Biblical and Theological Considerations and Questions

FORMAT 2 — FORUMS
    What Makes a Marriage Christian?
    Marriage and Culture
    Marriage and the Bible: A Bible Study
    History of a Liturgical Fragment

FORMAT 3 — STUDY GROUPS
    Discussion questions

Introduction

Purpose of this toolkit

The purpose of this toolkit is to help The Episcopal Church and its people discuss and study what we mean by marriage. What does it mean to be married? What does the Church have to say about marriage? What makes a marriage Christian? What is the role of the Church in marriage? In a rapidly changing culture in the United States, what values does the Church hold as indispensable to marriage? How can the Church continue to speak to people about relationships, faithfulness and life in Christ? And how does marriage serve as an icon of the love of Christ not just to the couple but to their larger communities?

These questions, and many more, are at the heart of the conversations around the Church on marriage. This toolkit is designed to promote and facilitate your conversations so that together — as the Body of Christ — we can be witnesses to Christ's love for each other, for the Church and for the world.

Who should use this toolkit?

These resources are designed for study groups, large and small, for adults and teenagers in the Church and in the wider communities around your Church. Suggestions include provincial and diocesan meetings; deanery clericus meetings and diocesan clergy conferences; Sunday morning congregational education offerings or special evening or Saturday classes. They can be used as one-time events with groups already in existence, such as Education for Ministry (EfM) groups, other Bible study classes, men's and women's groups, Episcopal Church Women (ECW), youth groups, young adult classes, or in partnership with a neighboring Episcopal Church or ecumenical partner.

Many of life's richest experiences come in conversation and fellowship with people from all walks of life. For these classes and groups, intentionally including as diverse a group of participants — people of different ages, races, cultures, genders, sexualities, marital/partnered status, cohabiting couples and singles (including, where possible, those who feel a special vocation to the single life) — is strongly encouraged.

How to use this toolkit

The resources in this toolkit have been organized in three suggested formats:

Format 1: Carry-On Conversations: This discussion format offers two design options: a 90-minute evening or Saturday program, or three 35-minute sessions.

Format 2: Forums: This format provides resources for four 45-minute forums designed for use on the typical Sunday morning Christian Formation format or with existing groups (such as ongoing small groups or EfM groups.) Any or all of them can be used as part of a series of classes or meetings; or as one-time, stand-alone classes.

Format 3: Study Groups: This format is intended for those who would like to "go deeper." It provides reflection questions for a study group that reads some or all of the seven essays on marriage included in Appendix 1 in the Report to the 2015 General Convention of the Task Force on the Study of Marriage.

Whichever format you choose, we recommend appointing both a group facilitator and a scribe.

The role of the facilitator is to:

- Create a welcoming, safe, and comfortable environment of dialogue, not debate.
- Talk as little as possible. The facilitator is not there to lecture, argue, rebut, revise, or otherwise to get in the way of people expressing their questions and feelings.
- Encourage conversation.
- Manage the conversation so that everyone has a chance to contribute. This includes inviting the introverts to speak, and inviting the extroverts to listen to others.

The role of the scribe is to:

- Provide notes — whenever possible, on newsprint or a whiteboard so that the full group can see what is being recorded.
- Free up the facilitator to focus on the people and the conversation.

The role of the bishop and the diocese

Bishops, among their other roles, are the chief teachers of the Church and their diocese. This is particularly true when the bishops meet together as the House of Bishops. The role of chief teacher and pastor includes the encouragement and advancement of opportunities for study and conversation on topics of particular importance to the Church and the world, including marriage.

The Task Force asks bishops across the Church to:

- Publicize and encourage the use of this toolkit throughout their diocese.
- Offer classes and discussion groups themselves as part of their parish visitations, conferences and retreats, and on their own staffs.
- Provide for the study of these materials with their General Convention deputation, with the clergy in their dioceses and at provincial meetings.
- Engage with their peers in studying and discussing these materials in preparation for the 2015 General Convention.
- Encourage diversity in groups.
- Be prayerful about the role of the Church in this area, and encourage others to follow their example.

The role of the clergy and laity

The clergy, among their other roles, are teachers and pastors in their particular churches. Like bishops, this includes the encouragement and advancement of opportunities for study and conversation on topics of particular importance to the Church and the world, including marriage. Members of the laity, like bishops, priests, and deacons, are called to represent Christ to the world. They bring to this important conversation the breadth and depth of their own experience of marriage — their own and/or those they've experienced in the context of relationship with family, friends, neighbors, and colleagues.

The Task Force asks clergy and laity across the Church to:

- Publicize and encourage the use of this toolkit in congregations and communities.
- For clergy in particular, we ask you to lead by example in supporting and providing contexts for the congregational use of these resources.
- For the laity in particular, we ask you to urge your clergy and lay leaders — diocesan and congregational — to utilize these resources.
- Be open and welcoming to different points of view.
- Encourage diversity by intentionally inviting and including a broad spectrum of participants.
- Be prayerful about the role of the Church in this area and encourage others to follow your example.

Publicizing your forums or event

- Three to four weeks prior to your event, advertise it to your congregation by bulletin announcements, verbal announcements, website, and social media (by creating a Facebook event, for example)
- Send a press release to your local newspapers and your diocese.
- Send an invitation to nearby congregations, and reach out to ecumenical partners.
- Send an email or letter of invitation to selected people in your congregation —remember to invite a diverse group of people.
- Send an invitation to other groups in your church asking if you can offer this study with them.

FORMAT 1:
Carry-On Conversations

Introduction

This format offers an outline for a 90-minute discussion group designed to be used as an evening or Saturday program — perhaps including a light meal or other refreshment. Alternatively, it can be divided into three 35-minute sessions held at different times. In addition to the designs for the two different approaches, a one-page handout for each topic is provided, along with a facilitator's guide, suggestions for ways to invite participation, and a form for reporting on your event.

We have also provided a separate PowerPoint presentation that walks you through the various components and provides some visuals that may be useful to you as you make use of this resource.

Until the summer of 2015, the PowerPoint will be available at the General Convention website for the Task Force on the Study of Marriage: http://www.generalconvention.org/ccab.

- Then, under "Find CCABs …," click on "Choose a category";
- Choose "Task Force of General Convention";
- Click on "Task Force on the Study of Marriage";
- Click on "Documents"; and
- Click on the downloadable "Study of Marriage Task Force PowerPoint Presentation for Carry-on Conversation."

After the summer of 2015, this Power Point will be removed from the General Convention website and can be obtained by contacting the Chair of the Task Force, Brian C. Taylor, at the email address, bctaylor@me.com.

Design Principles

This "carry-on" is designed for:

- Conversations that feature participation, engagement, and collaboration;
- A process that is open, welcoming, upbeat, stimulating, and flexible enough for a variety of settings, group sizes, and demographics.

Invitation Strategy

- Try to involve people who offer divergent points of view about marriage;
- Try to involve people who are single, newly married, married for a long time, in other partnered relationships, divorced, widowed, etc.;
- Try to involve people who are currently active in the Church, those who are less active, and those who have little or no affiliation with the Church; and
- Offer to do sessions for groups that are already meeting for another purpose.

Invitation Sample

Dear (Friend, Colleague, Church Member, etc.):

We invite you to participate in a church-wide conversation about marriage: its history, biblical and theological dimensions, and changing trends. In 2012, General Convention created a task force that has developed resources for this purpose. Using these resources, we are holding a 90-minute session (or three 35-minute sessions) on (day and date) at (time) at (location). We would be pleased if you could join us in this important conversation. Please let us know if you are interested and are available to participate.

- WHO: Everyone and anyone who is interested in marriage and the future shape of marriage;
- WHY: In 2012, The General Convention of The Episcopal Church created a task force to study marriage. Members of the Task Force are encouraging conversations about marriage throughout our Church. We invite you to participate in a conversation about the history of marriage, its biblical and theological dimensions, and changing norms and current trends.
- WHEN: _____ WHERE: _____

The Facilitator's Role

- Create a comfortable, welcoming environment.

- Encourage participation by all present.

- Explain the purpose of the event and time constraints.

- Outline the structure for the event and distribute materials.

- Avoid any temptation to lecture, explain, argue, rebut, revise, or otherwise get in the way of allowing people to express themselves. We want to hear from them!

- Consider appointing someone to record key responses from participants.

Designs (two options)

One 90-Minute Session
- Welcome, Prayer, and Overview
- One-Minute Story of a Relationship in Which You Have Seen the Image of God
- History of Marriage
- Changing Norms and Trends
- Biblical and Theological Dimensions
- Thank You and Closing Prayer

Three 35-Minute Sessions
- Welcome, Prayer, and Overview (each session)
- One-Minute Story of a Relationship in Which You Have Seen the Image of God (each session)
- Session One – History of Marriage
- Session Two – Changing Norms and Trends
- Session Three – Biblical and Theological Dimensions
- Thank You and Closing Prayer (each session)

FACILITATOR GUIDES

"Carry-On Conversation" Facilitator Guide for 90-Minute Session

Module	90-Minute Design (Suggested times are flexible.)
Welcome & Overview 5 mins.	• Gathering and introductions • Prayer for Guidance – #57 or #58 BCP page 832 • Overview and context for this conversation • Hand out packets with three one-page summary documents for use during the session
Stories of Relationships 5-10 mins.	• Guided by principles laid out in General Convention Resolution D039-2000, which names values that the Church upholds for its members in relationships: "fidelity, monogamy, mutual affection and respect, careful, honest communication, and the holy love which enables those in such relationships to see in each other the image of God." — Tell a one-minute story about your relationship or one you know well in which you have seen the image of God (in groups of three) — Invite people to record and send one-minute video to taskforceonmarriage@gmail.com AND/OR post written response to: www.facebook.com/A050taskforce
History of Marriage 20-25 mins.	• Use one-page summary of the key aspects regarding the history of marriage (pg 17, 18, 19). • Conversation and sharing of responses to these questions: (large group) QUESTIONS: What did you find surprising/affirming/unsettling about this historical synopsis? How does this history help inform our contemporary understanding of marriage? (Record key responses.)
Changing Norms & Trends 20-25 mins.	• Use one-page summary of key trends and changes in norms vis-à-vis marriage (pg 18). • Conversation and sharing of responses (in small groups or 5-6) QUESTION: How might these trends, and others of which you are aware, influence how the Church understands marriage?
Biblical & Theological Dimensions 20-25 mins.	• Use one-page summary of key biblical and theological themes or issues regarding how the Church understands marriage (pg 19). QUESTION: Which of these themes is most central to your understanding of Christian marriage? (small groups of 5-6)
Thanks & Prayer 5 mins.	Thank You Closing prayer: Lord's Prayer or one chosen by facilitator

V. DEARLY BELOVED: A TOOLKIT FOR THE STUDY OF MARRIAGE   251

"Carry-On Conversation" Facilitator Guide for Three 35-Minute Session

Module	Three 35-Minute Sessions Design (Adjust times to fit your needs.)
Welcome & Overview 5 mins.	Each time you gather, begin with: • Gathering and introductions • Prayer for Guidance – #57 or #58 BCP page 832 • Overview and context for this conversation
Stories of Relationships 5-10 mins.	Each time you gather, begin with this exercise: • Guided by principles laid out in General Convention Resolution D039-2000, which names values that the Church upholds for its members in relationships: "fidelity, monogamy, mutual affection and respect, careful, honest communication, and the holy love which enables those in such relationships to see in each other the image of God." — Tell a one-minute story about your relationship or one you know well in which you have seen the image of God (in groups of three) — Invite people to record and send one-minute video to taskforceonmarriage@gmail.com AND/OR post written response to: www.facebook.com/A050taskforce
Session One History of Marriage 20-25 mins.	• Use one-page summary of the key aspects regarding the history of marriage (pg 17). • Conversation and sharing of responses to these questions: (large group) QUESTIONS: What did you find surprising/affirming/unsettling about this historical synopsis? How does this history help inform our contemporary understanding of marriage? (Record key responses.)
Session Two Changing Norms & Trends 20-25 mins.	• Use one-page summary of key trends and changes in norms vis-à-vis marriage (pg 18). • Conversation and sharing of responses (in small groups or 5-6) QUESTION: How might these trends, and others of which you are aware, influence how the Church understands marriage?
Session Three Biblical & Theological Dimensions 20-25 mins.	• Use one-page summary of key biblical and theological themes or issues regarding how the Church understands marriage (pg 19). QUESTION: Which of these themes is most central to your understanding of Christian marriage? (small groups of 5-6)
Thanks & Prayer 5 mins.	Do this for each session: Thank You Closing prayer: Lord's Prayer or one chosen by facilitator

HANDOUT 1

Our Experience of Grace in Relationship

Guided by principles laid out in General Convention Resolution D039-2000, which names values that the Church upholds for its members in relationships: "fidelity, monogamy, mutual affection and respect, careful, honest communication, and the holy love which enables those in such relationships to see in each other the image of God..."

Break participants into groups of two or three for the purpose of telling a one-minute story about their relationship — or one they know well — in which they have seen the image of God. There is no need for the triads to report back to the larger group.

HANDOUT 2

Historical Considerations and Questions

The following considerations and questions are designed to offer an opportunity to explore together the history of marriage and reflect together on the questions it raises. Depending on the size of the group, conversations can happen in groups of two or three, in larger breakout groups, or with the whole assembly.

a. Among the several patterns we see repeated in history in regard to marriage, one essential element of marriage that almost always occurred was a process of betrothal.

> *Question:* What happens during a betrothal process to the couple and to the rest of the kinship and community network? Does contemporary Episcopal practice give due respect to the ancient practice of betrothal? Does this practice still have relevance in our contemporary understanding of marriage?

b. Different historical periods interpreted the marriage ritual in different ways. Eastern and Teutonic cultures believed that the marriage rite dramatically changed and blessed both the husband and the wife, while Romans believing that the wedding day was in fact the bride's day.

> *Question:* How do we still see this ancient question being played out in contemporary marriage practices? How does the concept of same-sex marriage further inform this ancient divergence of viewpoints?

c. For much of history, the expectation and necessity of formal, legal marriage was one left to those with power, status, and property. In our own day, we do not believe that economic or social status should have any impact on people's right to marry.

> *Question:* How does this change in the Christian understanding of who can marry change our contemporary understanding of the nature and purposes of marriage?

d. Throughout history, access to legal marriage has been closely related to the right to give consent – a right directly related to one's ability to act and choose autonomously. Only those with the right to act autonomously could exercise the right to choose marriage. Often this has meant that those who were oppressed and subordinated in a patriarchal and colonial context could not decide their own lives. Access to marriage became a means of controlling the powerless in a society.

> *Question:* Are there situations in contemporary society in which access to marriage is still being controlled by the powerful and privileged to the detriment of those with less power?

e. In much of the history of marriage, the decision to cohabitate without the legal sanction of civil and religious authorities was a means of expressing suspicion and distrust for the institutions of the church and the state, choosing less formalized models of authority and validity.

> *Question:* Is this still one of the reasons that so many couples in The Episcopal Church choose to cohabit rather than to marry today, or are there new reasons and rationales for cohabitation?

f. Since at least the time of Augustine, at various periods in history marriage has been understood as a sacramental rite. While The Episcopal Church acknowledges only two primary sacraments instituted by Christ (Baptism and Eucharist), The Episcopal Church also gives special honor to marriage as one of the historically recognized sacramental rites of the Church.

> *Question:* Who is the primary actor in a sacramental rite, the Christian(s) or God?

HANDOUT 3

Changing Norms in Contemporary Context

The cultural landscape continues to shift around many aspects of the institution of marriage — a shift evidenced by the statistics represented in the following data points illustrating examples of changing norms. Share these data points with participants and then discuss using the questions below.

1. Marriage as a precursor to childbirth is seen as a relic of the past by many young adults. From "Knot Yet: The National Marriage Project," University of Virginia, 2011.

2. In previous generations, marriage was seen as a cornerstone of launching into adulthood. Today, young adults are delaying marriage due to financial insecurity, fear of divorce, and a desire for career stability. Ibid.

3. Ninety percent of young adults feel they must be completely financially independent before they marry. Ibid.

4. The cohabitation rate of unmarried senior citizens is rising: up 50 percent since 2000. Ibid.

5. Sixty-five percent of all couples who eventually marry lived together before marriage. From Pew Research Study: "The Decline of Marriage and Rise of New Families," 2010.

6. The vast majority of adults in their twenties (80 percent) see marriage as an "important part of their life plan." "Knot Yet," University of Virginia.

7. The "ideal" for marriage has shifted from providing economic security to finding a "soul mate" — often with idealistic and unmet expectations. Ibid.

8. Marriage remains the norm for adults with a college education and good incomes; markedly less prevalent for those with less education or economic stability. Ibid.

9. In the past 7 years, 35-40 percent of all marriages began with on-line dating. "Emerging Adulthood: The Winding Road from Late Teens through the Twenties," Jeffrey Arnett; Oxford.

10. As of June 2014, 31 states prohibit same-sex marriage, 20 states and the District of Columbia allow same-sex marriage, and 47 percent of Episcopalians in 40 dioceses live in states or jurisdictions where same-sex marriage is legal. Office for Congregational Research, DFMS.

11. Two-thirds of all adults see living together as a necessary step to marriage. Cohabitation has become a routine substitute for marriage. Pew Research Study.

12. In 1960, two-thirds of all adults in their twenties were married. By 2008, that number was only 26 percent. Ibid.

13. Divorce rates leveled off in the US in 1980 to 45 percent of all marriages and has held steady for the past 35 years. For senior adults, the divorce rate has jumped 35 percent. "The All Or Nothing Marriage," Eli J. Finkel, a Professor of Psychology at Northwestern University, published in the *New York Times*, 2014.

Discussion Questions:

- The changing norms around marriage may challenge the way some of us have experienced dating and marriage. How does your experience differ or align with these current trends?
- Are there trends that strike you as impacting the institution of marriage positively? Others negatively?
- Discuss the impact of larger societal issues reflected in these statistics (i.e., feminism; civil rights; marriage equality and economic justice movements).
- Given the influence of social media on the changing landscape of human interaction, how do you understand its impact on courtship and marriage?
- What opportunities or challenges do you believe these trends will represent for the Church in our care and concern for all human relationships?

HANDOUT 4

Biblical and Theological Considerations and Questions

Each set of passages below — from the Celebration and Blessing of a Marriage and from Scripture passages assigned for use in that celebration — highlights a key theme or themes inherent in the Church's understanding of marriage. In small groups, take five minutes for each set, read through and savor the texts, and then reflect on the questions after each set of passages.

> *"...intended by God for their mutual joy ...to love and to cherish, until we are parted by death." (BCP 423, 427) "... for love is strong as death ..." (Song of Solomon 8:6) "As the Father has loved me, so I have loved you; abide in my love." (John 15:9) "[Love] bears all things, believes all things, hopes all things, endures all things. Love never ends." (1 Corinthians 13:7-8)*

How have you experienced the love of God in your life? In your relationships? What does it mean to "abide in love"? What helps you to do so?

> *"Established by God in creation ..." (BCP 423) "... not good that the man should be alone." (Genesis 2:18)*

What does it mean to be "alone"? What do these passages say to a newlywed couple? To a widow or widower? To a single person who feels called to a single life?

> *"intended by God ... for the help and comfort given one another in prosperity and adversity ... faithful ... as long as you both shall live ...to have and to hold from this day forward, for better for worse, for richer for poorer, in sickness and in health" (BCP 423, 424, 427) "live in love, as Christ loved us and gave himself up for us ... Be subject to one another out of reverence for Christ." (Ephesians 5:2,21)*

How have you experienced love in difficult times as well as happy times? How is mutual love played out in your life and in the lives of those you know?

FORMAT 2: Forums

This format provides resources for four 45-minute forums designed for use in a typical Sunday morning Christian Formation format or with existing groups (such as ongoing small groups or EfM groups.) Any or all of these sessions can be used as part of a series of classes or meetings or as one-time, stand-alone classes. Each handout is one or two pages long for easy distribution.

You may want to begin each session with the "Stories of Relationships" exercise described in Carry-On Conversations. This is not only a good ice-breaker, but also a way to help focus the conversation.

The first two resources follow the Describe/Listen/Reflect format and provide an opportunity to engage with the questions of what makes a marriage Christian, and the relationship between culture and marriage. The third resource is a Bible study on the passage from Ephesians that is the source for one of the dominant images in Christian marriage as a metaphor for the relationship between Christ and the Church. The final resource in this section offers an opportunity to examine the text of the opening to the marriage liturgy in the Anglican tradition.

FORUM 1

What Makes a Marriage Christian?

Describe

Many people get married in the courts with no religious ceremony. Vows of commitment are an integral part of civil and religious marriages. For those seeking God's blessing through ritual marriage in the Church, marriage rites also articulate values and obligations rooted in scripture and tradition. For example, The Blessing of a Civil Marriage (BCP 433) includes this charge to the couple:

> N. and N., you have come here today to seek the blessing of God and of his Church upon your marriage. I require, therefore, that you promise, with the help of God, to fulfill the obligations which Christian marriage demands.

The Celebration and Blessing of a Marriage (BCP, 423), declares that the covenant of marriage represents "the spiritual unity between Christ and his Church." It asks God to so bless "these your servants, that they may so love, honor, and cherish each other in faithfulness and patience, in wisdom and true godliness, that their home may be a haven of blessing and peace."

Listen

Using the questions below, discover what others in your group understand and experience with regard to the obligations of marriage.

- Why seek the blessing of God? Why seek the blessing of the Church? Is one OK without the other? What power (importance) is in such blessings? How does the blessing impact a marriage?
- How have you seen married couples fulfill these obligations?
- How have you witnessed this in other relationships?

Reflect

As you end this time together, consider what you will take away from listening to others' understandings of marriage.

- What have you heard today that especially made you think?
- What is one thing you'll do differently in the next week as a result of this reflection?
- In what aspect of this conversation will you seek God's guidance through prayer?

FORUM 2

Marriage and Culture

Describe

The institution of marriage has been shifting throughout history and continues to shift in our culture. Since the 1980s, 45 percent of marriages end in divorce; children of divorced parents often delay marriage or may be reluctant to get married; people frequently cohabit prior to or instead of marrying; and marriage equality is becoming increasingly common.

Individuals respond to these shifts in a variety of ways. Within our Church, some seek to reclaim and reassert what they understand to be a traditional view of marriage. Others in our Church seek to address these issues by revising its practices, including its liturgies.

Listen

Using the questions below, discover what others in your community understand and experience with regard to these cultural shifts.

- What did previous generations of your family (e.g., grandparents, parents) teach you about marriage? How did they define marriage? What examples of marriage did they set?
- What shifts in marriage are you seeing in your community?
- What do you see as the benefits to marriage, if any? To marriage blessed by the Church?

Reflect

As you end this time together, consider what you will take away from listening to others' understandings of marriage.

- What have you heard today that especially made you think?

- What is one thing you'll do differently in the next week as a result of this reflection?
- In what aspect of this conversation will you seek God's guidance through prayer?

FORUM 3

Marriage and the Bible: A Bible Study

The following passage (Ephesians 5:1-2, 21-33, NRSV) is commended for use as a reading in the BCP "Celebration and Blessing of a Marriage."

> *Therefore be imitators of God, as beloved children,20 and live in love, as Christ loved us and gave himself up for us, a fragrant offering and sacrifice to God.21 Be subject to one another out of reverence for Christ.22 Wives, be subject to your husbands as you are to the Lord.23 For the husband is the head of the wife just as Christ is the head of the church, the body of which he is the Savior.24 Just as the church is subject to Christ, so also wives ought to be, in everything, to their husbands.25 Husbands, love your wives, just as Christ loved the church and gave himself up for her, 26 in order to make her holy by cleansing her with the washing of water by the word,27 so as to present the church to himself in splendor, without a spot or wrinkle or anything of the kind — yes, so that she may be holy and without blemish.28 In the same way, husbands should love their wives as they do their own bodies. He who loves his wife loves himself.29 For no one ever hates his own body, but he nourishes and tenderly cares for it, just as Christ does for the church,30 because we are members of his body.31 "For this reason a man will leave his father and mother and be joined to his wife, and the two will become one flesh."32 This is a great mystery, and I am applying it to Christ and the church.33 Each of you, however, should love his wife as himself, and a wife should respect her husband.*

Reflection questions

- In the 1928 revision of the marriage rite, The Episcopal Church removed the wife's vow to "obey" her husband. How do you feel about this in relation to the biblical text? Is this a text you would want read or did have read at your own marriage? Why or why not?

- Verse 24 calls on wives to be "subject … to their husbands" "just as the Church is subject to Christ." How is the Church "subject" to Christ? As one's body is to one's head (vs. 23)? What does that mean?

- How is mutual obedience (vs. 21, "Be subject to one another") expressed in this passage? How do you understand it in your own relationship or marriage?

- The author sets up an analogy between Christ or Church and the organic Head or Body. In keeping with 1 Corinthians 12 (especially vs. 21: "The eye cannot say to the hand, 'I have no need of you,' nor again the head to the feet, 'I have no need of you.' ") What does this concept of organic unity say to you about marriage? Is the head of the body separate from the body?

- Verses 28-29 describe the wife as identical to the husband's own body, on the analogy of Christ and his Body, the Church. What, if anything, does this say to you about gender in relation to the body?

- To what extent do you see verse 33 as an echo of Leviticus 19:18 ("… love your neighbor as yourself…") included by Jesus in his Summary of the Law?

- Under Roman custom and law, the father of a family had almost unlimited authority over that family (*patria potestas*). In what way does a call for mutual submission and a husband's responsibility to love his wife in a sacrificial and tender way represent a movement away from that patriarchal model?

FORUM 4

History of a Liturgical Fragment

This forum offers a comparison of the opening of the marriage liturgy in historical contexts dating from the Medieval English rite of Salisbury (Sarum) up through the 1979 BCP.

Perhaps the most striking feature of the Sarum rite is the location: the couple stands with the minister for most of the liturgy at the entrance to the Church, entering it for the mass that follows and forming a part of the marriage rite. Note, however, that even our present BCP includes the option of celebrating marriage in a place other than a church.

As you compare the evolution of the marriage rite in the English/Anglican/Episcopal tradition, you'll note that the changes (both in terms of content and ordering) have been substantial, reflecting different attitudes and the prevailing "style" of liturgy.

One important feature of the marriage rites used in The Episcopal Church from its beginnings until the 1979 revision is the omission of the language about the "causes" or reasons for which marriage was said to have been instituted or established by God.

Note also the reordering of these reasons as well as the change in the sequence of references to creation, the metaphorical application of marriage to Christ and the Church, and the wedding at Cana.

Questions to consider

- What does the location of marriage "in the Church," as opposed to at its entrance, "in some proper house," or "another appropriate place" say to you?
- Would you feel your own marriage to be different if the location had been or were different?
- Does this say anything about the Church being used as a "venue" by people with little church connection? Or about any distinction between the sacred and the civil nature of marriage?

- What significance, if any, do you see in the reordering of the "causes" or reasons for marriage in the 1979 BCP? What about their absence from the marriage liturgy used in The Episcopal Church for almost 200 years (1789-1979)?

Sarum (tr. Hoskin)*	1662 BCP	BCP 1789/90
... the man and woman shall stand before the entrance of the church ...	... the persons to be married shall come into the body of the church ...	... the Persons to be married shall come into the Body of the church, or shall be ready in some proper house ...
Behold, brethren, we have come hither in the sight of God, the angels, and all his saints in the presence of the church, to join together two bodies, of this man and of this woman, [at the altar during the mass: ... when the beginnings of the universe were laid down... ... so excellent a mystery, that thou signifiest the sacrament of Christ and the Church ...] [at the blessing after mass: ... the six water jugs in Cana of Galilee ...]	DEARLY beloved, we are gathered together here in the sight of God, and in the face of this congregation, to join together this Man and this Woman in holy Matrimony; which is an honourable estate, instituted of God in the time of man's innocency, signifying unto us the mystical union that is betwixt Christ and his Church; which holy estate Christ adorned and beautified with his presence, and first miracle that he wrought, in Cana of Galilee; and is commended of Saint Paul to be honourable among all men: and therefore is not by any to be enterprised, nor taken in hand, unadvisedly, lightly, or wantonly, to satisfy men's carnal lusts and appetites, like brute beasts that have no understanding; but reverently, discreetly, advisedly, soberly, and in the fear of God;	DEARLY beloved, we are gathered together here in the sight of God, and in the face of this company, to join together this Man and this Woman in holy Matrimony; which is an honourable estate, commended of Saint Paul to be honourable among all men: and therefore is not by any to be entered into unadvisedly or lightly, but reverently, discreetly, advisedly, soberly, and in the fear of God.
	duly considering the causes for which Matrimony was ordained.	
[at the blessing of the wife during mass: May she be rich in children ... and see the sons of her sons all the way to the third and fourth generation ...]	First, It was ordained for the procreation of children, to be brought up in the fear and nurture of the Lord, and to the praise of his holy Name. Secondly, It was ordained for a remedy against sin, and to avoid fornication; that such persons as have not the gift of continency might marry, and keep themselves undefiled members of Christ's body. Thirdly, It was ordained for the mutual society, help, and comfort, that the one ought to have of the other, both in prosperity and adversity.	

* The Sarum liturgy has a short prologue that differs substantially from the 1662 version. However, other portions of the Sarum liturgy contain allusions similar to those in the 1662 prologue, and they are included in brackets, with an indication of where they fall in the liturgy.

V. DEARLY BELOVED: A TOOLKIT FOR THE STUDY OF MARRIAGE

BCP 1892	BCP 1928	BCP 1979
... the Persons to be married shall come into the Body of the church, or shall be ready in some proper house ...	... the Persons to be married shall come into the Body of the church, or shall be ready in some proper house ...	... the persons to be married ... assemble in the church or some other appropriate place ...
DEARLY beloved, we are gathered together here in the sight of God, and in the face of this company to join together this Man and this Woman in holy Matrimony; which is an honourable estate,	DEARLY beloved, we are gathered together here in the sight of God, and in the face of this company to join together this Man and this Woman in holy Matrimony; which is an honorable estate,	Dearly beloved: we have come together in the presence of God to witness and bless the joining together of this man and this woman in Holy Matrimony.
instituted of God in the time of man's innocency. signifying unto us the mystical union that is betwixt Christ and his Church: which holy estate Christ adorned and beautified with his presence and first miracle that he wrought in Cana of Galilee, and is commended of Saint Paul to be honourable among all men; and therefore is not by any to be entered into unadvisedly or lightly, but reverently, discreetly, advisedly, soberly, and in the fear of God.	instituted of God in the time of man's innocency. signifying unto us the mystical union that is betwixt Christ and his Church: which holy estate Christ adorned and beautified with his presence and first miracle that he wrought in Cana of Galilee, and is commended of Saint Paul to be honourable among all men; and therefore is not by any to be entered into unadvisedly or lightly, but reverently, discreetly, advisedly, soberly, and in the fear of God.	The bond and covenant of marriage was established by God at creation, and our Lord Jesus Christ adorned this manner of life by his presence and first miracle at a wedding in Cana of Galilee. It signifies to us the mystery of the union between Christ and his Church, and Holy Scripture commends it to be honored among all people.
		The union of husband and wife in heart, body, and mind is intended by God
		for their mutual joy; for the help and comfort given one another in prosperity and adversity; and, when it is God's will, for the procreation of children and their nurture in the knowledge and love of the Lord. Therefore marriage is not to be entered into unadvisedly or lightly, but reverently, deliberately, and in accord with the purposes for which it was instituted by God.

FORMAT 3: Study Groups

Read and discuss essays found in Appendix 1 of the Blue Book Report to General Convention 2015 of the Task Force on the Study of Marriage.

These study questions pertain specifically to particular essays on marriage that we have produced. You may use these study questions for individual or small groups or parish- or diocesan-wide forums. These questions may be used with any of our essays.

The essays in Appendix 1 of the Blue Book report are:

- A Biblical and Theological Framework for Thinking about Marriage
- Christian Marriage as Vocation
- A History of Christian Marriage
- Marriage as a Rite of Passage
- The Marriage Canons: History and Critique
- Agents of the State: A Question for Discernment
- Changing Trends and Norms in Marriage

Notes to the group facilitator:

1. This design is based on a 45-minute group discussion.
2. Ask people to read the essay(s) prior to the group meeting.
3. Because there are several essays in the Blue Book documents, each varying in length, you may want to study one essay per meeting. If you choose to discuss all essays at one session allow two-three hours.

4. It may be helpful to individuals and to your group discussion process to ask people to do questions 1-4 individually, writing down their answers prior to the full group discussion.

Questions:

1. What are two or three points in the essay that stood out for you?

2. How do these points affirm, challenge, or enlarge your personal understanding of marriage?

3. What do you think is the significance of this essay for you, your church, your community, your diocese or The Episcopal Church in the U.S.?

4. How has your understanding of marriage been changed by reading this essay? What will you do about it?

5. What are possible next steps for you, your church, and The Episcopal Church?

6. What can you — or your church or diocese — do to advance the discussion of the points in this essay?

Note: The essay on A History of Marriage contains its own discussion questions at the end of the text, which are more specific to its content. The facilitator may use either set of questions for discussion when considering that essay.

VI. Pastoral Resources for Preparing Couples for Marriage

adapted from Liturgical Resources 1, revised and expanded edition (2015)*

---

* Prepared by the Standing Commission on Liturgy and Music, 2009-2012

Contents

Pre-Marital Preparation: Introduction
    Presenters
    Session One: Getting to Know You and an Overview
    Session Two: Learning from the Past, Part 1
    Session Three: Learning from the Past, Part 2
    Session Four: Looking to the Future
    Session Five: Liturgical Decisions and Wrap-up

Handouts
    1. Declaration of Intention for Marriage (Canon I.18.4)
    2. About Presenters—For the Couple
    3. Information for Presenters
    4. Model Congregational Guidelines

Pre-Marital Preparation: Introduction

Below is a guideline for a five-session, pre-marital preparation that may be used along with the materials described above. These materials were originally prepared by the Standing Commission on Liturgy and Music during the 2009-2012 triennium as part of its work of developing theological and liturgical resources for blessing same-sex relationships. They have been revised for use with any couple.

Pre-marital preparation sets as its goal the strengthening of a lifelong, monogamous partnership rooted in Christ. General Convention Resolution 2000-D039 addresses the hope—the Church's and the couple's—for such relationships:

> *Resolved*, That we expect such relationships will be characterized by fidelity, monogamy, mutual affection and respect, careful, honest communication, and the holy love which enables those in such relationships to see in each other the image of God; and be it further
>
> *Resolved*, That we denounce promiscuity, exploitation, and abusiveness in the relationships of any of our members; and be it further
>
> *Resolved*, That this Church intends to hold all its members accountable to these values, and will provide for them the prayerful support, encouragement, and pastoral care necessary to live faithfully by them.

Ideally, sessions last 60 to 90 minutes each, and both partners should be present for all sessions (although the preparer may decide to meet with one of the individuals to address specific issues). Those with experience preparing couples may choose to adapt, combine, or reorder this outline.

Presenters

"Presenters" are people chosen by the couple to support and present them to the presider and the assembly during the marriage. Presenters may be friends, parents, family members, or drawn from the local congregation. This option gives a voice to important people in the life of the couple during the liturgy and enriches the experience for all present. Presenters can also serve an important role in supporting the couple before and after their marriage ceremony. The selection of a couple mature in their relationship can be particularly helpful to a couple starting life together. The couple, together with the clergy or lay preparer, should talk as soon as possible about selecting presenters, so that the prayerful work of the presenters can begin early on.

Two short handouts provided in this pastoral resource (one for the couple and one for presenters) detail the role of presenters and are intended for use at the conclusion of the initial preparation session. They are designed for use with "The Witnessing and Blessing of a Marriage." Congregations offering presenters for "The Celebration and Blessing of a Marriage" or "The Celebration and Blessing of a Marriage 2" can use these handouts by substituting the text of the presentation from the Additional Directions (BCP p. 437; above, p. 19).

Session One: Getting to Know You and an Overview

This session focuses on getting to know one another. It also starts to address the details of the rite, offering the couple and the clergyperson an opportunity to study the rites together, looking at their meaning and choices and affirming that the marriage blessing, grounded in God, is given through the Church. Some clergy, however, may prefer to do a very general overview of the rites in this session, then study them more intensely later in the process.

Addressing the practical issues of the marriage at the outset helps to build trust and allows the couple to open themselves to the substance of the next four sessions. By providing even a general overview of the rites, the preparer can address questions and alleviate anxieties about the actual day. The couple and clergyperson officiating will need to decide, either in this session or later in the preparation, which rite to use.

Session One includes a great deal of material, some of which may be moved to another session.
Handouts for this session include:

1. The liturgies "The Celebration and Blessing of a Marriage" (BCP, pp. 423-32); "The Witnessing and Blessing of a Marriage" (above, pp. 20); "The Celebration and Blessing of a Marriage 2" (above, pp. 10)

2. *Declaration of Intention* (found at the end of this outline)

3. *About Presenters—For the Couple* (found at the end of this outline)

4. *Information for Presenters* (found at the end of this outline)

Outline of Session One
- Pray together.
- Get to know one another (varies as to how well the preparer knows the couple).
- Explore the couple's religious backgrounds, their experiences with the church(es), and their reasons for being in this congregation.

- Reflect on the theological significance of the couple's relationship. The Declaration of Intention and the marriage liturgies may be useful in this discussion. (This reflection might be moved to a later session.)
- Review and ask the couple to sign the Declaration of Intention.
- Walk through the marriage rites, raising theological issues and naming liturgical choices:
    - Discuss the eucharist as normative in the service. However, including a celebration of the eucharist may not be appropriate if only one member of the couple is Christian.
    - Emphasize the difference between a civil service and the ecclesial blessing that is part of the marriage service.
    - Answer general questions regarding details of the service and the Church's practice.
    - Introduce the possibility of presenters.

At the end of the session, provide written handouts and suggest "homework" topics for the couple to think about for Sessions Two and Three:

- Families of origin and growing up in them
    - What worked and didn't work so well in their families of origin (this topic may also influence work in Session Four)
    - Family church/religious history as well as each individual's history—positive and negative—with the church/religion
- Marriages of family members, particularly parents
    - Parents' ways of dealing with conflict
    - Parents' styles of child-rearing
    - Family tolerance of children's sexual orientation or gender identity.

Session Two:
Learning from the Past, Part 1

This session provides a time for one member of the couple to speak and for the other to listen. Session Two opens with prayer, then looks back to focus upon the relationship of one partner with his/her family of origin, including exploring the marriage(s) of his/her parents and siblings and, if possible, grandparents and close friends. This discussion includes what the individual would or would not replicate from the past in his/her own ongoing and future relationships, particularly the relationship that is to be blessed. In addition, the individual can look at levels of acceptance of his/her relationship by his/her family and at other issues from family of origin and childhood.

The guiding assumption underlying this analysis is that certain issues are replicated from generation to generation, and that, once the issues are identified, individuals can choose to continue those patterns or deliberately alter them. This session works most effectively if the conversation flows naturally, rather than following a rigid interview, and if it includes the following important areas:

- Family: number and birth order of siblings
- Money: its role and influence in the family
- Sex: attitudes in family of origin about monogamy, fidelity, and the role of sex in relationship
- Alcohol and drugs: their places within the family as children grew
- In-laws: relationship with in-laws and greater family
- Children:
    - o agreement or disagreement between parents about child-rearing
    - o the individual's feelings about being a child in his/her family
- Conflict: parents' methods of arguing and disagreeing.

As the conversation concludes, the preparer invites the individual to identify what he/she would or would not replicate in his/her own adult relationship with the life partner. Following that, the silent partner is given the floor to comment on what he/she has heard and learned, especially any surprises.

Session Three: Learning from the Past, Part 2

This session continues the look back by extending the chance for the other member of the couple to speak about his/her family of origin. Both members of the couple need the opportunity to explore the topics and to hear each other's stories so that each can learn and appreciate more deeply what the other brings to their relationship.

Session Three, which also begins with prayer, duplicates with the second person the process with the first from Session Two. If time permits at the end, the couple might discuss the impact of family history on their own relationship.

Session Four:
Looking to the Future

This session, an opportunity to look at the relationship today and into the future, invites the couple to name areas in the relationship that appear strong and supportive while also opening a space to identify and address areas that may be problematic. Thoughts, questions, and new information from previous sessions may help determine where the couple is today and where their relationship and household may need attention in the future.

After opening with prayer, this session should include discussion of:

- The couple's relationship in general: in-depth exploration of where they have been and where they are now
- Role of sex and intimacy in the relationship (for example, potential changes of sexual behavior as a result of committing to a monogamous relationship)
- Role of alcohol and drugs in the relationship
- Money (for example, household finances and financial planning)
- Legal protections (for example, medical and financial durable powers-of-attorney, wills and living wills, insurance)
- Household roles (for example, who takes out the trash, who keeps the social calendar?)
- Communication:
    - How the couple talks things through
    - What happens when they disagree
- Concerns for the future
- Decision-making as a couple
- Dealing with families as individuals (one's own as well as one's partner's) and as a couple
- Support networks, now and in the future.

Session Four concludes with a discussion of the need for boundaries between generations so that the couple's life as a unit may be seen as distinct from older and younger generations.

Session Five:
Liturgical Decisions and Wrap-up

Session Five, focused on the marriage service itself, is an opportunity to make choices for the liturgy, based on the discussion at the first session. The depth of this discussion will be determined by what was or was not addressed in Session One. In addition, as the final session, Session Five serves as a time to consider questions that may have arisen from previous sessions.

Outline of Session Five

- Pray together.
- Address questions and concerns regarding previous sessions and other issues that have arisen.
- Review theological reflections in light of previous sessions and what is to come. The preparer can help the couple connect the spiritual practices of their life as a couple and the "staging" of the service. For example, will they process into the service together or separately, or will they be already in the worship space as the liturgy begins? Will they sit together during the Ministry of the Word or across the aisle from one another?
- Discuss details of the service itself:
  - Scripture (which passages speak particularly to the couple's life together?) and whether non-biblical readings may be included
  - Will the liturgy take place at the congregation's principal weekly celebration? Is celebration of the eucharist to be omitted for pastoral cause?
  - Other liturgical choices, especially:
    - Which collect will be used?
    - For the Witnessing and Blessing of a Marriage, which of the two vows will be used?
    - Will rings be exchanged, or, if rings have already been worn, are they to be blessed?
    - What music, if any, will be included? (The couple should consult with the congregation's musician.)

- Discuss presenters and their roles in supporting the couple in the service and in their ongoing life.

In closing, the preparer can assure the couple that they have done hard and important work together, work that is a gift both to the preparer and to the couple. The preparer can express his/her eager anticipation of the couple's marriage and of meeting their close and extended families, seeing them with their friends, and celebrating their relationship in the sight of God.

Handouts

1. Declaration of Intention
2. About Presenters—For the Couple
3. Information for Presenters
4. Model Congregational Guidelines

The *Declaration of Intention* requires the replacement of N.N. and N. N. in the first sentence with the couple's names.

Handouts 2 and 3 are designed for use with the liturgy "The Witnessing and Blessing of a Marriage." These handouts may be modified if one of the other marriage liturgies is to be used.

Handouts 2 through 4 are samples that may be adapted for the use of a specific congregation. In these, "N. Episcopal Church" should be replaced with the congregation's name, and a similar change made for "Episcopal Diocese of X."

HANDOUT 1

Declaration of Intention (Canon I.18.4)

We understand the teaching of the church that God's purpose for our marriage is for our mutual joy, for the help and comfort we will give to each other in prosperity and adversity, and, when it is God's will, for the gift and heritage of children and their nurture in the knowledge and love of God. We also understand that our marriage is to be unconditional, mutual, exclusive, faithful, and lifelong; and we engage to make the utmost effort to accept these gifts and fulfill these duties, with the help of God and the support of our community.

_____   _____
Signature   Signature

Date _____

SAMPLE HANDOUT 2

About Presenters—For the Couple

At N. Episcopal Church, we consider "The Witnessing and Blessing of a Marriage" to be a celebration supported by the congregation, much as candidates for baptism are supported by all the members of the Church. Just as those who are baptized are initiated into the full life of the Church, those who receive the Church's blessing upon their marriage are embraced in a new way in the faith community.

The Marriage Liturgy

The presentation takes place immediately after the sermon, as follows:

The couple comes before the assembly. If there is to be a presentation, the presenters stand with the couple, and the Presider says to them

Presider   Who presents N. and N. as they seek the blessing of God and the Church on their love and life together?

Presenters   We do.

Presider   Will you love, respect, and pray for N. and N., and do all in your power to stand with them in the life they will share?

Presenters   We will.

Choosing Presenters

There are a variety of possibilities for choosing presenters who will stand with you and present you at the liturgy. It can be helpful to choose at least one member of this faith community to walk with you through this process. If you are new to the congregation, the priest (or other person designated) can help you discern whom you might consider. The selection of a couple mature in their relationship can be particularly helpful if you are just beginning your life together. Often, couples will choose their own parents, children, or other supportive family members to be their presenters.

Presenters can pray for you during the period of preparation before your marriage, keep you connected to the congregation, and continue to support you in your ongoing covenanted life together.

Finally, in choosing, remember that these people will stand with you during the liturgy and present you at this rite. Also remember that, immediately after you are presented, the entire congregation will vow to support you as you, in turn, become a blessing and bear grace to the entire congregation.

Because presenters serve an important role before and after the marriage, you and your clergyperson should talk early about selecting presenters, so that your prayerful partnership may begin as soon as possible.

SAMPLE HANDOUT 3

Information for Presenters

At N. Episcopal Church, we consider "The Witnessing and Blessing of a Marriage" to be a celebration supported by the congregation, much as candidates for baptism are supported by all the members of the Church. Just as those who are baptized are initiated into the full life of the Church, those who receive the Church's blessing upon their marriage are embraced in a new way in the faith community.

At the marriage, you present the couple to the presider and to the assembly, as follows:

> The couple comes before the assembly. If there is to be a presentation, the presenters stand with the couple, and the Presider says to them
>
> *Presider* Who presents N. and N. as they seek the blessing of God and the Church on their love and life together?
>
> *Presenters* We do.
>
> *Presider* Will you love, respect, and pray for N. and N., and do all in your power to stand with them in the life they will share?
>
> *Presenters* We will.

As a presenter, your role begins even before the marriage. We encourage you to pray for the couple both privately and in the Prayers of the People at Sunday services during their period of preparation. You can continue to support their ongoing life by acknowledging the anniversary of their marriage and offering your presence whenever their household experiences times of difficulty or celebrates occasions of joy. If you are a member of the congregation, you also have a role in keeping them connected to others in the congregation.

As a presenter, you promise to support the couple as they become a blessing and bear grace to their families and friends, the Church, and the world. In this role, then, you are a witness to the blessing given and received in the marriage liturgy and carried forth by the couple into the world.

SAMPLE HANDOUT 4

Model Congregational Guidelines

NOTE: Most congregations adopt some form of marriage policy expressing norms and guidelines for couples preparing for marriage. All congregations may engage in a helpful and fruitful exercise to develop guidelines that reflect the Christian community in which they worship; the guidelines that are developed should apply to all couples. Obviously, such a policy is optional at the discretion of the clergy in consultation with the vestry or bishop's committee. As always with liturgical matters, final decisions are the responsibility of the clergy. Following is a model of a guideline that applies for all couples preparing for marriage. It may be modified to meet specific situations and needs.

Information for Couples Seeking Marriage at N. Episcopal Church

A. Introduction

The Christian community at N. Episcopal Church understands that relationships are complex and that making a lifelong commitment to a relationship through a marriage is a significant, exciting, and wonder-filled event in people's lives. We also believe that a Christian community that agrees to bless such a relationship needs to be intentional about supporting the couple as they prepare for the marriage and as they live out their lives.

We understand that committed, lifelong relationships, whether for gender-and-sexual-minority couples or different-sex/gender couples, are to be outward and visible signs of an inward, spiritual, and God-given love. In this context, N. Episcopal Church seeks to support all couples in their commitment to one another and to help make the love of God more visible for the whole community.

B. Guidelines

The following guidelines have been adopted by the lay and ordained leaders of N. Episcopal Church:

1. As required by the Canons of The Episcopal Church at least one member of a gender-and-sexual-minority couple must be baptized.
2. It is desirable that at least one member of the couple be an active member of this, or some other, Christian community. We hope this membership might include giving serious, prayerful consideration to supporting the congregation through time, talent, and/or treasure.
3. Approximately six months' notice should be given to allow for planning and pastoral preparation.
4. If the couple has no connection with N. Episcopal Church but wishes to have their marriage at N. Episcopal Church or to use the services of N. Episcopal Church's priest:
   - they should be able to show that at least one of the couple has active membership in another Episcopal or Christian congregation;
   - they need to complete marriage preparation with their own or other clergyperson or a qualified lay preparer;
   - they might consider making a financial contribution to N. Episcopal Church in thanksgiving for their marriage and for the ongoing support of the Church, its ministry and mission. A creative formula to calculate this contribution might be to consider a tithe (10 percent) of the budget for the entire celebration. [*Clergy have discretion here, as resources vary greatly from couple to couple. Also, if a couple is returning to Church for the first time, an unconditional welcome may be the best pastoral response.*]

In all cases, it is important that all concerned comply with the laws of the state, the Canons of the Episcopal Church, and the canons and policies of the Episcopal Diocese of X as well as the directives of the diocesan bishop, including compliance with diocesan policies for cases in which the relationship is not the first marriage for one or both people.

VII. Appendices

Contents

    1. Marriage Canons
    2. A Review of General Convention Legislation

1. Marriage Canons

From The Episcopal Church, Constitution and Canons, 2015

TITLE I: ORGANIZATION AND ADMINISTRATION

Canon 18: Of the Celebration and Blessing of Marriage

Sec. 1. Every Member of the Clergy of this Church shall conform to the laws of the State governing the creation of the civil status of marriage, and also these canons concerning the solemnization of marriage. Members of the Clergy may solemnize a marriage using any of the liturgical forms authorized by this Church.

Sec. 2. The couple shall notify the Member of the Clergy of their intent to marry at least thirty days prior to the solemnization; Provided, that if one of the parties is a member of the Congregation of the Member of the Clergy, or both parties can furnish satisfactory evidence of the need for shortening the time, this requirement can be waived for weighty cause; in which case the Member of the Clergy shall immediately report this action in writing to the Bishop.

Sec. 3. Prior to the solemnization, the Member of the Clergy shall determine:

(a) that both parties have the right to marry according to the laws of the State and consent to do so freely, without fraud, coercion, mistake as to the identity of either, or mental reservation; and

(b) that at least one of the parties is baptized; and

(c) that both parties have been instructed by the Member of the Clergy, or a person known by the Member of the Clergy to be competent and responsible, in the nature, purpose, and meaning, as well as the rights, duties and responsibilities of marriage.

Sec. 4. Prior to the solemnization, the parties shall sign the following Declaration of Intention:

We understand the teaching of the church that God's purpose for our marriage is for our mutual joy, for the help and comfort we will give to each other in prosperity and adversity, and, when it is God's will, for the gift and heritage of children and their nurture in the knowledge and love of God. We also understand that our marriage is to be unconditional, mutual, exclusive, faithful, and lifelong; and we engage to make the utmost effort to accept these gifts and fulfill these duties, with the help of God and the support of our community.

Sec. 5. At least two witnesses shall be present at the solemnization, and together with the Member of the Clergy and the parties, sign the record of the solemnization in the proper register; which record shall include the date and place of the solemnization, the names of the witnesses, the parties and their parents, the age of the parties, Church status, and residence(s).

Sec. 6. A bishop or priest may pronounce a blessing upon a civil marriage using any of the liturgical forms authorized by this Church.

Sec. 7. It shall be within the discretion of any Member of the Clergy of this Church to decline to solemnize or bless any marriage.

CANON 19: Of Regulations Respecting Holy Matrimony: Concerning Preservation of Marriage, Dissolution of Marriage, and Remarriage

Sec. 1. When marital unity is imperiled by dissension, it shall be the duty, if possible, of either or both parties, before taking legal action, to lay the matter before a Member of the Clergy; it shall be the duty of such Member of the Clergy to act first to protect and promote the physical and emotional safety of those involved and only then, if it be possible, to labor that the parties may be reconciled.

Sec. 2. (a) Any member of this Church whose marriage has been annulled or dissolved by a civil court may apply to the Bishop or Ecclesiastical Authority of the Diocese in which such person is legally or canonically resident for a judgment as to his or her marital status in the eyes of the Church. Such judgment may be a recognition of the nullity, or of the termination of the said marriage; Provided, that no such judgment shall be construed as affecting in any way the legitimacy of children or the civil validity of the former relationship.

(b) Every judgment rendered under this Section shall be in writing and shall be made a matter of permanent record in the Archives of the Diocese.

Sec. 3. No Member of the Clergy of this Church shall solemnize the marriage of any person who has been the husband or wife of any other person then living, nor shall any member of this Church enter into a marriage when either of the contracting parties has been the husband or the wife of any other person then living, except as hereinafter provided:

(a) The Member of the Clergy shall be satisfied by appropriate evidence that the prior marriage has been annulled or dissolved by a final judgment or decree of a civil court of competent jurisdiction.

(b) The Member of the Clergy shall have instructed the parties that continuing concern must be shown for the well-being of the former spouse, and of any children of the prior marriage.

(c) The Member of the Clergy shall consult with and obtain the consent of the Bishop of the Diocese wherein the Member of the Clergy is canonically resident or the Bishop of the Diocese in which the Member of the Clergy is licensed to officiate prior to, and shall report to that Bishop, the solemnization of any marriage under this Section.

(d) If the proposed marriage is to be solemnized in a jurisdiction other than the one in which the consent has been given, the consent shall be affirmed by the Bishop of that jurisdiction.

Sec. 4. All provisions of Canon I.18 shall, in all cases, apply.

2. A Review of General Convention Legislation

Introduction

The legislative history here shows the development of General Convention deliberations about the place of gay men and lesbians in the life of the Church, particularly with regard to the blessing of their faithful, monogamous, lifelong relationships. Successive conventions have both acknowledged the work of their predecessors and reached new decisions.

Resolution texts are from the website of the Archives of the Episcopal Church: http://www.episcopalarchives.org/e-archives/acts/.

Minneapolis, 1976: For the first time, General Convention adopted a resolution that acknowledged and affirmed the presence of persons of homosexual orientation in the Church.

Resolution 1976–A069:

Resolved, the House of Bishops concurring, That it is the sense of this General Convention that homosexual persons are children of God who have a full and equal claim with all other persons upon the love, acceptance, and pastoral concern and care of the Church.

Anaheim, 1985: General Convention reaffirmed the 1976 resolution and encouraged dioceses to deepen understanding.

Resolution 1985–D082:

Resolved, the House of Bishops concurring, That the 68th General Convention urge each diocese of this Church to find an effective way to foster a better understanding of homosexual persons, to dispel myths and prejudices about homosexuality, to provide pastoral support, and to give life to the claim of homosexual persons "upon the love, acceptance, and pastoral care and concern of the Church" as recognized by the General Convention in 1976.

Phoenix, 1991: General Convention affirmed the traditional understanding of marriage as between a man and a woman, and acknowledged "discontinuity" between that teaching and the experience of many members of the Episcopal Church.

<u>Resolution 1991–A104:</u>

Resolved, the House of Deputies concurring, That the 70th General Convention of the Episcopal Church affirms that the teaching of the Episcopal Church is that physical sexual expression is appropriate only within the lifelong monogamous "union of husband and wife in heart, body, and mind" "intended by God for their mutual joy; for the help and comfort given one another in prosperity and adversity and, when it is God's will, for the procreation of children and their nurture in the knowledge and love of the Lord" as set forth in the Book of Common Prayer; and be it further

Resolved, That this Church continues to work to reconcile the discontinuity between this teaching and the experience of many members of this body; and be it further Resolved, That this General Convention confesses our failure to lead and to resolve this discontinuity through legislative efforts based upon resolutions directed at singular and various aspects of these issues; and be it further

Resolved, That this General Convention commissions the Bishops and members of each Diocesan Deputation to initiate a means for all congregations in their jurisdiction to enter into dialogue and deepen their understanding of these complex issues; and further this General Convention directs the President of each Province to appoint one Bishop, one lay deputy and one clerical deputy in that province to facilitate the process, to receive reports from the dioceses at each meeting of their provincial synod and report to the 71st General Convention; and be it further

Resolved, That this General Convention directs the House of Bishops to prepare a Pastoral Teaching prior to the 71st General Convention using the learnings from the diocesan and provincial processes and calling upon such insight as is necessary from theologians, theological ethicists, social scientists and gay and lesbian persons; and that three lay persons and three members of the clergy from the House of

Deputies, appointed by the President of the House of Deputies be included in the preparation of this Pastoral Teaching.

Indianapolis, 1994: General Convention added sexual orientation, along with marital status, sex, disabilities, and age as categories to which non-discrimination in Church membership is assured.

Resolution 1994–C020:

Resolved, the House of Bishops concurring, That Title I, Canon 17, Section 5 be amended as follows:

No person shall be denied rights, status [in], or [access to] an equal place in the life, worship, and governance of this Church because of race, color, [or] ethnic origin, national origin, marital status, sex, sexual orientation, disabilities or age, except as otherwise specified by [this] Canon.

Indianapolis, 1994: General Convention called for a study of "the theological foundations and pastoral considerations involved in the development of rites honoring love and commitment between persons of the same sex."

Resolution 1994–C042:

Resolved, the House of Deputies concurring, That the 71st General Convention direct the Standing Liturgical Commission and the Theology Committee of the House of Bishops to prepare and present to the 72nd General Convention, as part of the Church's ongoing dialogue on human sexuality, a report addressing the theological foundations and pastoral considerations involved in the development of rites honoring love and commitment between persons of the same sex; and be it further

Resolved, That no rites for the honoring of love and commitment between persons of the same sex be developed unless and until the preparation of such rites has been authorized by the General Convention; and be it further
Resolved, That the sum of $8,600 be appropriated to support this work, subject to funding considerations.

Philadelphia, 1997: General Convention reaffirmed the traditional understanding of marriage and called for continuing study.

Resolution 1997–C003:

Resolved, That this 72nd General Convention affirm the sacredness of Christian marriage between one man and one woman with intent of life-long relationship; and be it further

Resolved, That this Convention direct the Standing Liturgical Commission to continue its study of theological aspects of committed relationships of same-sex couples, and to issue a full report including recommendations of future steps for the resolution of issues related to such committed relationships no later than November 1999 for consideration at the 73rd General Convention.

Denver, 2000: General Convention acknowledged relationships other than marriage.

<u>Resolution 2000–D039:</u>

Resolved, That the members of the 73rd General Convention intend for this Church to provide a safe and just structure in which all can utilize their gifts and creative energies for mission; and be it further

Resolved, That we acknowledge that while the issues of human sexuality are not yet resolved, there are currently couples in the Body of Christ and in this Church who are living in marriage and couples in the Body of Christ and in this Church who are living in other life-long committed relationships; and be it further

Resolved, That we expect such relationships will be characterized by fidelity, monogamy, mutual affection and respect, careful, honest communication, and the holy love which enables those in such relationships to see in each other the image of God; and be it further Resolved, That we denounce promiscuity, exploitation, and abusiveness in the relationships of any of our members; and be it further

Resolved, That this Church intends to hold all its members accountable to these values, and will provide for them the prayerful support, encouragement, and pastoral care necessary to live faithfully by them; and be it further

Resolved, That we acknowledge that some, acting in good conscience, who disagree with the traditional teaching of the Church on human sexuality, will act in contradiction to that position; and be it further

Resolved, That in continuity with previous actions of the General Convention of this Church, and in response to the call for dialogue by the Lambeth Conference, we affirm that those on various sides of controversial issues have a place in the Church, and we reaffirm the imperative to promote conversation between persons of differing experiences and perspectives, while acknowledging the Church's teaching on the sanctity of marriage.

Minneapolis, 2003: Acknowledging continuing differences, General Convention recognized "that local faith communities are operating within the bounds of our common life as they explore and experience liturgies celebrating and blessing same-sex unions."

Resolution 2003–C051:

Resolved, That the 74th General Convention affirm the following:

1. That our life together as a community of faith is grounded in the saving work of Jesus Christ and expressed in the principles of the Chicago–Lambeth Quadrilateral: Holy Scripture, the historic Creeds of the Church, the two dominical Sacraments, and the Historic Episcopate.

2. That we reaffirm Resolution A069 of the 65th General Convention (1976) that "homosexual persons are children of God who have a full and equal claim with all other persons upon the love, acceptance, and pastoral concern and care of the Church."

3. That, in our understanding of homosexual persons, differences exist among us about how best to care pastorally for those who intend to live in monogamous, non-celibate unions; and what is, or should be, required, permitted, or prohibited by the doctrine, discipline, and worship of The Episcopal Church concerning the blessing of the same.

4. That we reaffirm Resolution D039 of the 73rd General Convention (2000), that "We expect such relationships will be characterized by fidelity, monogamy, mutual affection and respect, careful, honest communication, and the holy love which enables those in such relationships to see in each other the image of God," and that such relationships exist throughout the church.

5. That we recognize that local faith communities are operating within the bounds of our common life as they explore and experience liturgies celebrating and blessing same-sex unions.

6. That we commit ourselves, and call our church, in the spirit of Resolution A104 of the 70th General Convention (1991), to continued prayer, study, and discernment on the pastoral care for gay and lesbian persons, to include the compilation and development by a special commission organized and appointed by the Presiding Bishop, of resources to facilitate as wide a conversation of discernment as possible throughout the church.

7. That our baptism into Jesus Christ is inseparable from our communion with one another, and we commit ourselves to that communion despite our diversity of opinion and, among dioceses, a diversity of pastoral practice with the gay men and lesbians among us.

8. That it is a matter of faith that our Lord longs for our unity as his disciples, and for us this entails living within the boundaries of the Constitution and Canons of The Episcopal Church. We believe this discipline expresses faithfulness to our polity and that it will facilitate the conversation we seek, not only in The Episcopal Church, but also in the wider Anglican Communion and beyond.

Anaheim, 2009: The General Convention directed the Standing Commission on Liturgy and Music to "collect and develop theological and liturgical resources" for blessing same-gender relationships.

Resolution 2009–C056:

Resolved, the House of Deputies concurring, That the 76th General Convention acknowledge the changing circumstances in the United States and in other nations, as legislation authorizing or forbidding marriage, civil unions or domestic partnerships for gay and lesbian persons is passed in various civil jurisdictions that call forth a renewed pastoral response from this Church, and for an open process for the consideration of theological and liturgical resources for the blessing of same-gender relationships; and be it further

Resolved, That the Standing Commission on Liturgy and Music, in consultation with the House of Bishops, collect and develop theological and liturgical resources, and report to the 77th General Convention; and be it further

Resolved, That the Standing Commission on Liturgy and Music, in consultation with the House of Bishops, devise an open process for the conduct of its work inviting participation from provinces, dioceses, congregations, and individuals who are engaged in such theological work, and inviting theological reflection from throughout the Anglican Communion; and be it further

Resolved, That bishops, particularly those in dioceses within civil jurisdictions where same-gender marriage, civil unions, or domestic partnerships are legal, may provide generous pastoral response to meet the needs of members of this Church; and be it further

Resolved, That this Convention honor the theological diversity of this Church in regard to matters of human sexuality; and be it further Resolved, That the members of this Church be encouraged to engage in this effort.

Indianapolis, 2012: In Resolution A049, the General Convention commended the resource "I Will Bless You, and You Will Be a Blessing" for study and use, authorized the liturgy for provisional use, and called for a process of review and further development of the theological resources. In addition, in Resolution A050, the General Convention called for a task force to explore understandings of marriage, including attention to legislation authorizing or forbidding same-sex marriage.

Resolution 2012–A049

Resolved, the House of Deputies concurring, That the 77th General Convention commend "Liturgical Resources I: I Will Bless You and You Will Be a Blessing" for study and use in congregations and dioceses of The Episcopal Church, with the following revisions:

> Throughout "I Will Bless You and You Will Be a Blessing" change "same-gender" to "same-sex"
>
> Blue Book p. 184: change "Resources for Blessing Same-Gender Relationships" to "Resources for The Witnessing and Blessing of a Lifelong Covenant in a Same-Sex Relationship"
>
> Blue Book p. 240: Add rubric after first rubric, stating: "At least one of the couple must be a baptized Christian."
>
> Blue Book p. 240: In paragraph 2, line 1, delete "at least one of whom is baptized"
>
> Blue Book p. 241: In Presider's address to the assembly, delete "come what may" (paragraph 1, line 9)
>
> Blue Book pp. 241–242: In Presider's address to the assembly, delete all of paragraph 2 ("Ahead of them ... calls us all to share.")
>
> Blue Book p. 242: In Presider's address to the assembly, change "let us pray, then," (paragraph 3, line 1) to "Therefore, in the name of Christ, let us pray."
>
> Blue Book p. 245: After the bidding for peace in their home and love in their family, add the following bidding: "For the grace, when they hurt each other, to recognize and acknowledge their fault, and to seek each other's forgiveness and yours: Lord, in your mercy (or Lord, in

your goodness) Hear our prayer."

Blue Book p. 246: Change rubric that begins "After a time of silence" to the following: "The leader may add one or more of the following biddings."

Blue Book p. 247: In Commitment (both forms) line 7, change "I will honor and keep you" to "I will honor and love you"

Blue Book p. 248: In first form of blessing rings, change line 2 to "as signs of the enduring covenant"

Blue Book p. 248: In Blessing of the Couple, add rubric between first and second paragraphs: "The Presider continues with one of the following"

Blue Book p. 248: In Blessing of the Couple, add third paragraph after the "Amen": "or this / God, the holy and undivided Trinity, bless, preserve, and keep you, and mercifully grant you rich and boundless grace, that you may please God in body and soul. God make you a sign of the loving-kindness and steadfast fidelity manifest in the life, death, and resurrection of our Savior, and bring you at last to the delight of the heavenly banquet, where he lives and reigns for ever and ever. Amen."

Blue Book p. 257: In paragraph under E. Vocation, change "1 Samuel 18" to "1 Samuel 3"; and be it further

Resolved, That the 77th General Convention authorize for provisional use "The Witnessing and Blessing of a Lifelong Covenant" from "Liturgical Resources I: I Will Bless You and You Will Be a Blessing" beginning the First Sunday of Advent 2012, under the direction and subject to the permission of the bishop exercising ecclesiastical authority; and be it further

Resolved, That bishops, particularly those in dioceses within civil jurisdictions where same-sex marriage, civil unions, or domestic partnerships are legal, may provide generous pastoral response to meet the needs of members of this Church; and be it further

Resolved, That bishops may authorize adaptation of these materials to meet the needs of members of this Church: and be it further

Resolved, that the provision of Canon I.18.4 applies by extension to "Theological Resources for Blessing Same-Sex Relationships," namely, "It shall be within the discretion of any Member of the Clergy of this Church to decline to" preside at any rite of blessing defined herein; and be it further

Resolved, That this convention honor the theological diversity of this church in regard to matters of human sexuality, and that no bishop, priest, deacon or lay person should be coerced or penalized in any manner, nor suffer any canonical disabilities, as a result of his or her conscientious objection to or support for the 77th General Convention's action with regard to the Blessing of Same-Sex Relationships; and be it further

Resolved, That the theological resource for the blessing of a lifelong covenant be further developed by the Standing Commission on Liturgy and Music over the 2013–2015 triennium with specific attention to further engagement with scripture and the relevant categories and sources of systematic theology (e.g., creation, sin, grace, salvation, redemption, human nature); and be it further

Resolved, That the Standing Commission on Liturgy and Music include the work of diverse theological perspectives in the further development of the theological resource; and be it further

Resolved, That the Standing Commission on Liturgy and Music develop an open process to review "I Will Bless You and You Will Be a Blessing," inviting responses from provinces, dioceses, congregations, and individuals from throughout The Episcopal Church and the Anglican Communion, and from our ecumenical partners, and report to the 78th General Convention.

Resolution 2012–A050

Resolved, the House of Deputies concurring, That the 77th General Convention direct the Presiding Bishop and President of the House of Deputies to appoint a task force of not more than twelve people, consisting of theologians, liturgists, pastors, and educators, to identify and explore biblical, theological, historical, liturgical, and canonical dimensions of marriage; and be it further

Resolved, That the task force consult with the Standing Commission on Constitution and Canons and The Standing Commission on Liturgy and Music to address the pastoral need for priests to officiate at a civil marriage of a same-sex couple in states that authorize such; and be it further

Resolved, That the task force consult with couples living in marriage and in other lifelong committed relationships and with single adults, and be it further

Resolved, That the task force consult with other churches in the Anglican Communion and with our ecumenical partners, and be it further

Resolved, That the task force consider issues raised by changing societal and cultural norms and legal structures, including legislation authorizing or forbidding marriage, civil unions, or domestic partnerships between two people of the same sex, in the U.S. and other countries where The Episcopal Church is located; and be it further

Resolved, That the task force develop tools for theological reflection and norms for theological discussion at a local level; and be it further

Resolved, That the task force report its progress to the 78th General Convention; and be it further

Resolved, That the General Convention request the Joint Standing Committee on Program, Budget and Finance to consider a budget allocation of $30,000 for the implementation of this resolution.

Salt Lake City, 2015: In Resolution A054, the General Convention authorized two liturgies for marriage for trial use and the use of "The Witnessing and Blessing of a Lifelong Covenant," thus allowing the marriage of same-sex couples in civil jurisdictions where such marriages are legal. In addition, Resolution A036 revised the marriage canon (Canon I.18; the revised text appears above in Appendix 2), and Resolution A037 requested dioceses and parishes to use the study materials produced by the Task Force on the Study of Marriage established by the 2012 Convention, and called for an expanded task force to continue to study marriage.

Resolution 2015-A036:

Resolved, the House of Deputies concurring, That Canon I.18 is hereby amended to read as follows:

~~CANON 18: Of the Solemnization of Holy Matrimony~~

Canon 18: Of the Celebration and Blessing of Marriage

Sec. 1. Every Member of the Clergy of this Church shall conform to the laws of the State governing the creation of the civil status of marriage, and also ~~to the laws of this Church governing~~ *these canons concerning* the solemnization of *marriage* ~~Holy Matrimony~~. *Members of the Clergy may solemnize a marriage using any of the liturgical forms authorized by this Church.*

~~Sec. 2. Before solemnizing a marriage the Member of the Clergy shall have ascertained:~~

~~(a) That both parties have the right to contract a marriage according to the laws of the State.~~

~~(b) That both parties understand that Holy Matrimony is a physical and spiritual union of a man and a woman, entered into within the community of faith, by mutual consent of heart, mind, and will, and with intent that it be lifelong.~~

~~(c) That both parties freely and knowingly consent to such marriage, without fraud, coercion, mistake as to identity of a partner, or mental reservation.~~

~~(d) That at least one of the parties has received Holy Baptism.~~

~~(e) That both parties have been instructed as to the nature, meaning, and purpose of Holy Matrimony by the Member of the Clergy, or that they have both received such instruction from persons known by the Member of the Clergy to be competent and responsible.~~

Sec. 2. The couple shall notify the Member of the Clergy of their intent to marry at least thirty days prior to the solemnization; Provided, that if one of the parties is a member of the Congregation of the Member of the Clergy, or both parties can furnish satisfactory evidence of the need for shortening the time, this requirement can be waived for weighty cause; in which case the Member of the Clergy shall immediately report this action in writing to the Bishop.

~~Sec. 3. No Member of the Clergy of this Church shall solemnize any marriage unless the following procedures are complied with:~~

~~(a) The intention of the parties to contract marriage shall have been signified to the Member of the Clergy at least thirty days before the service of solemnization; Provided, that for weighty cause, this requirement may be dispensed with if one of the parties is a member of the Congregation of the Member of the Clergy, or can furnish satisfactory evidence of responsibility. In case the thirty days' notice is waived, the Member of the Clergy shall report such action in writing to the Bishop immediately.~~

~~(b) There shall be present at least two witnesses to the solemnization of marriage.~~

~~(c) The Member of the Clergy shall record in the proper register the date and place of the marriage, the names of the parties and their parents, the age of the parties, their residences, and their Church status; the witnesses and the~~

~~Member of the Clergy shall sign the record.~~

~~(d) The Member of the Clergy shall have required that the parties sign the following declaration:~~

~~(e) "We, A.B. and C.D., desiring to receive the blessing of Holy Matrimony in the Church, do solemnly declare that we hold marriage to be a lifelong union of husband and wife as it is set forth in the Book of Common Prayer.~~

~~(f) "We believe that the union of husband and wife, in heart, body, and mind, is intended by God for their mutual joy; for the help and comfort given one another in prosperity and adversity; and, when it is God's will, for the procreation of children and their nurture in the knowledge and love of the Lord.~~

~~(g) "And we do engage ourselves, so far as in us lies, to make our utmost effort to establish this relationship and to seek God's help thereto."~~

Sec. 3. Prior to the solemnization, the Member of the Clergy shall determine:

(a) that both parties have the right to marry according to the laws of the State and consent to do so freely, without fraud, coercion, mistake as to the identity of either, or mental reservation; and

(b) that at least one of the parties is baptized; and

(c) that both parties have been instructed by the Member of the Clergy, or a person known by the Member of the Clergy to be competent and responsible, in the nature, purpose, and meaning, as well as the rights, duties and responsibilities of marriage.

Sec. 4. Prior to the solemnization, the parties shall sign the following Declaration of Intention:

We understand the teaching of the church that God's purpose for our marriage is for our mutual joy, for the help and comfort we will give to each other in prosperity and adversity, and, when it is God's will, for the gift and heritage of children and their nurture in the knowledge and love of God. We also understand that our marriage is to be unconditional, mutual, exclusive, faithful, and lifelong; and we engage to make the utmost effort to accept these gifts and fulfill these duties, with the help of God and the support of our community.

Sec. 5. At least two witnesses shall be present at the solemnization, and together with the Member of the Clergy and the parties, sign the record of the solemnization in the proper register; which record shall include the date and place of the solemnization, the names of the witnesses, the parties and their parents, the age of the parties, Church status, and residence(s).

Sec. 6. A bishop or priest may pronounce a blessing upon a civil marriage using any of the liturgical forms authorized by this Church.

~~Sec. 4~~ *Sec. 7. It shall be within the discretion of any Member of the Clergy of this Church to decline to solemnize or bless any marriage.*

and be it further

Resolved that this canon shall become effective on the First Sunday of Advent, 2015.

Resolution 2015-A037:

Resolved, the House of Deputies concurring, That the 78th General Convention requests dioceses and parishes use the study materials on marriage provided in the last triennium by the Task Force on the Study of Marriage, namely the "Dearly Beloved" toolkit and the appended essays in their Blue Book report to this Convention; and be it further

Resolved, That the 78th General Convention directs the Presiding Bishop and President of the House of Deputies to appoint jointly an expanded Task Force on the Study of Marriage to continue this work, consisting of not more than 15 people, including theologians, ethicists, pastors, liturgists, and educators, who represent the cultural and theological diversity in the Church; membership should include some of the Task Force on the Study of Marriage appointed in 2012, some from dioceses outside the United States, and young adults; and be it further

Resolved, That the Task Force explore further those contemporary trends and norms identified by the Task Force on the Study of Marriage in the previous triennium, specifically regarding those who choose to remain single; unmarried persons in intimate relationships; couples who cohabitate either in preparation for, or as an alternative to, marriage; couples who desire a blessing from the Church but not marriage; parenting by single or and/or unmarried persons; differing forms of family and household such as those including same-sex parenting, adoption, and racial diversity; and differences in marriage patterns between ethnic and racial groups; and be it further

Resolved, That the Task Force consult with (i) individuals and couples within these groups about their experience of faith and church life; and (ii) the results of diocesan and parochial study of "Dearly Beloved" toolkit; and be it further

Resolved, That the Task Force explore biblical, theological, moral, liturgical, cultural, and pastoral perspectives on these matters, and develop written materials about them which represent the spectrum of understanding in our Church and which include responses from theologians, ethicists, pastors, liturgists, social scientists, and educators who are not members of the expanded Task Force, and whose perspectives represent the spectrum of understandings on these matters in our Church; and be it further

Resolved, That the Task Force study and monitor, in consultation with the Standing Commission on Liturgy and Music, the impact of same-sex marriage and rites of blessing on our Church; the continuing debate about clergy acting as agents of the state in officiating at marriages; and any other matters related to marriage by action of or referral by this Convention; and be it further

Resolved, That the Task Force report and make recommendations to the 79th General Convention; and be it further

Resolved, That the Task Force provide educational and pastoral resources for congregational use on these matters that represent the spectrum of understandings on these matters in our Church; and be it further

Resolved, That the General Convention request the Joint Standing Committee on Program, Budget and Finance to consider a budget allocation of $90,000 for the implementation of this resolution.

<u>Resolution 2015-A054:</u>

Resolved, the House of Deputies concurring, That the 78th General Convention commend "Liturgical Resources I: I Will Bless You and You Will Be a Blessing, Revised and Expanded 2015," as found in the Blue Book, Liturgy Supplemental Materials: Appendices of the Report of the Standing Commission on Liturgy and Music (BBLSM), pp. 2-151, with the following revisions:

> BBLSM p. 84: In The Commitment, change the rubric to read "Each member of the couple, in turn, takes the right hand of the other and says"

VII. APPENDICES

BBLSM p.84: After "I N., give myself to you, N." add ", and take you to myself."

BBLSM p. 85: At the Pronouncement, change the rubric to read "The Presider joins the right hands and says"

BBLSM p. 87: In Concerning the Service, change the second paragraph to read "At least one of the couple must be a baptized Christian, and the marriage shall conform to the laws of the state and canons of this church."

BBLSM p. 88: Under Gathering, change the rubric to read "The couple joins the assembly."

BBLSM p. 89: Change "In marriage according to the laws of the state [or civil jurisdiction] of X" to "In marriage [according to the laws of the state or civil jurisdiction of X]"

BBLSM p. 89: Change "Solemnize their marriage according to the laws of the state [or civil jurisdiction] of X" to "are married [according to the laws of the state or civil jurisdiction of X]"

BBLSM p.94: After "I N., give myself to you, N." add ", and take you to myself."

BBLSM p. 95: At the Pronouncement, change the rubric to read "The Presider joins the right hands of the couple and says"

BBLSM p. 95: Replace "I pronounce that they are married according to the laws of the state [or civil jurisdiction] of X" to "I pronounce that they are married [according to the laws of the state or civil jurisdiction of X]"

BBLSM p. 100: At The Marriage, change the rubric to read "Each member of the couple, in turn, takes the right hand of the other and says"

for study and use in congregations and dioceses of The Episcopal Church; and be it further

Resolved, That the 78th General Convention authorize for use "The Witnessing and Blessing of a Lifelong Covenant" from "Liturgical Resources I: I Will Bless You and You Will Be a Blessing, Revised and Expanded 2015" (as found in Supplemental Materials: Appendices of the Report of the Standing Commission on Liturgy and Music, pp. 77-86, as amended)" beginning the First Sunday of Advent 2015; under the direction and with the permission of the bishop exercising ecclesiastical authority; and be it further

Resolved, That the 78th General Convention authorize for trial use in accordance with Article X of the Constitution and Canon II.3.6 "The Witnessing and Blessing of a Marriage," and "The Celebration and Blessing of a Marriage 2," from "Liturgical Resources I: I Will Bless You and You Will Be a Blessing, Revised and Expanded 2015" (as found in Supplemental Materials: Appendices of the Report of the Standing Commission on Liturgy and Music, pp. 87-105) beginning the First Sunday of Advent 2015. Bishops exercising ecclesiastical authority or, where appropriate, ecclesiastical supervision will make provision for all couples asking to be married in this Church to have access to these liturgies. Trial use is only to be available under the direction and with the permission of the Diocesan Bishop; and be it further

Resolved, That bishops may continue to provide generous pastoral response to meet the needs of members of this Church; and be it further

Resolved, That the provision of Canon I.18.4* applies by extension to "Liturgical Resources I: I Will Bless You and You Will Be a Blessing, Revised and Expanded 2015," namely, "It shall be within the discretion of any Member of the Clergy of this Church to decline to" preside at any rite contained herein; and be it further

Resolved, That the provisions of Canon I.19.3 regarding marriage after divorce apply equally to all the rites of "Liturgical Resources I: I Will Bless You and You Will Be a Blessing, Revised and Expanded 2015," in accordance with guidelines established by each diocese; and be it further

Resolved, That this convention honor the theological diversity of this Church in regard to matters of human sexuality; and that no bishop, priest, deacon or lay person should be coerced or penalized in any manner, nor suffer any canonical disabilities, as a result of his or her theological objection to or support for the 78th General Convention's action contained in this resolution; and be it further

Resolved, That the Standing Commission on Liturgy and Music continue to monitor the use of this material and report to the 79th General Convention; and be it further

Resolved, That the 78th General Convention direct the Secretary of General Convention, and the Custodian of the Standard Book of Common Prayer in consultation with the outgoing Chair of the Standing Commission on Liturgy and

Music and the Chairs of the Legislative Committees to whom this legislation is referred, to finalize and arrange for the publication with Church Publishing of the material (in English and Spanish) contained in "Liturgical Resources 1: I Will Bless You and You Will Be a Blessing, Revised and Expanded 2015" as approved by the 78th General Convention, no later than the first Sunday of Advent 2015, these materials to be available electronically at no cost.

*Canon I.18.4 refers to the 2012 Constitution and Canons; a comparable provision is contained in Canon I.18.7 of the 2015 Constitution and Canons.

www.ingramcontent.com/pod-product-compliance
Ingram Content Group UK Ltd.
Pitfield, Milton Keynes, MK11 3LW, UK
UKHW021833140426
5217IPUK00021B/1415